I0889755

Crime and Media in Contemporary France

Comparative Cultural Studies
Steven Tötösy de Zepetnek, Series Editor

Comparative Cultural Studies is a contextual approach in the study of culture in all of its products and processes. The framework of comparative cultural studies is built on tenets of the disciplines of comparative literature and cultural studies and on notions borrowed from a range of thought including literary and culture theories, (radical) constructivism, communication theories, and systems theories. In comparative cultural studies focus is on theory and method as well as application, and attention is on the how rather than on the what. Colleagues interested in publishing in the series are invited to contact the editor, Steven Tötösy de Zepetnek, at <clcweb@purdue.edu>.

Volumes in the series include:

Comparative Central European Culture. Ed. Steven Tötösy de Zepetnek. ISBN 1-55753-240-0.

Comparative Literature and Comparative Cultural Studies. Ed. Steven Tötösy de Zepetnek. ISBN 1-55753-290-7.

Sophia A. McClennen, *The Dialectics of Exile: Nation, Time, Language, and Space in Hispanic Literature.* ISBN 1-55753-315-6.

Comparative Cultural Studies and Latin America. Ed. Sophia A. McClennen and Earl E. Fitz. ISBN 1-55753-358-X

Jin Feng, *The New Woman in Early Twentieth-Century Chinese Fiction.* ISBN 1-55753-330-X.

Comparative Cultural Studies and Michael Ondaatje's Writing. Ed. Steven Tötösy de Zepetnek. ISBN 1-55753-378-4.

Camilla Fojas, *Cosmopolitanism in the Americas.* ISBN 1-55753-382-2.

Imre Kertész and Holocaust Literature. Ed. Louise O. Vasvári and Steven Tötösy de Zepetnek. ISBN 1-55753-396-2.

Deborah Streifford Reisinger, *Crime and Media in Contemporary France.* ISBN 978-1-55753-433-0.

Deborah Streifford Reisinger

Crime and Media in Contemporary France

Purdue University Press
West Lafayette, Indiana

Printed in the United States of America.

ISBN 978-1-55753-433-0

Library of Congress Cataloging-in-Publication Data

Reisinger, Deborah Streifford, 1969-
Crime and media in contemporary France / Deborah Streifford Reisinger.
p. cm. -- (Comparative cultural studies)
Includes bibliographical references and index.
ISBN 978-1-55753-433-0 (alk. paper)
1. Crime--France. 2. Mass media and crime--France. 3. Violence--France.
4. Motion pictures and literature--France. I. Title.
HV6967.R44 2007
364.944--dc22

2006034435

Contents

Acknowledgments

A number of persons have been instrumental in the writing of this book, in ways they may or may not realize. I thank, above all, Martine Antle for her extraordinary guidance throughout the long stretches of research and writing; she believed in this project from its inception and was instrumental in helping it find a place. I must also thank individual colleagues, friends, and mentors for reading and discussing these topics at length: Dominique Fisher, Sahar Amer, Joanne Hershfield, Sophie Adamson, Anne Garretta, Jody Argote, Richard Golsan, and Keith Reader posed insightful questions and gave invaluable feedback at various stages of this project. I have presented portions of this book at a range of conferences and academic venues, and I am especially grateful to those colleagues and students for their perceptive comments. I thank my family, and in particular my father, who has been a tremendous source of support and inspiration. Last but not least, I thank the anonymous reviewers of my manuscript and the editor of the Purdue series of Books in Comparative Cultural Studies, Steven Tötösy de Zepetnek, for his interest in and support of my work. I dedicate this book to Udo, my partner in life and in love, who has been more supportive than I could have ever dreamed possible. His kindness, encouragement, and perspective continue to amaze me.

Note: A portion of chapter 2 was published in *South Central Review* 17.4 (Winter 2000): 84–99 with the title "Murder and Banality in the Contemporary *Fait divers*."

Chapter One

Crime and Sensation in Contemporary France

The late 1980s and early 1990s were an era of heightened crime awareness in France, a precursor for the hyper-focus on security and *délinquance* that would characterize the turn of the century. With the introduction of the word "serial killer" into the French language, the emerging popularity of "reality TV," and an increasingly pervasive media discourse focused on public insecurity, French society consumed crime as fast as the media could reproduce it. While stemming in part from American cultural capitalism, French society has nonetheless incorporated and followed similar trends in the perception and representation of crime. Yet, as Tricia Rose explains, "Crime and violence have become the central focus of popular attention, not because more and more people are the victims of crime, but because more [people] vicariously experience violence through the repetition of tabloid, televised news, and other reality-based programming" (149). In other words, criminal acts have not actually multiplied, but the increased mediation of crime has heightened the public's perception of violent acts and in turn increased its concern. It is this mediated (omni)presence of crime that I will interrogate throughout this book, through an analysis of the complex processes of production, reception, and artistic rearticulation that contribute to the representation of violence in contemporary French society. Through their appearance in a variety of media forms that circulate with increasing velocity, violent images and discourse have become a defining part of the public's daily news diet. The rapid and constant circulation of these images combines to create what Bill Nichols calls an "aesthetics of immediacy" that threatens conventional historiography. As he explains, "The aesthetics of immediacy, conjured in a timeless, spaceless telescape of mediated reality, drowns out the descriptions that urge us to further actions beyond exclamation or dismay. Its claims of authenticity, its construction of an endless 'now,' its preference for the chronicle, the random and unforeseen over the order and cohesion of historiography, and the problem solving discourses of a technocratic order all come at a time when master narratives are a target of disparagement" (59).

By focusing on the immediate, the media absolves itself of its role in creating and baiting a fearful public, and instead shifts the blame elsewhere. During the 1980s, movies, books, and plays depicting violent acts fell under the media's increasing scrutiny and were blamed for their negative influence on children, young adults, and criminal offenders. Ironically, the same media that produces these violent images has been the largest mouthpiece for its criticism: newspapers devote articles to increasingly violent discourse, television shows critique the cinema's realistic portrayal of murder, and news magazines interrogate the brutality of violent images. These attacks on artistic depictions of violence are relative only to literature's long relationship to violence, however, as these criticisms are recycled arguments that have long plagued art and literature. Since its emergence, literature has been associated with the crime story; we need only turn to the Bible for early examples. In French literature in particular, writers such as Villon, Stendhal, and Flaubert have re-inscribed murder in their works, and the twentieth century provides no exception: Jarry, Breton, Prévert, Camus, Gide, Sartre, Genet, Duras, and Le Clézio and have all authored texts based on real crime stories. Like its literary counterpart, French cinema has focused on real crime since its inception. One of the most famous silent films is *L'Histoire d'un crime* (Ferdinand Zecca, 1901), based on an 1882 display of photographs at the Musée Grevin in Paris in which a woman asks her husband to kill her lover. Other examples include *Nouvelles en trois lignes* (Félix Fénéon, 1906), *La Danse héroïque* (Alice Guy, 1914), *Le Feu follet* (Louis Malle, 1963), *Stavinsky* (Alain Resnais, 1963), *Que la bête meure* (Claude Chabrol, 1969), and *Moi, Pierre Rivière* (René Allio, 1979), which later became the subject of a book edited by Michel Foucault (*Moi, Pierre Rivière ayant égorgé ma mère, ma sœur et mon frère,* 1973). Clearly, it is not new to fictionalize crime. What *is* new is how more recent works critique the mediatization of the crime story by calling into question the sensationalized interpretation of reality. Bertrand Tavernier's 1995 film *L'Appât*, for instance, retells the story of three middle-class teenagers who spend their days watching violent American films and eventually turn to killing to make extra money. The film is based on the 1991 case that shook the country and set in motion a national debate about the "new wave" of motiveless crimes. The French media focused blame on Oliver Stone's film *Natural Born Killers* (1990) for inciting the teenagers to commit the crimes, exemplifying how artists (and their works) are increasingly held responsible for the reactions of their audience members. Tavernier's film, however, does not make this explicit connection, and while he rather matter-of-factly presents the events as they happened, he was nonetheless criticized for not condemning the murders in a clearer manner. When his film was later broadcast on FR2 television, it was broadcast at the odd hour of 9:40 p.m. and was framed by two debates about the role of violence in society. This kind of criticism and negative attention paid to artistic works is not new, however, as literature and the creative arts have frequently been the target of moral criticism. In the 1800s and early 1900s, critics castigated literature as a moral deterrent, and it became a convenient place to lay blame for changing (and often "weakening") social values. Painting, music, and the plastic arts have been condemned for inciting dubious behavior, and we find echoes of the cinema's dangerous effect on youth in the 1930s and 1950s. The principal difference today lies in the contemporary media's ability to diffuse these debates to the general public. So while literature and film continue to re-write crime, the response to these new works depicting violence has often been hypercritical, with conservative politicians denouncing their negative influence on children and generating public outrage, protests, trials, and even censorship. This research thus focuses on the apex of where the controversy lies: at the junction of crime, media, politics, and art.

In a close examination of the Paulin and Succo cases, two highly sensationalized news stories (*faits divers*) in France in the 1980s, this book analyzes media representations of these crimes to demonstrate how the press endeavors to manipulate public response to violent crime and heighten public anxiety. As examples of a perceived growing wave of motiveless crimes during this time, the Paulin and Succo cases are exemplary illustrations of the media's efforts to manipulate public sensibility about crime. Turning to the artistic representation of these two *grandes affaires criminelles*, I examine Claire Denis's film *J'ai pas sommeil* (1994), based on the Paulin case, and Bernard-Marie Koltès's play *Roberto Zucco* (1990), based on the Succo case. Both Denis's and Koltès's rewritings of the crime story appeared within ten years of the occurrences of the *faits divers*, which allows us to examine them in the historical context of the *affaires*. Furthermore, while these rewritings do not stray very far from the facts, each represents a deliberately fictionalized interpretation of the *fait divers*. In other words, neither artist claims to retell the crimes exactly as they happened or to offer a biographical account of the criminal's life; rather, each alters its protagonist's name, invents characters who interact with him, and opts to omit the criminal's death, refusing the cathartic closure offered by the real case. This characteristic distinguishes these rewritings from works like *L'Appât* or Cédric Kahn's film *Roberto Succo* (2001), which eschew artistic interpretation to retell the crimes just as they happened. When Kahn explained why he chose to base his film on a journalistic account of the *affaire* instead of on Koltès's work, he explained that "it was the interpretative part, the artist's role, that transforms the *fait divers* that bothered me" ("la part d'interprétation, la part de l'artiste, qui transforme le fait divers, me gênait") (Kahn 1). It is exactly this interpretative role of the artist that I am interested in exploring, for it best addresses how we might imagine a new way of exploring the *fait divers*.

In an analysis of the respective representations of these crime stories, it is clear that rather than justifying criminal acts, as they have so often been accused, Denis and Koltès interrogate and challenge contemporary society's relationship with crime. Desensationalizing, deconstructing, and recontextualizing the *fait divers*, these rewritings subvert the dominant media discourse about crime, which constructs the criminal as a (racial, sexual, psychological) Other, in opposition to the (white, straight, sane) public. In contrast, Denis and Koltès incite the reader or spectator to experience the criminal as a person rather than a monster, and the crimes in their historical and cultural contexts rather than as singular events that occur in a virtual social vacuum. Although Denis and Koltès do not suggest that we may "know" the

Other, their rewritings destabilize boundaries between the public and the criminal, effectively neutralizing the criminal's difference. Through an analysis of both media and artistic response to the sensational Paulin and Succo affairs, then, this book highlights the importance of the *fait divers* as a contemporary social signifier and site of discursive struggle. Both of the *faits divers* I examine took place during the 1980s, a period that was marked by the Socialists' return to power (under François Mitterand), and the rise of the National Front, an extreme right-wing political group led by Jean-Marie Le Pen. While this categorization is somewhat simplistic in that it does not include or preclude the existence of the many political groups that fall outside of this paradigm, these parties dominated the media, and their very public quarrels significantly marked the cultural discourse of this period. The Left, for instance, focused on creating new laws integrating immigrants, while the Right formulated a discourse founded on racist principles designed to thwart immigration. These opposing tendencies led to radically different representations of the *fait divers*, with judgments often turning on issues of ethnicity and sexuality. Perhaps most importantly, this shift in political dynamics was magnified by and through the media, whose representations of these ideological struggles characterized France in the 1980s.

During this time period, the notion of *insécurité* (insecurity, or anxiety about crime) dominated headlines and news stories throughout France, particularly in conservative newspapers. While this concept of public peril exists in other countries, in France this fear takes on particular significance. As Hughes Lagrange points out, "the theme of insecurity appeared in several western European countries from the middle of the 1970s. But it is in France where it has the most effect on public opinion and finds the most resonance in the whole of social life" (unless noted otherwise, all translations are mine) ("le thème de l'insécurité est apparu dans plusieurs pays d'Europe occidentale à partir du milieu des années 70. Mais c'est en France qu'il acquiert le plus d'emprise sur l'opinion, trouve le plus de résonance dans l'ensemble de la vie sociale") (122). In general terms, the notion of *insécurité* has been largely constructed by conservative politicians, with conservative newspapers like *Le Figaro* reflecting and promoting these fears. As Ellen Willis affirms, "crime has always been an issue of the Right. Fear of crime, while it has not solely propelled the Right into power, has contributed significantly to creating a generalized anxiety about insecurity and social breakdown" (54). France is no exception, as several criminal researchers have pointed out (see Mucchielli). But what is this feeling of *insécurité*, and how may it be characterized? Asked how he would define *sécurité*, the Minister of the Interior at the time, Pierre Joxe, explained: "To be safe is to be sheltered and to know it. Or believe it. It is to be reassured. It is therefore very subjective: who can say he is, or believe himself to be safe from death?" ("Être en sécurité, c'est être à l'abri et le savoir. Ou le croire. C'est être rassuré. C'est donc très subjectif: qui peut se dire, ou se croire à l'abri de la mort?") (Guilledoux 178). In an interview that followed Joxe's comments, Robert Pandraud (the delegated Minister of Security) described *sécurité* as "the protection of people and things, as well as civil peace" ("la protection des personnes et des biens, ainsi que la paix civile") (181). The contrast between *feeling safe* and actually *being protected* highlights an important distinction in how the government reacts to and attempts to prevent crime. On the one hand, it asks people to take responsibility to build communities, and on the other, it attempts to establish a police state to ensure the psychological comfort of its citizens. Stemming from an overall feeling of fear, then, the public's relationship to crime and insecurity rests on a combination of social factors. As Lagrange indicates, *insécurité* feeds on economic instability, crises of identity, and changes in urban sociability, issues of growing importance in the 1980s (122). Above all, it is the media's depiction of these components that informs the public and endeavors to shape its perception of crime.

Feelings of *insécurité* are exaggerated by senseless crimes that defy rationality. Both the Paulin and Succo *affaires* are characterized by the "senseless" and "cool" manner in which the murders were committed; neither criminal gave a reason for his violent actions, nor was the public able to assign meaning to their acts. Unlike the *crimes de délinquance* committed by "troubled youth," which have remained at a steady rate for the last century, these motiveless murders seem to have drastically increased over the last two decades. While this statistical increase reflects new technologies that allow police to track and solve murders (Mucchielli 16), the sheer number of these murders provides fodder for fear-inspired stories about crime waves. These distinct crimes thus represent the growing menace of motiveless murders, which has heightened public insecurity in a new and different way. The notoriety and prominence of these two *affaires* in the public sphere (ranging from front-page stories and magazine issues to television specials and political commentary) allow us to examine a broad range of public response to this particular type of murder and its mediation. By linking these cases together and placing them in the larger political and social context of the 1980s, then, it is clear that the *fait divers* is used as a tool for upholding dominant ideology: that is, by creating a climate of insecurity, state authority is constructed, legal control is expanded, and alternative politics are quieted. In this way, writes criminologist Ray Surette, "the media establish powerful frames for perceiving the world while they control the distribution of shared social knowledge" (xvii). The rise of the right wing and the increasing public saturation of crime by the media also provoked resistant readings of these crimes that highlight how the *fait divers* is manipulated to promote political, social, and cultural ideology. Analyzing all of these factors (media representation, political response, critical reaction, public controversy), we see how these authors and filmmakers directly subvert the media's alliance with political groups which shape our fascination with and increasing appetite for reports depicting crime. These artistic works highlight how the media—and society as a whole—use the criminal to frame larger debates.

Given the new media environment, then, what is the significance and role of the *fait divers* in contemporary society? How does the media construct and feed the public's fascination with these crime stories? Jean Baudrillard sensationally claims that the *fait divers* has become "absolute banality," that in contrast with earlier periods, when it was considered exceptional, today's *fait divers* is forgotten soon after its initial media appearance. Calling it an ordinary fascination ("la fascination ordinaire") ("Cool Killers" 143), Baudrillard concludes that "It is no longer spectacular in the sense that there's no scene or scenography, but it's very fascinating . . . cancer, tuberculosis led to a whole kind of romanticism. One could still make things literary, now no, it's simply obscene, there's nothing left to do" ("Ça n'est plus spectaculaire au sens où il n'y a plus de scène ni de scénographie, mais c'est très fascinant . . . le cancer, le tuberculose, ont donné lieu à tout un romantisme. On pouvait encore littérariser ces choses, maintenant non, c'est simplement obscène, il n'y a plus rien à faire") ("Cool Killers" 143). Thus, according to Baudrillard, the ordinary nature of today's *fait divers*, due in part to its mediation and proliferation, stalls its ability to achieve an important stature. Given Baudrillard's subsequent conclusion, that such banality cannot be made cinematic or literary, what is the effect of the literary or cinematic text that does reenact the contemporary *fait divers*? How does this work address the media's impact on the crime story, and what kinds of critical negotiations might arise for readers and spectators of these rewritings? In looking at the artistic rearticulations of the crime story, this book addresses a component of crime discourse that is habitually neglected; indeed, Baudrillard's previous statement denies the very possibility of such a literature. Although the artist's role in influencing the public discourse is frequently discounted and likewise difficult to determine, the importance of incorporating artistic productions into discussions about crime cannot be understated. The artist's role in interpreting and challenging the dominant discourse on crime merits an in-depth examination, something that has not yet been accomplished.

Both *J'ai pas sommeil* and *Roberto Zucco* were accused of presenting "detached" or "non-judgmental" portrayals of the criminal, prompting some reviewers to question whether these rewritings signal a general trend towards the depiction of the criminal as a hero. Although the subject of media headlines and public rumor and discussion, the "heroization" of criminals is rarely the subject of academic research, as evidenced by the small number of articles and books devoted to this subject. One exception is Paul Kooistra's work (*Criminals as Heroes: Structure, Power, and Identity,* 1989), which traces the making of three American criminals into heroes (Jesse James, Butch Cassidy, and Billy the Kid). According to Kooistra, few criminals actually attain the status of criminal-heroes, which he defines as persons who "violate the law but who represent a 'higher' justice. . . . The legitimacy of the state is not challenged, only the corrupt practices of the oppressors of the people. Regardless of how many men they have murdered or robberies they committed for personal gain, these are attributes imputed to the heroic criminal" (9). According to this definition, which finds echoes in Hobsbawm (1969) and Quinney (1975), a hero must represent a higher law, signifying justice at its finest. Consequently, neither criminal in the cases that I examine corresponds to this definition, as their crimes fall into the category of motiveless acts and senseless killings. Yet despite this departure from Kooistra's accepted definition, we cannot ignore the labels of hero that befall many of today's criminals, and Roberto Succo in particular.

As Ralph Hyatt claims in an article bemoaning the "hypnotic attraction" of evil, criminals too often figure as contemporary heroes. As Hyatt explains, "Typically, adoration is reserved for God and divine-like beings. We revere parents, siblings are held dear, spouses loved, and friends admired, but adoration, which connotes a quality of worship, is the emotion set aside for the supernatural—or those, like heroes, who seem to approach the supernatural. . . . What is most interesting, if not bothersome, is that not only have our examinations in these matters been watered down embarrassingly, but the most unqualified—namely criminals—indiscriminately have been elevated to the status of hero" (36). Hyatt's focus on the sweeping elevation of criminals to heroes suggests that contemporary society is undergoing a change in its definition of heroism. Indeed, he provocatively asks, "Is the definition of 'hero' significantly changing before our very eyes? Will historians in the next millennium pinpoint the word's altered meaning to this century?" (36). Hyatt's questions are more reminiscent of media sensationalism than careful research, however, and his determinations are mere speculations, not based on any statistics, but rather on general impressions. If we look to history, there is a steady number of French criminals raised to a "heroic" status, although few of these fit Kooistra's definition of a criminal-hero: Gilles de Rais, Violette de Nozières, Henri Landru, Marcel Petiot, Marcel Barbeault, the Papin sisters. In fact, although many of their crimes were committed during the first half of the twentieth century, these early criminals have more in common with Hyatt's understanding of modern criminals. Instead of attempting to prove an increased public interest in criminals, then, my research counters this mainstream discourse and instead points to how this kind of sensational propaganda is reproduced in the media to generate public alarm and *insécurité*. Looking to how artistic representations of these criminal affairs subvert the media's efforts to control public sentiment, we will see that Denis and Koltès contest these dominant readings, which stress the immediacy of crime. While each rewriting presents a unique representation of the public's relationship to the crime story, they together form a body that speaks to issues neglected by the mainstream media, whose sensational and shallow representations of the crime story foster reaction (about *insécurité*, immigration, and ethnicity) over reflection (about why such crimes occur, our role in them, and how they are articulated). Contrary to popular criticism, then, these works neither render the crime "spectacular," nor do they restore it a banality *à la Baudrillard*. Instead, the poignant questions that they pose recenter the *fait divers* in a political and cultural context that encourages reflection about how we read crime in today's contemporary culture. The public's response to these texts, whether in the form of protest or disregard, stands testimony to the artist's ability to accurately reflect reality.

Redefining the *Fait divers*

The term *fait divers* does not have an English counterpart. Its closest translation is "news item" or "news brief," but this does not adequately describe the term, which is distinguished by its negative reputation. Although first termed in 1859 with the emergence of the popular press, *faits divers* have been traced back to Gutenberg's invention of the printing press in 1453, when they first became items of popular interest (Lever 3). In contrast with historical news, the *fait divers* typically represents news of minor importance; it may include items such as murders, suicides, and accidents, as well as more humorous or odd coincidences. In his book *De la fable au fait divers* (1991), Christian Vandendorpe divides the *fait divers* into two categories: *affective*, those events whose themes include the monstrous, supernatural, horrific, magical, and bloody; and *cognitive*, events which conjure up emotions of surprise, incredulity, laughter, and tragedy (13). In this book, I focus on these *affective* crimes, and I examine strictly sensational *faits divers* that have received the broadest attention by the media and therefore the public. Often called monstrous, these *grandes affaires* are particularly unsettling for the public because of their horrific and often inexplicable nature. In his seminal essay "Structure of the *Fait-Divers*" (1964), Roland Barthes also separates the *fait divers* into two categories, those defined by a causal relationship (*relation de causalité*) and those characterized by their coincidental nature (*relation de coïncidence*). Explaining that the *fait divers* is distinguished by its closed structure, Barthes notes that its nature is self-referential. He writes, "It contains all its knowledge in itself: no need to know anything about the world in order to consume a *fait-divers*. It refers formally to nothing other than itself" (186). Here Barthes's definition applies primarily to the coincidental *fait divers* rather than the large-scale crimes that become *affaires*, and a distinction between the two should be emphasized. Nonetheless, this statement remains problematic in that it seems to advocate reading the *fait divers* as an a-historic item that occurs in a vacuum, when in fact the news brief (or "filler," as it is often translated) communicates profoundly about society. So although the *fait divers* does not refer *formally* to anything else, a more profound look into its structure, presentation, and reading proves that it connotes substantial information about the contemporary world. In this ambiguous zone that Barthes describes, "the event is experienced as a sign whose content is nonetheless uncertain" (194). While Barthes concludes that the *fait divers* is meaning without significance, he nonetheless classifies it as literature, "even if that literature is reputed to be bad" (194). Barthes's conclusion, that the *fait divers* is meaning with an uncertain significance, is similar to Baudrillard's statement that the *fait divers* no longer holds the public fascination. Like Barthes, Baudrillard notes that "the content of the messages, the signified of the signs, are largely immaterial" (*Consumer Society* 34). However, Baudrillard breaks from Barthes by stating that "we are not engaged in them, and the media do not involve us in the world, but offer for our consumption signs as signs, albeit signs accredited with the guarantee of the real" (34). Where Barthes and Baudrillard part ways, then, is in the meaning of the *fait divers*. While Barthes writes that "a crime without a cause is a crime that is forgotten" (189), Baudrillard claims that the *fait divers* is forgotten because it *has no meaning*. In other words, Barthes finds that the *fait divers* disappears because we cannot determine its cause. He explains that "this is why, in the *fait-divers*, contrary to the novel, a crime without a cause is not so much inexplicable as unexplained: the causal 'delay' does not aggravate the crime, it destroys it . . . the *fait-divers* then vanishes, precisely because in reality its fundamental relation is exhausted" (189). By differentiating between a crime that is not explained and one that is unexplainable, Barthes makes an important distinction that is glossed over by Baudrillard. Barthes acknowledges that the *fait divers* is not often read at a deeper level, but Baudrillard erroneously insists that the possibility of such a reading no longer exists, a point that I will return to in chapter 2. This difference, although seemingly minor, is significant to how the *fait divers* is processed by society.

In stressing that the *fait divers* is not read profoundly by the larger public, Barthes does not preclude that it cannot or should not be studied in this manner; rather it is important to not confuse the critic with the reader. As he elaborates, "an ideology and a psychoanalysis of the *fait-divers* are possible, but they would concern a world of which knowledge is never anything but intellectual, analytical, elaborated at second-hand by the person who speaks of the *fait-divers*, not by the person who consumes it" (186). On the other hand, Barthes assumes an uninformed reader, and today's public is far more media-savvy than his contemporaries. While it is therefore safe to presume that a significant segment of the population may not analyze the crime news in depth, it is wrong to assume that this kind of analysis does not take place. Jack Katz has shown that the evidence is in fact otherwise: readers do *not* ignore crime news or read with only superficial interest. His research shows that the public's recall of crime stories far exceeds recall of stories on other matters such as education, state government, and Middle East politics (57). So while the content may not be clearly defined and we may not know what the signs mean, we *are* trying to make meaning.

Exactly what purpose the *fait divers* serves and what interest it arouses have been the subject of historical, sociological, and psychological inquiry in recent years. Beginning with Barthes's 1964 essay, French critics began to define the *fait divers* and situate its function within the printed media. Its popular roots and familiar language make the *fait divers* easily accessible to the general public, but while its universality assures its familiarity, it also creates a distance, for the *fait divers* always happens to someone else. As Sylvie Dion has shown, the *fait divers* is fascinating precisely because of this illusion of proximity (47). At the same time, however, the *fait divers* may represent a split with society. Auclair explains that "the crime story stems from some rupture of the ordered universe where man finds his security but with fear he nevertheless dreams of transcending" ("le fait divers est toujours de quelque rupture de l'univers réglé où l'homme trouve sa sécurité mais dont avec crainte il rêve cependant de s'affranchir") (44). The public thus uses the crime story to escape the mundane world. Along these lines, we may see the *fait divers* as a neutralizing component of the hegemonic discourse, relating society's mores while at the same time reinforcing its conservative values. In other words, the *fait divers* functions as a sedative, stabilizing public action by reminding society of the consequences of its actions. Katz has posited similarly that the media's portrayal of murder provides the occasion for mass reactions against deviance. Fulfilling the public's appetite for news, such stories "instruct readers on the nature of the limits of personal competence and sensibility," while also offering them the chance to generalize and dialogue about crime. He explains that "crime is made news by a modern public searching for resources to work out sensibilities routinely made problematic in everyday modern life" (48). The *fait divers* thus provides a kind of instructive entertainment. Drawing on these various approaches, this project presupposes that the public's fascination with the *fait divers* derives from a natural human interest, one that has been documented for centuries. Although the public uses the *fait divers* for a variety of reasons (amusement, historical vividness, the calming effects of watching evil in others, the increasing circulation and availability of these stories), I am primarily interested in the media's role in shaping this public fascination, as it has significantly changed in recent years.

In contrast with earlier periods when the *fait divers* was announced in public squares or appeared solely in newspapers, today's public is daily witness to the proliferation of these countless sound bites, stemming from not only from the printed press, but also from radio and television, and now the Internet. Barthes wrote in 1964 that the earlier definition of the news brief "does not account for the extraordinary promotion of the *fait-divers* in today's press" (185). Since his article, media forms have continued to evolve, as reflected in the new location of the *fait divers* in the newspaper. Until very recently, most French newspapers maintained a special section devoted to *faits divers*, but today we find that *faits divers* are rarely confined to a specific area of the paper. Instead, the crime story is diffused throughout the contemporary newspaper, where it has become generic news. Likewise, television, which previously dedicated a portion of the news to *faits divers*, often opens its nightly news reports with these items, and has now begun devoting entire programs to the *fait divers*. Beginning in 1990 with *La Trace* (TF1), French "reality shows" about crime have proliferated; more recent programs, such as *État de Choc* (M6), *Le Droit de savoir: Faits divers* (TF1), *Ça arrive près de chez vous* (FR2), and *Faites entrer l'accusé* (FR2), attest to the public's growing fascination with the *fait divers*. In contrast with the literary and cinematic works that I will investigate, however, reality TV never calls into question the nature of the crime; it merely reproduces it, projecting the recorded images onto screen. As Nichols confirms, "it is never critical of the hierarchy" (59). Instead, it is the public debate in the French press about the so-called danger of these shows that informs my research, for the artists who rewrite the *fait divers* are accused of this same crime. While Nichols writes that "reality TV may be as sensational as it wishes; it may be as seemingly de-centered, a-historical, and futureless as it chooses" (59), the public reaction is not so clear. The critical response to these new programs suggests that the public is not yet at ease with ahistorical, fluid representations of crime. According to French media critic Hugh Dauncey, who presents the first overview of French reality television, the reality show is primarily problematic in its unfaithful representation of reality; it is the filmed reconstructions of events, for instance, that have received the most criticism from government officials. In relating the controversy surrounding the reality show *Témoin no. 1*, Dauncey writes that "the presence of *gendarmes* and *juges* live in the studio is seen by some as encouraging an unacceptable confusion in the minds of the viewers between what remains a reality show (however serious) and the normal legitimate procedures of policing and justice" (91). It is thus the confusion created between reality and fiction that causes discomfort among critics, or the "blurring of boundaries" that is mirrored in press reports.

The principal point of convergence with media and literature is that both are concerned with notions of truth. The media, while increasingly under scrutiny for its ability to accurately portray events, is nonetheless imbued with a stronger sense of truth than is literature. This is due in part to the journalistic focus on the details of the crime itself. Rarely does a *fait divers* attempt to delve into the psychology of the criminal; the perpetrator is instead carefully constructed as an Other and cast aside in his difference (here I use the term Other to refer to how the conservative media in particular posits the criminal in inverse relation to the general public). In this space, where he becomes an object of fascination and repulsion, the criminal is spoken *for* rather than spoken *with*, classified and labeled by his crimes alone. As Kristeva writes of the Other, "You are the object of fascination: one notices you, one talks about you, one hates or admires you, or both at the same time. But you are not an ordinary Mr. and Mrs. Nobody. You are a problem, a desire—positive or negative, never neutral" (39). As I will show, institutions "Other" the criminal by gazing at him through clinical, judicial, and mediated structures that construct him in diametric opposition to the public. Foucault reveals that the notion of the criminal is a product of certain procedures and rules that form the discourse of the penal system, a discourse that is recirculated by the media. Having labeled and cast out the criminal according to a binary system of classification, then the media turns to other details of the *fait divers*. It concerns itself with the who/when/where/what and wow of the crime, and in this way, the media leads the reader to invent his or her own psychology of the criminal (the "why"), based on often irrelevant but leading or weighted details that posit the criminal's radical Otherness. Newspapers will often include extraneous information, such as a criminal's sexual identity (if he is not heterosexual), ethnic background (if he is not white) or religious orientation (if he is not Christian), in order to elicit a reaction from its readers. Tabloid-like newspapers such as *France-Soir* attempt to elicit emotion from their readers and push them to draw conclusions about the crime, while *Le Monde* routinely omits these extraneous and provocative details. It is perhaps this two-dimensional depiction of the criminal that intrigues the literary author or filmmaker to rewrite the crime story, for although they are the writers of these *affaires*, Denis and Koltès are also and perhaps more fundamentally readers of the *fait divers*. Both artists attest to having read many of the same newspaper articles cited in this book, which they reportedly used to create their own interpretations of the *affaires*. On one level, then, we may analyze *J'ai pas sommeil* and *Roberto Zucco* as responses to the *fait divers* that offer a distinct understanding of the crime story. On a secondary level, the characters within these two rewritings represent an additional level of interpretation by presenting the crime story prior to its mediation. *J'ai pas sommeil* and *Roberto Zucco* thus function as *mises-en-abîme* of how the *fait divers* is mediated. If we look at how as *readers* of the *fait divers* Denis and Koltès portray how their characters interact with the criminal, we see how the *fait divers* may be freely interpreted by the public.

In one way, then, the artist's focus on the criminal mirrors public fascination with the *fait divers*. Aware of the attraction and repulsion of the *fait divers*, these artists capitalize on the reader's or spectator's interest, which is later thwarted through detached and nonjudgmental depictions of the criminal. For this reason, literature and film may be at their most popular when they tap into these moments of public fascination by questioning the place of "evil" in humankind, and there are numerous examples that attest to this interest. On the other hand, the author and filmmaker whom I study move beyond the reality-show depiction of the *fait divers* by fleshing out the criminals, a distinction that marks a significant departure from films and television shows that "represent the increasing commodification of crime and crime-related consumables at the expense of escalating racial divisions and escalating fears about crime" (Tunnel 118). Whether we read these artistic depictions of the criminal as sympathetic, neutral, or condemning, Denis and Koltès present a fresh and subversive look at the criminal. Challenging the sketch-like personage that the media creates, they encourage the reader or spectator to confront the criminal in a different manner that rewrites his Otherness. Radically, the characters in *J'ai pas sommeil* and *Roberto Zucco* ignore the media's intermediary role as a determiner of public meaning, and they choose to personally interact with the criminal. In refusing to cater to the media's binary depiction of the murderer, Denis and Koltès present a new relationship between the criminal and the public.

Theorizing the *Fait Divers*

The prevalence, or rather the omnipresence, of the *fait divers* in contemporary society is pivotal to this study because of my focus on reception and rearticulation. Continuously rewritten and recirculated by a variety of media, the "truth" of the sensationalized *fait divers* is in constant flux. In fact, there is no one "truth" that may be culled from the *fait divers*, but rather a large number of historically significant readings. Each new piece of information that is printed, televised, filmed, or spoken about the crime story serves to alter and shape the public's understanding of it; the discourse surrounding the event thus determines our sense of what is real. In examining how meaning is made through the sensational *fait divers*, then, it is most useful to employ what may be termed a context-activated cultural studies model to engage with the crime story and its rewritings (here I borrow both Tony Bennett's conception of the "activated text" and Janet Staiger's explanation of a "context-activated theory"). This approach emphasizes my conviction that the text is not a vessel of inherent meaning, and that the wide variety of responses to it are structured by a complex set of cultural, social, and political systems. Examining as texts both the discourse surrounding the *fait divers* and its artistic rewritings, this model is effective in its emphasis on the fluid nature of the *fait divers*. My understanding of this approach—whereby the text is viewed as a process rather than a finite object—is greatly informed by John Fiske, Michel Foucault, Tony Bennett, and Janet Staiger, critics whose research in discourse, media, and cultural studies illustrates how we might begin to read these crime stories and their artistic rewritings as sites of discursive resistance.

In *Media Matters* (1997), Fiske analyzes how several American "media events" (the term suggests the overlap between "real" events and their representations) are circulated, read, and contested in the context of contemporary techno-struggles. Fiske's work is significant because it takes into account the power struggles inherent in media representations of these events. Emphasizing that the media does not merely "circulate discourse and make it available for analysis, [but] it also produces knowledge and applies power" (217), Fiske reminds us that the power to speak, to know, and to see are politically and technologically connected. Thus, we cannot separate the *fait divers* from the discourses that produce it. By stressing discourse's relationship to power ("it is never conducted on a level field") (6), Fiske explains that "the way an event is put into discourse is never determined by the nature of the experience, but always by the social power to give it one set of meanings rather than another" (4). In other words, we must always look to the set of social practices that constructs contemporary ideology. Fiske's approach to reading media events echoes Michel Foucault's work on discourse and power. Foucault asserts that there are three primary systems of exclusion that influence discourse: prohibited words (*la parole interdite*), the division of madness (*le partage de la folie*), and the will to truth (*la volonté de vérité*). The production of discourse is thus controlled, selected, organized, and redistributed by institutional procedures whose aim is to expose the innate danger and, accordingly, power of discourse. As Foucault writes, "this will to truth, like the other systems of exclusion, relies on institutional support: it is both reinforced and accompanied by whole strata of practices" (*Archeology of Knowledge* 219). In the case of the sensationalized *fait divers*, the media capitalize on the criminal's difference to Other him, placing him outside the realm of the norm. Once the criminal is characterized as an Other in this binary system of exclusion, he becomes an object of fascination, which in turn leads to the production of a *volonté de vérité*. The public's desire not only to know about the *fait divers*, but to know "the truth," is thus heightened by the combined practices of the media, police, and judicial systems, which insist upon a single meaning. Ironically, it is the multiple effects of this system that further distance the public from the truth.

Using this approach to analyze France's representations of the crime story in the 1980s, it is clear how the *fait divers* functions as a strategic tool for political manipulation. This method plainly demonstrates that the *fait divers* does not contain meaning in itself, but rather shifts in meaning according to the discourses that create and contest it. As Surette writes, these struggles for meaning involve "claims and claimsmakers who compete with one another to have their particular construction of reality widely accepted" (xvi–xvii). Surette stresses that "claimsmakers do more than draw attention to particular social conditions, they shape our sense of what the problem is" (xvii). When we examine how these various "claimsmakers" (law enforcement, politicians, judges, psychiatrists, journalists) reflect contemporary political and cultural struggles by vying for public attention, we must pay very close attention to discourse; we must analyze both what is said and what is not. Like Fiske's emphasis on how discourse produces meaning, Rose underscores the importance of differentiating between the facts of criminal cases and the discourses that produce them. As Rose writes, "In this whirlwind of produced, heightened, and repeated anxieties, it is essential to take a step back and distinguish between criminal acts and the social languages used to talk about crime and criminals. It is important not to lose sight of the fact that these are not one and the same. In other words, crimes taking place are not the same thing as the perception of these crimes, nor are they equivalent to the process of counting, naming, categorizing and labeling criminal activity" (150). Underlining the role of discourse in creating meaning, Rose reminds us to separate the actual events from their circulation in the media. This distinction echoes Ellen Willis's important distinction between "crime" and "crime": "'Crime,' the social issue, the social crisis, the source of recurrent and escalating waves of panic, revulsion, fury and angst—is not the same as crime. . . . The acts that count as crime in the public's imagination . . . are those in which the collision of particular criminals with particular victims is unpredictable, uncontrollable, seemingly arbitrary and meaningless" (51–52). Only by deconstructing the diffusion of the crime or *fait divers* can we analyze the production of the event and begin to uncover the many layers that cloak its symbolic relevance.

For the purposes of this study, I have contained my examination of the media's transmission of the *fait divers* to widely circulating press reports about the crime stories. In contrast with the *presse de masse* or *presse de sensation* (i.e., *France-Soir*, *France-Dimanche*, *Paris-Match*), *Le Monde* and *Le Figaro* are considered *presse sérieuse* or *presse blanche* (Auclair 149). While these *presse blanche* representations of crime are considerably more neutral than their sensational counterparts, their relative objectivity often masks a specific political ideology. This more narrow focus allows me to look at how the country's most dominant discourses use the *fait divers* as a terrain of struggle and resistance for political and cultural meaning. In analyzing these conflicting discourses, then, I center my analysis on *Le Monde* and *Le Figaro*, whose generally opposing reports of these *faits divers* wholly illustrate how political discourse creates meaning; *Le Figaro*'s steady references to *insécurité*, for instance, starkly contrast *Le Monde*'s focus on combating racism and xenophobia. Similar to how discourse functions in the media, the artistic text that reinscribes the *fait divers* must be examined not as a self-contained entity, but rather as one that shifts in meaning according to who reads it and under what conditions it is read (or viewed). In practice, then, the reader's relationship to the text, and the discourse produced in relation to it, function to influence the reader's interpretation of the work. Whether, for example, the reader experiences the text before or after having read its reviews, has talked to his or her neighbors about the text, maintains a strong political or cultural affiliation, or is familiar with the events that prompted the work all sway the reader's interpretation of the play or film. While it is of course impossible to account for all of these factors, it is nonetheless critical to take them into consideration if we wish to arrive at a more accurate understanding of the text's reception. We cannot say that the text controls its readers, but on the contrary, that it is the product of what its readers and their experiences bring to it: the "meaning" lies somewhere in between the text and its readers.

This work is rooted in the framework of comparative cultural studies, as defined by Steven Tötösy de Zepetnek. As Tötösy writes, this approach "is performed in a contextual and relational construction and with a plurality of methods and approaches. . . . In comparative cultural studies it is the processes of communicative action(s) in culture and the how of these processes that constitute the main objectives of research and study" ("From Comparative Literature Today toward Comparative Cultural Studies," 235–67). Unlike traditional comparative studies, which focus on metaphorical argumentation, then, this approach is tied to the applications of these notions, so rather than centering my arguments on personal or hypothetical interpretations, my analysis is both contextual and empirical. In looking at the "how" rather than the "what," this approach examines what happens to these particular cultural products. How are they watched or read, and by whom? How are they criticized, discussed, and absorbed—or rejected? And, perhaps most importantly, in what ways do they become part of the culture at large?

Tony Bennett's work on James Bond as a cultural icon serves as an excellent model as to how to approach this kind of broad cultural study. Bennett challenges the idea that a text contains a predetermined meaning and demonstrates that *all* information relating to the text shapes how its readers interpret its meaning. In "Text and Social Process: The Case of James Bond," Bennett elaborates on this notion of the "activated text," which he also terms the "living life of the text." He explains that "to study the connection between literary phenomena and social processes requires that everything that has been said or written about a text, every context in which it has been inscribed by the uses to which it has been put, should, in principle, be regarded as relevant to and assigned methodological parity within such a study" (9). In accordance with Bennett's and Tötösy's frameworks of comparative cultural studies, which I use throughout this work, I have tried to look at all information produced about the textual rewritings of the Paulin and Succo *affaires*, including reviews, press releases, and interviews with the authors. There are nonetheless difficulties inherent in this analytical approach. Audience response is difficult to determine and may not accurately be discovered through ticket sales and critical reaction; instead, the production and distribution of a film or literary work bear considerably on response and relative interest, as do the political and cultural discourses of the historical moment. I therefore investigate a variety of factors that may influence reception and response, hoping to at least account for the wide diversity of factors that come into play and thus avoid the simplistic causal relationship that my project calls into question. Bennett refers to these other texts as "incrustations" (citing Pierre Macherey), emphasizing that they have been built up around a text and are thus inseparable from it (9). Looking at *J'ai pas sommeil* and *Roberto Zucco*, we discover that these works are "encrusted" with reviews and interviews that influence public response, often before the public's first encounter with the text; this notion of incrustation will be particularly helpful in examining the response to *Roberto Zucco*, whose production was shrouded with protests, political posturing, and media hype. In keeping with Bennett's approach, then, I analyze not merely these texts about the *fait divers*, but also the public debate (or lack thereof) about their meaning and production. Like Fiske's emphasis on examining what is voiced as well as what is not, I include speculation (based on political and social circumstances) about what did and did not happen (why, for instance, *Roberto Zucco* was protested and *J'ai pas sommeil* not). In this manner, the literary text or film is examined not as a finished product, but as a component in a system of relations that includes both production and reception.

Janet Staiger echoes Bennett's notion of the "activated" or "living life" of the text in her book *Interpreting Films* (1992). Staiger calls Bennett's research "context-activated," stating that in this theory, "readers are equally significant in creating meaning, that historical context is very significant for the interaction, and that meaning or significance is 'in' that contextual interaction" (36). In explaining the importance of employing what she terms "historical interpretive strategies," Staiger writes that "cultural artifacts are not containers with immanent meaning, that variations among interpretations have historical bases for the differences, and that differences and change are not idiosyncratic but due to social, political, and economic conditions, as well as to constructed identities such as gender, sexual preference, race, ethnicity, class, and nationality" (xi). Thus, rather than focusing on a single meaning laid in a text, Staiger suggests that we look at the many levels of meaning that a text may convey. Not only must these be studied and imagined, but above all related to a variety of spectator positions that influence reception; in examining *J'ai pas sommeil*, for instance, it is important to examine the critical response of some homosexual men who were angered at Denis's portrayal of a gay serial killer. While Staiger and Bennett share similar theoretical concerns that are useful to my project, I find Staiger's emphasis on reception studies particularly well-articulated for taking into account the varied public response to these two works. Staiger illustrates that reception studies "does not attempt to construct a generalized, systematic explanation of how individuals might have comprehended texts, or possibly someday will, but rather how they actually have understood them" (8). She thus distinguishes reception studies from the majority of reception theory and reader-response criticism, which focuses on reader psychologies and ahistorical textual analysis. While acknowledging the importance of these approaches in advancing critical research about readers, Staiger finds these views largely problematic because of their reliance on "ideal" (or imaginary) readers. This distinction points to another important argument of this model, the distinction between real and imaginary spectators. Staiger labels "ideal readers" those who are "exemplary" in that they behave in established manners, learn about themselves through the text, and reflect the author's ideology (25). Moreover, these ideal readers do not reflect the experiences of real readers (who act according to specific personal, cultural, and political circumstances), but instead reveal "more about the critic and the critical method than about the activities of readers" (26). Many critics who refer to ideal readers do not distinguish between (or among) gender, class, race, or sexuality, instead assuming that all readers in a group do the same thing. Furthermore, they do not differentiate earlier readers from today's media-savvy public, which is more cynical because of its exposure to the media. Instead of resorting to these ambiguous methods, then, Staiger advocates creating a space for describing the relations among texts and historical readers, or among films and actual spectators. I therefore use this model to look at how various audiences—rather than imaginary spectators—have actually responded to these works.

One problem that arises in this approach is how we may determine *any* meaning in these texts. Having stated that each reader's own experiences function in combination with a variety of cultural and political factors to influence his or her reading, how do we center our analysis on a dominant reading (and is this even necessary?)? Moreover, how can we discuss the significance of these texts, which rewrite the *fait divers*? They, too, are subject to personal and social factors that the artists themselves cannot determine. Here I draw upon Stuart Hall's idea of the "preferred reading" or dominant interpretation of the work (35). Hall argues that due to a text's properties (e.g., narration, chronology, characterization), we may arrive at a "preferred reading" that is most consistent with dominant ideology. This idea furthermore allows us to talk about dominant readings of the *fait divers* without negating alternative subject positions, for Hall's precision emphasizes that these preferred readings can be refused by readers or spectators. Most importantly, Hall's idea of a "preferred reading" allows me to address conclusions *within* a politically and culturally motivated historical context, which is not inconsistent with my overall approach. Using Staiger's model of "real" audiences and Bennett's notion of an "activated" text, my project moves beyond what Bennett calls "the world of texts" (3) to explore the complex set of relationships between creation, production, and interpretation that make up the construction of the *fait divers*. Within this framework of cultural studies, I have integrated analyses of social conditions (governmental response to crime, political discourse about how to combat crime), audience response (critical reaction, public protest), and textual analysis (discourse, both cinematic and literary) to complete my research. Endeavoring to look at all the "incrustations" that create the larger text, I find this model particularly useful, as it allows me to consider 1) how media representations of the *fait divers* reflect the struggle to create dominant political, historical, and cultural meanings, 2) how artistic rewritings of the *fait divers* create new representations that contest dominant readings of the crime, and 3) how readers and spectators may use these incrustations to shape their understanding of the crime story. By using this broad approach, I am able to assess the multiple layers of meaning that contribute to the status of the *fait divers* as a site of discursive and social struggle.

While there has been important research done on the *fait divers* in the last twenty years, there remain significant gaps of knowledge that have not been addressed. As I have shown, critics have begun a broad examination of the *fait divers* as a genre, with researchers exploring the sociological and psychological role of the *fait divers* in history as well as in the present day. Crime has become a popular topic, and France is no exception to this trend. The following publications provide just a sample of recent works that detail this rising interest in the crime story: *Fait divers en République* (M'sili, 2000), *Le Nouvel Almanach du crime et des faits divers* (Bourgoin, 2001), *La France des tueurs en série* (Vézard, 2002), *Médias et violences urbaines* (Peralva and Macé, 2002), *Dans la tête du tueur: Sur les traces de Francis Heaulme* (Abgrall, 2002) and *Vertigo*'s special edition on the *fait divers* (June 2004). While much is made of the widespread problem of crime, very little, on the other hand, has been said about alternative readings of the *fait divers* that subvert and interrogate the media's representations of crime. The weaving of literature and film with the *fait divers* in French studies is one such area that has been almost entirely neglected. With the exception of British scholar David Walker's *Outrage and Insight: Modern French Writers and the "Fait divers"* (1995) and US-American Joel Black's *The Aesthetics of Murder: A Study in Romantic Literature and Contemporary Culture* (1991), the subject remains virtually untouched. Walker gives an admirable review of the *fait divers* throughout the nineteenth and twentieth centuries, but his coverage of the crime story stops at the 1970s and moreover does not touch on the intertextuality between the *fait divers* and its rewritings. Black's study focuses on writers and filmmakers from various nationalities to show how they have made crime into an aesthetic object; some of these works are based on actual *faits divers* and others on fictional crimes. His presentation of murder as an object of study beyond the moral-rational and towards the aesthetic-critical offers ample proof of the importance of such an approach, but his focus on artists who deliberately turn murder into "beautiful acts" remains outside the range of my investigation; although Denis and Koltès have been accused of aestheticizing crime, their works instead implicate the media in this role. Therefore, while these studies offer much-needed insight into an essentially void area of study, my own work goes well beyond the scope of current research, both expanding and revising earlier studies. This book thus addresses the *fait divers* from a new perspective that both enhances current research and breaks new ground.

My initial interest in this project stems from concerns about the media's increased dominance and proliferation in recent years; French critics and scholars such as Baudrillard and Bourdieu apprise and warn the public of this growing public menace on a regular basis. In *On Television*, for instance, Bourdieu writes that "so much emphasis on headlines [*faits divers*] and so much filling up of previous time with empty air—with nothing or almost nothing—shunts aside relevant news, that is, the information that all citizens ought to have in order to exercise their democratic rights" (18). Some critics have expressed a fear that the media's increasing power strips readers of their critical abilities, making the general public dangerously susceptible to this media rhetoric. Unable to decipher these manipulative messages, the public is presumably in danger of falling prey to this narrow view of the world, one that adheres to the status quo, refuses other voices, and promotes a fear-inspiring agenda that paralyzes the public. My resistance to this view is not that the media does not maintain and continue to gain increasing power in the public arena; certainly, its growing diffusion and proliferation is undeniable. Rather, I take issue with the implied assumptions about the public's inability to decipher media discourse. Thus, while I show throughout this project that the media—and the conservative media in particular—endeavors to manipulate public sentiment, I do not believe that readers/spectators necessarily accept, espouse, or replicate these views. Indeed, it is my belief that contemporary readers and spectators are much more analytical and even cynical than they are often perceived and depicted. Both of the artistic rewritings that I examine in this project embody this perspective, offering examples of characters that resist the media and rebel against law enforcement.

When I began this project, I adopted the working title of "Listening to the Other," with the idea of highlighting how Denis and Koltès create a new space for theorizing the criminal. I wanted to emphasize how these artists offer the criminal a voice, which is silenced in the majority of media reports. As this project has evolved, however, I have found that this title no longer suggests what I wish to express, and it may even connote the opposite of what I had intended. In an article entitled "Speaking for Others," critic Linda Alcoff explains that "to promote 'listening to' as opposed to speaking for essentializes the oppressed (or silenced) as nonideologically constructed subjects" (22). Thus, the criminal is not *listened to* but rather *spoken for*, which again implies an element of inequality that I do not find to be present in these rewritings. Rather, Denis and Koltès create characters that speak *to* the criminal, which may be metaphorically seen in their gestures and regard as well as in their words. Alcoff references Gayatri Chakravorty Spivak's article "Can the Subaltern Speak?" (which prefers this "speaking to") and concurs that "we should strive to create wherever possible the conditions for dialogue and the practice of speaking with and to rather than speaking for others" (23). Indeed, I find that these questions of "speaking to" and "speaking for" are at the heart of the controversy surrounding these literary and cinematic rewritings. These new rewritings subvert the most vocal claimsmakers (media, politicians, law enforcement) who practice "speaking for" in a binary system that silences other voices. In examining how the public has thus far responded to Denis's and Koltès's rewritings, then, this book attempts to answer questions that are often fluid and intangible, such as how the artist affects the reception and perception of crime, what the significance of the author's or filmmaker's returning to the crime holds, and above all, what the role of the *fait divers* is in a society increasingly saturated with mediated crime reports. In activating these *faits divers* within their many textual incrustations, I highlight the symbiotic relationship of politics, history, media, literature, criticism, and film. It is out of the desire to emphasize this interdependence that I began this project, and these *affaires* attest to the relationship between the artist and society at a time when literature is being increasingly removed from its sociological and historical origins. By analyzing these crimes in the broadest contexts of their activitations, I endeavor to show that the *fait divers* remains not only an important site of discursive struggle, but also a significant site for reader resistance in an age of increasing media and state control.

Chapter Two

Mediating Crime

As an account of a serial killer, the Paulin *affaire* represents a relatively new addition to contemporary French criminality. The term "serial killer" first appeared in France in 1980, and although the term "tueur en série" is now part of the French language, its entrance into French printed discourse as an English word makes its origins unmistakable. Current articles on serial killing in French interchange the two terms, and while this shift reflects the French government's stricter regulations on the use of English terms, I believe that this change also points to an integration of the concept into French culture at a more fundamental level. Until very recently, serial killing has been referred to as an "American crime" (see Levin and Fox), a correlation that seems to be confirmed by the relatively small number of serial killers in France in comparison to the United States. According to Hickey's 1990 research of serial killers worldwide, there were only three French serial killers in the twentieth century: Henri Landru (who killed over ten women between 1915 and 1922), Marcel Petiot (who committed over twenty-seven murders in the early 1940s), and Thierry Paulin (who murdered at least twenty women between 1984 and 1987) (259). Jenkins has attributed these differences to more relaxed libel laws and a greater awareness of serial killing in the United States (41). The French National Police's resident psychoanalyst and criminologist, Pierre Leclair, concurs with Jenkins, stating that "Germs existed before the invention of the microscope. Serial killers have always existed. Americans have the merit of having been the first to define and quantify the phenomenon" ("Les microbes existaient avant l'invention du microscope. Les tueurs en série ont toujours existé. Les Américains ont le mérite d'avoir été les premiers à définir et à quantifier le phénomène") (Vézard 13). In fact, there has been a string of serial killers recently uncovered in France. Some of the most mediated figures include Francis Heaulme (who killed ten people between 1984 and 1992), Patrice Alègre (son of a policeman who killed at least seven women between 1989 and 1997), Guy George ("le tueur de l'est parisien," who murdered seven women between 1991 and 1998), and Emile Louis (who killed between seven and seventeen young women between 1975 and 1999).

The relative jump in the percentage of this kind of murder has prompted a series of books that question the American nature of the crimes. Most point to France's outdated system of tracking criminals, which actually contributed to the delayed capture of Thierry Paulin. Despite the increased interest in serial killers, much of the information known about them is uncertain. As Hickey confirms in *Serial Murderers and Their Victims*, "much of what we 'know' about serial murder is based on misinformation and myth construction" (1). The serial killer is defined primarily by his keen intelligence and sheer disregard for human life; this indifferent attitude is particularly disconcerting for a public accustomed to assigning meaning to crime. In the Paulin *affaire*, for instance, the murderer's ability to dodge the police allowed the media to feed the public's growing alarm for over four years, turning this *fait divers* into an indicator of larger social problems, such as *insécurité* and racial tension.

In this chapter, I analyze the media's response to the Paulin *affaire,* reviewing the characteristics of this *fait divers* and how it was read and interpreted by the press, cultural critics, politicians, and law enforcement. Although this chapter explores a variety of media response to the events, I focus primarily on the daily newspapers *Le Monde* and *Le Figaro*, whose distinct and often opposing accounts of the *affaire* best illustrate how crime is manipulated to achieve specific political outcomes. By illustrating how Paulin is employed as a social signifier for racial and immigration issues, I show that Jean Baudrillard's reading of the *affaire* as "une banalité absolue" represents a shallow determination that mirrors the media's cursory examination of crime.

From *Fait Divers* to *Affaire*

In October of 1984, Germaine Petitot opened the door of her apartment in the 18th *arrondissement* to two young men, who bound, gagged, and beat her until she told them where her meager stash of money was hidden. Although Petitot survived the assault, she was too traumatized to remember the faces of her aggressors. Just hours after she was found, police uncovered the bodies of Anna Barbier-Ponthus, 83; and Germaine Cohen-Tanouji, 75, in the nearby 9th *arrondissement,* where they had been suffocated with a pillow. Two days later, while investigating an arson, firemen found the body of Suzanne Foucault, 89, who had been beaten and suffocated with a plastic bag. At this time, the events had not yet reached the front pages of the newspapers, primarily because the police had not been able to connect the murders to the same perpetrator. One month later, in early November 1984, police found the body of 71-year-old Iona Seicaresco, who had been brutally beaten and strangled to death with an electric cord. Several days later, again in the 18th *arrondissement*, 84-year-old Alice Benaïm was found. She was force-fed bleach, and then suffocated with a towel. After the deaths of these five women, the press was alerted to the possible connection. The following day, another woman was found strangled, her skull cracked. Between 9 and 12 November 1984, three more women were found. Jeanne Laurent, 82; Marise Choy, 84; María Mico-Díaz, 84; and Paule Victor, 77, were discovered during this time. Throughout the three-year period of Paulin's crime spree, the *affaire* ebbed and receded in relation to the number of crimes committed, allowing the crimes to be defined as a series of three waves (October–November 1984, December 1985–June 1986, and November 1987). For months at a time, Paulin did not commit any murders, prompting the media to cease coverage of the killer and the public to resume its regular activities.

The grisly Paulin *affaire* thus entered the French press as a brief *fait divers* announcing the discovery of an elderly woman's murder. As more and more victims began to surface, however, the mounting tension and fear caused by these crimes transformed the ensuing events into a full-blown *affaire* that effectively eclipsed other *faits divers* of its time. The news of Paulin's capture, for instance, overshadowed several other horrifying *faits divers* that warranted the press's attention (*l'affaire Grégoire*, *l'affaire Boutboul*, and *les médecins de Poitiers*). Paulin's crimes quickly became featured on the front page of several major newspapers, including *Le Figaro* ("Les Tueurs des vieilles dames"). Most other front-page headlines discussing the crimes in *Le Figaro* were linked to fear and *insécurité:* "Lost confidence" (Peyrefitte, "Confiance perdue") (12 November 1984); "France is scared" ("La France a peur") (13 November 1984), "Insecurity: The government's back against the wall" ("Insécurité: Le pouvoir au pied du mur") (14 November 1984). In contrast with this coverage, *Le Monde* never gave front-page coverage to the *affaire.* Television broadcasts, on the other hand, multiplied their newscasts on the "monster," and the police recommended that older women not go out alone and not open their doors to anyone. What the Paulin murders possessed that these other *faits divers* did not were several exceptional details that served to highlight the excessive and unique nature of the killings: the sheer number of the murders (at least twenty are known), the age of the victims (all were women between 69 and 85 years of age), and the random and seemingly motiveless nature of the crimes (Paulin usually stole no more than 500 francs—less than 100 dollars—from his victims). Yet the interest in the unknown killer was not limited to simple media coverage and public rumor. During the period of Paulin's crimes, the media transformed the imaginary killer into an inhuman beast, and the unknown murderer became known as the "monstre de Montmartre." For over four years, the police searched unsuccessfully for Paulin, as his pattern of killing in spurts allowed him to divert them from his trail for months at a time. Sensationalizing the events, the press not only revealed a desire to create and feed the production of news, but it also reflected the political climate of the time. As I shall illustrate, the reasons for sensationalizing the *affaire* are rooted in a deeper political and cultural context of *insécurité.* Paulin's crimes coincided perfectly with the ascendance of the National Front, which gained upwards of 12 percent of the vote during this time, making the public's growing fear of Paulin invaluable fodder for the Far Right.

The sensationalistic portrayal of a crime begins with its appearance as a *fait divers* on the first page. By placing the *fait divers* on the front page, the newspaper confirms that it has the public's best interests in mind. If there is a killer in its midst, the public should be alerted so that it may react accordingly; to not tell would be dishonest, and the press both relies and prides itself on its candor in informing the people of the most important news of the day. On a secondary level, however, the media employs the *fait divers* to tap into society's interest in crime. As Lyon and Sanders write, "since the audience has little interest in routine or everyday happenings . . . the media displays a strong tendency to focus on atypical events" (26). Whether this public curiosity is created by or merely confirmed by the media is the subject of continued debate, but the media's focus on the spectacular in crime plainly capitalizes on public fear. Focusing on the serial killer's extreme behavior, the popular press turns him into an invisible phantom and monster. Su C. Epstein explains this labeling as a common practice in media representations of serial killers, which together work to create a dominant understanding of the killer as inhuman. She explains that "Referring to such criminals as 'monsters' and 'evil' encourages people to think of the serial killer as unnatural, unreal, and inhuman. Referencing the unique 'skill' of the serial killer and focusing on the fact that these criminals engage in their crimes undetected for long periods of time also encourage the public to view the killer as superhuman and unique" (73). Epstein explores the portrayal of fictive serial killers in film, concluding that the mythic monster created in cinema leads to a blurring of the real and the fake. Although people are usually aware of these distinctions, Epstein explains that the serial killer's special status seems to confuse the public; she cites examples of police who have released serial killers because they did not fit the mythic persona sketched by the media.

The creation of this monster then allows the public to more readily indulge its curiosity. In addition to allowing the public to access its fantasies, this label also assures the killer's guilt. As Lillo writes, this label reinforces "a condemnation without appeal that excludes all possibility of a pardon" ("une condamnation sans appel et exclut toute possibilité de pardon") (23). With the serial killer safely at a distance, made to seem very unlike people the public may encounter, his atrocities are not as difficult to accept. The result is a fascination with the killer that transcends the bonds of the ordinary; as Richard Tithecott writes, "the serial killer, both repulsive and attractive, verges on the sacred" (5). The sensationalism inherent in this kind of depiction may thus be linked to the discourse employed by the media. In describing how television similarly employs sensationalism to attract viewers, Bourdieu writes in *On Television* that "The principle that determines this selection is the search for the sensational and the spectacular. Television calls for *dramatization*, in both senses of the term: it puts an event on stage, puts it in images. In doing so, it exaggerates the importance of that event, its seriousness, and its dramatic, even tragic character" (18–19). Although Bourdieu's example refers to the sensational practices characteristic of television, the press employs similar strategies to ignite the reader's curiosity. In the *fait divers*, the repetitive categorization of Paulin as a monster is representative, if not typical, of how the media treats crime in a binary fashion. This portrayal seems to reassure the public and criminal researchers alike, who are no more immune to this tendency toward labeling; Levin and Fox, for instance, authors of *Mass Murder: America's Growing Menace*, refer to multiple murderers as "evil people" (210). Thus, the idea of imagining Paulin as a regular person, like anyone else on the street, is too unsettling for a public accustomed to simple portrayals of good and evil. Tithecott further explains that by categorizing the criminal as evil, we place him beyond the realm of scientific investigation, which has proved unsuccessful in explaining serial killing (21). It is not that the public cannot comprehend a more complicated depiction of the criminal, but rather that years of viewing the criminal in a binary fashion, in combination with the popular press's practice of encouraging reaction instead of reflection, have created a public comfort zone that functions to empower the criminal; this view is also taken by Foucault, who writes of the *binarization* of the criminal. While media representations of the "assassin du XVIIIe" provoke public fear, this fear is balanced with a dose of curiosity, as Paulin's monster-like description makes him distinct enough that he does not personally threaten our sense of right and wrong. Thus the label of monster at once augments and calms public fear, as the public is immediately reassured of Paulin's difference as an Other.

In analyzing the atmosphere of public fear, we might consider what purpose the production of this fear serves. Why generate fear in the masses—only to sell newspapers and promote the self-reflexive capitalistic enterprise of the media? Certainly, each catchy headline piques the passerby's curiosity and creates in him or her a potential customer, hooking the reader into following the *affaire:* What new details were uncovered today? Were there any more murders? Do the police have any leads? Familiar with the public's seemingly endless interest in violence and crime, *Le Figaro* in particular seizes upon this knowledge and feeds its diffusion. Its coverage of the Paulin *affaire*, in contrast with *Le Monde*'s, exemplifies this daily barrage, which continues despite the absence of any new information. Like a soap opera, the public thus learns to follow the *affaire* with morbid fascination. One view of the press's role explains that these portrayals of violence "enhance the power of those with a vested interest in the status quo" (Lyon and Sanders 26). These criminal researchers elaborate that "media images of misbehavior 'cultivate' in members of the audience a belief that the larger social environment is dangerous and frightening. In this view social control is enhanced because frightened citizens are more easily manipulated and are willing to trade away civil freedoms for the safety offered by established authorities and the institutions of which they are a part" (Lyon and Sanders 26). Thus, while the "monster of Montmartre" excites our fear and curiosity, his presence serves a didactic purpose as well, reminding women of their vulnerable nature and fragile existence. In one article, entitled "The Monster" ("Le Monstre"), for instance, *Paris Match* printed several full-page pictures of Paulin drinking and dancing while in drag. The text reads, "Never has horror gone so far. No remorse at all, however, would come to haunt the nights of these monsters" ("Jamais horreur n'était allée si loin. Aucun remords, pourtant, ne venait hanter les nuits de ces monstres") (Lejeune, "Le Monstre"). The use of extreme descriptors (never/*jamais*, so far/*si loin*, not any/*aucun*, monsters/*monstres*) exemplifies the magazine's sensational depiction of the *affaire*. In this particular case, it reminds society that grandmothers are defenseless beings who are frequently taken advantage of, thus fulfilling the conservative mainstream's view that old women should not work, live alone, or even shop alone. The implementation of 24-hour hotlines, escort services, and continued coverage of the "events" work, then, not only to ensure the safety of these women, but also to secure their fear. Providing a striking backdrop for the brutality of the killings, these warnings contribute to the vulnerable image of older women in the proverbially anonymous big city where the crimes took place. The most troubling aspect of this *affaire* is that the crimes are *not* committed against "Others" or even at random; rather, the killing of elderly women constitutes a menace for *all* older women. According to several accounts in *Le Figaro*, older women *did* in fact live in fear of Paulin; headlines such as "The Great Fear of Old Women" ("La Grande Peur des vieilles dames") (Dupochonelle 11) and testimony from scared elderly women attest to this. Ironically this situation was the press's own doing; without their warnings to stay inside and their recounting of terrible details of the murders, these women would not know to be afraid. While the media would likely respond that it is simply trying to make the public aware of the potential threat to its health, it is unclear whether their warnings actually saved any lives.

This fear instructs not only the elderly population, but the general population as well. In the reporting of the *affaire*, for instance, Paulin becomes a monster that the entire country fears: as headlines in *Le Figaro* concluded: "France is afraid" ("La France a peur") (1). Every citizen in the entire country, it seems, is now at risk, despite the fact that all of the murders involved elderly women in only two *arrondissements* of Paris. As one article insisted, "We wrote it yesterday: violence against elderly, the most cowardly and abject form of criminality, is developing all over France" ("Nous l'écrivions hier: l'agression contre les personnes âgées, la plus lâche et la plus abjecte forme de criminalité, se développe un peu partout en France") ("Les Assassins du XVIIIe" 12). Another headline in *Le Figaro* proclaimed: "French public under the shock of insecurity" ("Les français sous le choc de l'insécurité") (Huet 6). Erroneously informing the reader that all of France is scared, these statements functionally extend anxiety beyond Paris, where all of Paulin's crimes were committed. Thus, as Lyon and Sanders have deduced, "social control is enhanced because frightened citizens are more easily manipulated and are willing to trade away civil freedoms for the safety offered by established authorities and the institutions of which they are a part" (26). Frightened and insecure, citizens are desperate for a sense of protection, even if this means giving up their freedom.

The "Dramatic Rise of Insecurity in France"

Le Figaro's use of the *fait divers* to create public anxiety effectively transforms what is primarily a personal concern (individual insecurity) into a political concern (about Mitterand's politics, the police force, the death penalty). The creation and elevation of this fear creates a crescendo effect that over time runs the risk of engendering a high public disapproval rate of the current political regime. *Le Figaro*'s insistence on the government's inability to protect its citizens testifies to the politically strategic use of the *fait divers*. The resulting relationship with the public is one of a gamble: betting on their ability to capture Paulin (a fine bet, as odds are that he will eventually be captured), police and politicians wager that the creation of public fear will ultimately serve to bolster their existence. In other words, by injecting fear into the public consciousness, the police bet that the capture of the criminal will restore public confidence in the criminal justice system. Lyon and Sanders explain this process as the following: "The media and criminal justice agencies are linked in a reciprocal relationship. Media attention is directed at certain atypical, but dramatic criminal acts. These portrayals generate and direct public concerns while shaping the steps taken by criminal justice agencies to appear responsive to these concerns. Agencies then devote major resources to cases that typify the forms of crime that have come to be central to the public agenda. . . . Working with the media, agencies consequently present these successes as indicating their interest in the public welfare and their general effectiveness as guardians of the social order" (29). This complex relationship highlights the manipulation of public emotion to justify political ends. When the news of the first murders reached the press in late 1984, for instance, *Le Figaro* seized the opportunity to attack Mitterand's policies. In a front-page editorial on November 10, 1984, *Le Figaro* concluded that "everyone knows that delinquency is on the rise, contrary to what Mr. Joxe and Mr. Badinter impudently affirm" (Ministers of the Interior and Justice Department under Mitterand, respectively). Suggesting that Joxe and Badinter were deceiving the public, *Le Figaro* encouraged distrust of the ruling Socialist Party. In an interview quoted in its pages, Jean-Pierre Bloch, councillor of the 18th *arrondissement*, stated that he attributed the six murders to "the government's complete inability to face insecurity" ("l'incapacité totale du gouvernement à faire face à l'insécurité") (Delsol 13). In subsequent articles linking the killings to governmental responsibility, the newspaper declared, "The state is incapable of assuming the first of its duties, the protection of its people" ("l'état est incapable d'assumer le premier de ses devoirs, la protection des personnes") (Nirascou, "Les Bornes franchis" 1). Blaming France's purported fears about the killer on the socialist government, the same journalist explains that "France is scared. Above all, she is upset. Upset to find that the socialist power, deaf and blind, refuses under its extraordinary principles to take the necessary measures" ("La France a peur. Elle est surtout excédée. Excédée de constater que le pouvoir socialiste, sourd et aveugle, refuse au nom de principes funambulesques, de prendre les mesures que s'imposent"). This outright attack on the party in power demonstrates how the *fait divers* is positioned for discursive struggle by opposing camps.

Stirring up public fear, *Le Figaro* roused latent racism. In the article entitled "18th Arrondissement: The Time of Fear" ("XVIIIe: Le temps de la peur"), journalist Françoise Lemoine quoted an elderly man who shouted at Socialist Party secretary Lionel Jospin, "We must leave France to those who work and send the others back!" ("Il faut laisser la France à ceux qui travaillent et renvoyer les autres!"), a statement largely reminiscent of the slogans of National Front leader Jean-Marie Le Pen. Lemoine's next paragraph secured the conservative slant of her article, which she began by claiming that "it's true that the 18th has a strong concentration of immigrants, including a lot of unemployed and a certain number of people who choose to not work" ("il est vrai que le XVIIIe connaît une forte concentration d'immigrés, parmi lesquels beaucoup de chômeurs, et un certain nombre d'oisifs par vocation"). Speculating as to the race and social class of the killer, *Le Figaro*'s intentions are clear: to maintain a racist and classist view of crime that perpetuates the suspicion of difference. In accordance with its conservative social views, the paper relays to the public their belief that immigrants (who are invariably unemployed) are the cause of crime. This is a prime example of how criminals are profiled on stereotypes rather than statistics. As Jean-Claude Baillon writes, "the wanted sketch of the aggressor is drawn: he will be young or an immigrant, one thinks. The statistics are there: he is French and an adult" ("le portrait robot de l'agresseur est dessiné: il sera jeune ou immigré, croit-on. Les statistiques sont là: il est français et adulte") (6). Yet another article in *Le Figaro* took a vague hypothesis ("the police conjecture that these killings were from one particular gang, most likely drug addicts") ("la Police estime que ces assassinats sont le fait d'une seule et même bande, vraisemblablement des drogués") and fabricated the sensational headline "The Assassins of the 18th Arrondissement: Undoubtedly Drug Addicts" ("Les Assassins du XVIIIe: Sans doute des drogués" 12). As Lyon and Sanders astutely point out: "While there is, of course, a relationship between illegal drugs and many criminal acts, the simplistic presentation of this connection by conservative political leaders and its essentially uncritical acceptance by the mass media have been largely responsible for creating a moral panic in which 'drugs = crime' is the key equation" (36). The association of crime and drugs in this case thus resonates with what the public already "knows" and therefore strengthens preexisting racial stereotypes.

In reinforcing public fear and social stereotyping, sensationalistic crime reports also lead the public to the erroneous conclusion that it can control the amount of crime in its midst by electing particular political parties. By promoting stereotypes that certain groups of people cause crimes (drug users and immigrants), the media prepares the public to act on its knowledge. Articles denouncing "relaxed" social policies and calling for more police control testify to this practice, and they further encourage the public to react. Suggesting that crime can be controlled by electing officials who are acutely aware of the public's safety, these press reports jockey the public's fear into political action. *Le Figaro*, for instance, used Paulin's eventual capture to stress the need for a larger police force. Police commissioner Taillanter was quoted in its pages as saying, "Today, the perception [of the police] is too easygoing. This lack of command has cracked the shell of our civilization" ("Aujourd'hui la représentation [de la police] est trop bienveillante. Le laisser-aller a fait craquer le vernis de notre civilisation") (Lesinge 11). This logic solidifies the status quo, serving to validate the necessity of additional law enforcement in the public's eyes. This argument is most resolutely countered by *Le Monde*, which stated that "the prevention of aggressions against the elderly cannot be assured only by the police" ("la prévention des agressions contre les personnes âgées ne peut pas être seulement assurée par les services de police") (Ambroise-Rendu 13). Quoting the police prefect Guy Fougier to bolster its argument, *Le Monde*'s reporter wrote, "It would be good if neighbors, doormen, and shopkeepers who know older women would equally worry about their safety and engage them in a dialogue to help them protect themselves better" ("Il serait bon que les voisins, les concierges, les commerçants qui ont pour clients de vieilles dames, s'inquiètent également de leur sécurité, engagent avec elles un dialogue et les aident à mieux se protéger").

By showing the public of what and why it should be fearful, and by later declaring that police have apprehended the criminals, the law is reinforced and proven effective. The need for protection thus proven by creating and feeding public fear, the police may then easily fulfill the requisite role of reassuring the public by proving that they are in fact the most reliable people for the job. Thus, the use of a fear-inducing discourse creates allied support for the Right, which strongly advocates for police control. In the Paulin case, then, as the public fear of the "monster" began to rise, the inhabitants of the 18th *arrondissement* conveyed their outrage to Interior Minister Pierre Joxe, who prompted the director of police to order one hundred and twenty additional *gardiens de paix* to occupy the area. Moreover, five hundred additional men were hired to patrol the area night and day, highlighting the immediacy of the crime story and the temporary nature of this remedy. Proceeding from older women's fears to all of France's fears to a general anxiety with the government, *Le Figaro* built its case to include, on November 15, a debate about reintroducing the death penalty: "this series of terrible dramas has reopened the debate about the death penalty in France" ("cette série de drames terribles a relancé en France le débat sur la peine de mort") ("Peine de mort" 1). The manufacturing of public fear thus peaks to legitimize the need for the death penalty in the public's eyes, showing that the *fait divers* never merely portrays criminal accounts.

In response to *Le Figaro*'s exploitation of these crimes to incite public outrage, *Le Monde* replied directly to the attack on the government with several articles addressing the Right's manipulation of the *affaire* for its purposes. Whereas most readers do not read both papers and thus do not experience these variant readings, debates such as these treat the public to the press's biases, demonstrating how the *fait divers* becomes a literal site of discursive struggle. Following *Le Figaro*'s endorsement of the death penalty, *Le Monde*'s front-page headlines proclaimed "The Opposition and the Death Penalty: Fear exploited" ("L'Opposition et la peine de mort: La peur exploitée") (Gendre 1). Attempting to show its readers how fear becomes the purveyor of wrongful blame, Lhomeau and Plenel demanded, "Who is responsible? The assassins, or those who are expected to protect the victims?" ("Qui est responsable? Les assassins, ou ceux qui sont supposés protéger les victimes?") (1). President Mitterand is also quoted here, stating that "it is vital to appease passions; if we live on exasperation, where will France go?" ("il faut apaiser les passions; si l'on vit d'exaspération, où ira la France?"). Mitterand's efforts to calm passions were not successful, however, and the hostilities between the two newspapers raged, further sensationalizing the *affaire*. In an article appearing in *Le Monde* on 17 November 1984, journalist Thomas Ferenczi echoed Mitterand's efforts to return to a clearer understanding of how the *fait divers* had become a political pawn ("Faits divers" 2). Explaining that older women are a sort of specialty of the Right, who find in them a large electoral clientele and a certain image of the universal human condition, Ferenczi emphasized how the Right had clung to the Paulin *affaire*. He then elaborated how the Left had convened around a *fait divers* concerning the death of a Turkish worker and activist; in this *fait divers* the Left finds elements such as worker's rights, capitalist exploitation, and workplace violence. Reasoning that while the tendency may be to become indignant about the politicization of the *fait divers*, Ferenczi wrote that the resulting drama nevertheless serves to advance reflection and propose solutions to the problems raised. Nonetheless, he concluded that the reactions also serve to double the acts of violence with violent words, something that hardly calms the excited mood of the country. The appearance of this article in *Le Monde* implies the paper's neutrality, inferring that it does not, as Mitterand implied, stir up emotion, but rather reports facts. While the article may be read as an account of *Le Monde*'s journalistic integrity, Ferenczi nonetheless addresses the press's important role in shaping the news, adding a welcome voice of self-consciousness to the sensational press reports. Comparing this *affaire* to earlier *faits divers* in France's history, media coverage of the murders prior to Paulin's capture was relatively typical: sensational headlines marked most press coverage of the *affaire*, with *Le Monde*'s reporting less dramatic but nonetheless steady.

The Politics of the Other

On 3 December 1987, Thierry Paulin was at last apprehended for the murders of over twenty elderly Parisian women. The police involvement in his capture is especially noteworthy, as Paulin had managed to narrowly evade their search for over three years despite an increase in the number of officers on the case. Held in custody in the south of France for a misdemeanor theft over a year prior to his capture in 1987, Paulin had been released because no physical description of him was yet available. When he was finally caught, it was due to an extraordinary stroke of luck, an element of the *fait divers* that Barthes terms "le miracle de l'indice" or the miracle of the clue ("Structure" 191–92). On 25 November 1987, Paulin attacked and semi-suffocated 84-year-old Berthe Finaltéri. Unbeknownst to Paulin, Finaltéri survived the attack and was able to furnish the police with a detailed description of both Paulin and his lover/sometime co-conspirator Mathurin, allowing the police to draw up a sketch of the two men. Several days later, on 1 December, after Paulin had killed two more women (Rachel Cohen and Geneviève Germont), commissioner Francis Jacob was talking with a group of merchants about "the monster" when a man resembling the police sketch walked past him. Reportedly following his instinct, Jacob asked the man for his identification papers. As a dark-skinned immigrant, Paulin is said to have assumed that the request was customary, and he cooperated with the policeman (Imbrohoris 78). Once at the police station and alerted that the police knew of the murders, Paulin confessed to the crimes just as calmly; as Imbrohoris sensationally relays, "without the slightest difficulty, without the least remorse, Paulin talks. Confesses. Explains" ("sans la moindre difficulté, sans le moindre remords, Paulin parle. Avoue. Commente. Explique") (78). During the inquest, Paulin explained all the gaps in the police department's knowledge, from why he stopped killing for a time (he had found another job) to why he began killing women in the 14th *arrondissement* (he had moved); Paulin merely failed to explain why he felt the desire to kill. Finally, Paulin denounced his lover, Jean-Thierry Mathurin, who was immediately arrested and jailed. On 20 December 1991 Mathurin was condemned to life in prison, with a minimum eighteen-year jail sentence. Charged with eight murders, six to which he confessed, Mathurin fainted upon hearing his sentence.

Following Paulin's arrest, journalists, social critics, and politicians offered their professional opinions of his behavior, as well as their speculations as to his motivations for the killings. These descriptions of Paulin in the media deserve particular attention, as his Otherness became the focus of nearly every report about him, highlighting how the *fait divers* is used to perpetuate racial stereotypes and distance the criminal from the general public. Paulin's Otherness is present, then, not only in the fictional *representation* of him prior to his arrest (as witnessed in *Le Figaro*'s assumptions about the 18th *arrondissement* and the label of monster); in the discovery of his identity following his arrest, the murderer *himself* is Othered. An immigrant from Martinique, Paulin was a homosexual, HIV-positive, unemployed, drug-using transvestite. As might be expected, the media capitalized on this difference. In a wide variety of publications, Paulin is introduced by his difference: "the 24-year-old West Indian and the 22-year-old Guyanese" ("l'Antillais de 24 ans et le Guyanais de 22 ans") ("Les Tueurs avouent" 1), "Thierry Paulin and Jean-Thierry Mathurin, two young drug addicts" ("deux jeunes drogués") (Puyalte 10), "The Assassin with an earring" ("L'Assassin à la boucle d'oreille") (Muller 104), "Mulatto, Bleached Hair, Homosexual, Transvestite, and Drug Addict, Thierry Paulin" ("Mulâtre, décoloré, homosexuel, travesti, et drogué, Thierry Paulin") ("Le Monstre"). This initial focus on Paulin's skin color and sexuality clearly left a lasting impression, as evidenced in more recent reports of Paulin's killings, where the emphasis on his nationality (and, by association, skin color) surfaces as an unnecessary and almost absurd detail. In a film review of *J'ai pas sommeil*, Alain Riou calls Paulin "this West Indian transvestite" ("Paulin, ce travesti antillais") (66). In another review, the writer summarizes the *affaire* in the following manner: "A West Indian, Thierry Paulin, homosexual, dealer, transvestite, occasional prostitute, was arrested and accused in December 1987. The accomplice (a white man) was judged" ("Antillais, Thierry Paulin, homosexuel, dealer, travesti, prostitué à l'occasion, fut arrêté et inculpé en décembre 1987. Le complice [un Blanc, celui-là] fût jugé") (Siclier 19). Mathurin, incidentally, is not white, but in Denis's film he was portrayed as a white man, an error that demonstrates how incrustations of the *fait divers* alter the facts of the original event.

The importance of Paulin's skin color thus became the subject of political debate, with the National Front insisting that the Socialist Party's anti-racist campaigns had effectively delayed Paulin's capture. Following Paulin's arrest, National Front Rhône deputy Bruno Gollnisch stated that the police search for Paulin was delayed because the authorities were afraid of appearing racist. In other words, had the police deliberately searched out a person of color, the chances that he would have been caught would have been greater. This overt racism contrasts with the veiled version commonly seen in the media, but together the two serve to highlight society's attempts to produce an identity-based approach to crime. Whereas the Right-wing leader (who received considerable press for his statements) claims that race is in a sense responsible for crime, the media inextricably but subtly links Paulin's Otherness to his crimes. Thus, Paulin is portrayed not as having a troubled childhood, a characteristic common to serial killers, but rather as a young homosexual from Martinique, as if these adjectives might help explain his crimes. However, not all newspapers responded to Paulin's capture in this manner, a distinction that created an atmosphere of blame and retaliation between France's largest news dailies.

The day after Paulin's arrest, *Le Figaro*'s headlines read "The Killers Confess to 13 Murders of Old Women" ("Les Tueurs avouent treize meurtres de vieilles dames" 1). The criminals were identified: "Thierry Paulin, a 24 year old Martiniquan and Jean-Thierry Mathurin, a 22-year-old Guyanese" ("Thierry Paulin, un Martiniquais de vingt-quatre ans et Jean-Thierry Mathurin, un Guyanais de vingt-trois ans"). Page 10 of the newspaper was devoted to the arrest, with four separate articles detailing the *affaire*. The same day, in the bottom right-hand corner of page 13, *Le Monde*'s comparatively small headline stated, "Arrest of two men *suspected* of the murder of several old women" (my emphasis) ("Arrestation de deux hommes soupçonnés du meurtre de plusieurs vieilles dames"). The criminal was introduced as "a young man, originating from Fort-de-France (Martinique), Thierry Paulin, 24 years of age" ("un jeune homme, originaire de Fort-de-France [Martinique], Thierry Paulin, vingt-quatre ans"); there were no other articles accompanying these five paragraphs. In fact, the capture of Paulin never reached the front pages of *Le Monde*. Rather, two days later Jean-Marc Théolleyre wrote an article entitled "Morbide fascination," which appeared next to an article about Paulin's arraignment. Théolleyre wrote of Paulin and Mathurin that "What we know, what is said of them, is not done to inspire other sentiments: homosexuality, a tendency toward drug abuse, regular patronizing of night cabarets, that is what we retain of a portrait that remains fuzzy. All that hardly sheds light on the motivations and above all this indifference, this routine of killing" ("Ce que l'on sait, ce que l'on dit d'eux, n'est pas fait pour inspirer d'autres sentiments: une homosexualité, des inclinations à la toxicomanie, des fréquentations ordinaires de cabarets nocturnes, voilà ce que l'on retient pour un portrait encore bien flou. Tout cela n'éclaire encore guère sur les mobiles et surtout sur cette indifférence, cette accoutumance mise à tuer") (13).

Stating that the combination of the lack of explanation surrounding the *affaire* with several details of the criminals' identities led the public to draw conclusions that linked the men's characteristics to their crimes, the article essentially denounces the conservative press's coverage of the *affaire*. Two days later, *Le Figaro* responded with a front-page attack: "The strange attitude of the left-wing press towards an out-of-the-ordinary criminal affair" ("L'Etrange attitude de la presse de gauche à propos d'une affaire hors du commun"). In the accompanying article, Debieuvre declared that "One of the most symptomatic criminal affairs of our times seems to hardly interest the left-wing press" ("Une des affaires criminelles les plus symptomatiques de notre époque ne paraît guère intéresser la presse de gauche") (12). Giving a day-by-day account of the liberal press's response to the *affaire*, *Le Figaro* took aim at Théolleyre's article, written "to justify the direction of the paper over this affair" ("pour justifier la discrétion du journal sur cette affaire") (Debieuvre 12). In a gesture of sarcasm, Debieuvre quoted the article at length and condemned the reporting of other leftist papers, *L'Humanité*, *Libération*, and *La Croix*. In another article that appeared on the same page, Gérard Nirascou accused these same newspapers of giving space to other *faits divers* but not this one, proving that the press focused on the Paulin *affaire* not because of its scruples, but because "Paulin and Mathurin were from Martinique and Guadeloupe respectively. The company they kept was more masculine than feminine. On occasion they did not hesitate to use stimulants that the law denounces, but which abound in certain areas. Such a profile does not perhaps correspond, in the eyes of some, to the ideal assassin and to crimes that are worthy of interest" ("Paulin et Mathurin étaient l'un martiniquais, l'autre guyanais. Leurs fréquentations étaient plus masculines que féminines. A l'occasion ils n'hésitaient pas à user de stimulants que la loi réprouve, mais fort répandus dans certains milieux. Un tel profil ne correspond peut-être pas, aux yeux de certains, à l'assassin idéal et à des crimes dignes d'intérêt") ("Les 'Bons' Morts" 12). After accusing the liberal press of reverse-racism, Nirascou acerbically concluded that "there would be 'good' deaths and then the others: 'the good ones.' Those who can serve an ideological combat; and the others, old women for example" ("il y aurait de 'bons' morts et les autres: les 'bons'. Ceux qui peuvent servir un combat idéologique; et les autres, les vieilles dames par exemple"). Denying its own ideological slant, transparent in its front-page campaign against *insécurité*, *Le Figaro* claimed to expose the ulterior motives of the Left. The resulting picture portrayed a glowingly neutral and scrupulous *Le Figaro* against the backdrop of a conniving *Le Monde*. In response to *Le Figaro*'s unequivocal critique of its journalistic decisions, *Le Monde* responded with a small bolded box devoted to the rapidly embroiling *affaire*. Entitled "French citizens" ("Citoyens français"), it began "*Le Figaro* of December 7 accuses *Le Monde* of Machiavellian scheming. After declaring that we did not devote a long article to Thierry Paulin's arrest, it asks if this "discretion" isn't due to the fact that Paulin is from Martinique and his accomplice from Guadeloupe. Let us reassure our friend. *Le Monde* does not distinguish between French citizens . . . and it is not because the Paulin affair has only just begun, from a judiciary standpoint, that we should distinguish between the victims: they all have the right to the same compassion" ("*Le Figaro* du 7 décembre prête au *Monde* de machiavéliques desseins. Après avoir constaté que nous n'avons pas consacré de longs développements à l'arrestation de Thierry Paulin, il se demande si cette 'discrétion' ne tiendrait pas au fait que Paulin est martiniquais et son complice guyanais. Rassurons notre confrère. *Le Monde* ne distingue pas entre citoyens français . . . Et ce n'est pas parce que l'affaire Paulin ne fait que commencer, sur le plan judiciaire, qu'il faudrait distinguer entre les victimes: elles ont toutes droit à la même compassion") ("Citoyens français" 16). This scathing response fired back at *Le Figaro* by implying that its coverage had been sensationalistic as well as racist. Although the exchange between the two newspapers stopped here, its effects continued to linger, generating subsequent discussion about the enduring significance of the Paulin *affaire* and the importance of understanding the motives of the killers.

While charges of racism characterized the media's representation of Paulin and invariably led the public to link Paulin's unknown motives to his difference, psychiatric experts endeavored to make sense of the brutal killings in their own fashion. These classifications show how societal institutions label the criminal in an effort to know and thus control him. Serge Bornstein, the expert psychiatrist in Mathurin's trial, offered a Freudian explanation of the crimes. He is quoted as concluding that "With Paulin, there is no constraint before the forbidden. He is big game, a great predator. . . . There was a loathing disgust for women and especially old women. Beyond the lure of winnings, it's the murder of the grandmother at a symbolic level" ("Chez Paulin, il n'y a aucun frein aux interdits. C'est un grand fauve, un grand prédateur. . . . Il avait un dégoût méprisant des femmes et surtout des vieilles femmes. Au-delà de l'appât du gain, c'est le meurtre de la grand-mère au niveau symbolique" (Peyrot 10). Bornstein's assessment of Paulin's behavior is founded in a long tradition of efforts to understand inexplicable behavior, which Foucault has plainly documented. Legal and medical professions have traditionally worked in partnership to determine not only *that* a suspect had committed a crime, but also the reasons *why* he committed it. Black explains that "the medical and the legal professions understandably have trouble accepting the possibility of pure, motiveless murder because they tend to view individuals as autonomous willing agents who act in their own self-interest" (137). It is thus unsurprising to read the psychiatrist's diagnosis of Paulin, but its conclusion discloses nothing, merely appeasing our curiosity by assigning an explanation. In labeling Paulin a predator and a beast, Bornstein thus adds himself to the list of others who have dehumanized Paulin.

Reading Baudrillard as "une banalité absolue"

Among the experts who offered their opinions of Paulin was Baudrillard, who presented the public with a broader critical look at the contemporary *fait divers*. Having declared in 1970 that the *fait divers* had become the principal category of thought

(*Consumer Society* 34), Baudrillard returned to the subject in 1989, this time using the Paulin *affaire* to substantiate his earlier claims. In both televised and printed interviews, the critic pronounced that the *fait divers* no longer holds meaning in a society increasingly saturated with representations of crime. Basing his assessment entirely on Paulin's disappearance from the press's front-page stories, which he claims ignored Paulin's existence soon after he was caught, Baudrillard stated that Paulin's crimes were not spectacular in and of themselves. In an interview that appeared in the French journal *Autrement* (1989), Baudrillard concluded that the Paulin *affaire* amounted to "ordinary fascination" ("la fascination ordinaire") ("Cool Killers" 143). It is on this erroneous assumption that Baudrillard bases his argument, which I view as containing three fundamental errors: 1) that Paulin's multiple ethnicity (*métissage*) makes him indefinable and thus invisible, 2) that this invisibility ensures his banality, and 3) that the "coolness" of his crimes signals the end of the *héroisation des criminals*. By closely examining these aspects of Baudrillard's argument, it is clear that Paulin's disappearance, which itself remains debatable, is linked to the presence rather than the absence of political and historical meaning. Instead of disappearing, Paulin emerges as an undeniable signifier for contemporary society's struggle with the Other. Further, in several of his works, Baudrillard discusses the extinction of history and politics (see, for instance, *Cool Memories*, *The Perfect Crime*, and *The Transparency of Evil*). This understanding of history is problematic in that it denies correlation and context in favor of solitary events that take place in a void of meaning, replacing relationships with representation. In his interview with Michel Marcus ("Cool Killers"), Baudrillard states that "There is no more history, only events" ("Il n'y a plus d'histoire, que des événements" 145). He asserts that Paulin's crimes exemplify the banality of contemporary crime. "In the traditional *fait divers*, there is something exceptional, a transcendence. With Paulin, we know that it is absolute banality. In Paulin's personage, there is a hybrid part of the anomalous figure without a cultural or sexual identity" ("Dans le fait divers traditionnel, il y a de l'exceptionnel, de la transcendance. Avec Paulin, on sait que c'est la banalité absolue. Dans le personnage Paulin, il y a un côté métissage de la figure anomalique sans identité culturelle, sexuelle") (144). Attributing Paulin's apparent vanishing to his indeterminable identity, Baudrillard turns Paulin into a signifier for social unease. Because he is an HIV-positive, cross-dressing, light-skinned black man, Paulin does not fit neatly into any of society's categories; instead, his difference situates him elsewhere, theoretically making it difficult to define or represent him. Baudrillard explains that "Paulin does not know who he is, he can play at any game, disguise himself, change sex. He renders every characteristic fluid, therefore agonizing for representation and identification. Paulin would be the anti-hero of *métissage*. Unidentifiable people become incarnations of the system" ("Paulin ne sait pas qui il est, il peut jouer sur tous les tableaux, se déguiser, changer de sexe. Il rend toute caractéristique flottante, donc angoissante pour la représentation et l'identification. Paulin serait un anti-héros du métissage. Les gens non-identifiables deviennent des incarnations du système") ("Cool Killers" 144).

Baudrillard infers that if Paulin knew himself, he would have one socially recognizable identity that the public might be more apt to remember—if, for instance, he had been a heterosexual white man, his *représentation* would be simpler, and his criminal nature might have allowed him to reach the "heroic" status that other criminals have achieved. In other words, the sheer difficulty of representing Paulin allows him to be swept back into the system. By singling out Paulin's Otherness and blaming the public's forgetfulness on his nonrepresentability, however, Baudrillard places himself in the same camp as the public he defines. In addition, his assumption that Paulin "does not know who he is" might also be construed as pejorative. In *The Perfect Crime* (1995), for instance, Baudrillard again uses the Paulin *affaire* to explain his theories of viruses and hate: "Take Paulin, the man from Guadeloupe who went around murdering old ladies a few years ago. A monstrous individual, but cool, with no apparent hatred" (146). Strangely, Baudrillard seems to exemplify him who does not know who he is. Paulin is not from Guadeloupe, but rather from Martinique. Similarly, in calling him "monstrous," Baudrillard dehumanizes Paulin for the sake of sensation as much as the media. Falling into the trap he has set, himself incapable of defining Paulin in his Otherness and in the senselessness of the murders, Baudrillard concludes that Paulin must not have an understanding of himself or his acts. "I don't think that Paulin considers himself as an anarchist or someone avenging a lost cause. Nor can we give him any meaning or significance" ("Je ne pense pas que Paulin se considère comme un anarchiste ou un être vengeur d'une cause perdue. Nous non plus ne pouvons lui donner de sens, de signification") ("Cool Killers" 145). Thus, because Baudrillard the sociologist cannot find meaning in Paulin's acts, he assumes that Paulin's acts *have* no meaning. In fact, the impossibility of assigning motive is a characteristic of all serial killers and constitutes part of their definition. Therefore, while this remains an important factor to examine in studying public response to the Paulin *affaire*, Baudrillard's use of this information to transform Paulin into the signifier for a societal shift does not make sense. Instead, his biased conclusion may be attributable to Paulin's Otherness as much as it may clarify Baudrillard's own views about crime. In the long-held binary opposition of the criminal as either bluntly stupid or brilliantly clever, which Foucault has so clearly outlined, Baudrillard groups Paulin into the former category, refusing him the possibility of reflecting on his crime. Lumping himself with the public, which ostensibly treats Paulin's murders as "la fascination ordinaire," Baudrillard confirms the trivialization of crime and murder.

While Baudrillard's hypothesis merits attention because it contributes to the discourse and rhetoric surrounding the serial killer , it remains extremely problematic in its vague generalizations and lack of documentation. In order for Baudrillard to prove his theory that Paulin's banality is caused by a difficulty in defining him, it would first be necessary to demonstrate a history of success in defining serial killers. Quite to the contrary, however, research shows that the fascination with "cool killers" lies in their very inscrutability; as criminologist O'Reilly-Fleming writes, "serial killers are still little understood, yet generate immense fascination for the general public" (1). A defining characteristic of the serial killer is thus his invisibility, both literally and figuratively. As Richard Tithecott explains, "For the serial killer 'on the loose,' this is what separates him from the average murderer. Invisibility gives him the status of being 'lost,' of being threateningly free. In an age in which the value of images perhaps exceeds the value of words, the search for the serial killer is the search for visual identification rather than explication. However, when he is caught we cannot look at him for long; we feel the need to turn away. He is taboo" (6). This explanation accounts for the "disappearance" of Paulin from the liberal press, whose coverage of the *affaire* was extensive while Paulin was eluding the police but considerably diminished after his capture, hinting that Paulin's taboo lies in his image. Tithecott's next statement reveals another clue to the divergent media responses to the *affaire*. He continues, "His image says everything and nothing, for it is 'normality' which stares back at us" (6). The normality to which Tithecott refers is the typical serial killer, a middle-class white man. United States Federal Bureau of Investigation figures show that the vast majority of serial killers worldwide are white men. Tithecott's argument centers on our failure to explore correspondences between the meaning given to serial killing and the meaning of masculinity and of whiteness in America, uncovering the possibility that serial killing is not, in fact, in opposition to the moral structure of society (5). This thesis is thought-provoking and persuasive, and its suppositions point to Paulin's racial difference as a factor in the liberal media's silence. If it is the killer's whiteness that forms a reflective mirror, allowing us to live out the opposing denial and celebration of his normality, then Paulin's difference shifts the mirror and denies the celebratory component. With little to reflect the majority's gaze, Paulin becomes a signifier for race, class, and sexuality, rather than the changing face of crime. In other words, if it is normality that makes us turn away, then *Le Monde*'s assertion that it does not distinguish between people of different ethnicities and lifestyles holds ground. If, on the other hand, Paulin is not perceived as "normal," and if his difference as a homosexual, HIV-positive immigrant defines rather than describes him, then *Le Figaro*'s claims that it is merely covering the *affaire* ring false. In examining Baudrillard's argument that Paulin's fluid identity serves as a determinant for his media disappearance, it seems that while his hypothesis that Paulin's identity plays a role is plausible, his argument is poorly structured. Far from being slippery or "angoissante pour la représentation," Paulin is *too* tangible. His so-called disappearance from the press was not merely due to a difficulty in defining him, as Baudrillard alleges; as I have illustrated, the attention the Paulin *affaire* received differed considerably from conservative to liberal newspapers, underlining the important role of politics in the representation of *faits divers*. By ignoring the extensive coverage of Paulin in *Le Figaro*, *Le Matin*, and *France-Soir* and by neglecting to distinguish between the conservative and liberal press's responses, Baudrillard disregards a key element of the media's reaction. A fundamental reason for Paulin's initial disappearance is that his identity *too closely* resembles the current vision of a monster. Although his normality stares back at us (i.e., he is not a literal monster), his identity nonetheless closely mirrors the imaginary object of *insécurité*, the feared Other: the young drug user, the unemployed immigrant, the HIV-positive homosexual. Without a displacement of the criminal or a mirror in which to see ourselves, the criminal temporarily disappears, too close for comfort. Thus, what may be read as the liberal press's reluctance to handle the outcome of the Paulin *affaire* speaks instead to a social racism and general discomfort with ethnic and sexual issues that is equally evidenced in *Le Figaro*'s insistence on Paulin's identity.

In a parallel effort to turn Paulin into a signifier for a changing society, Baudrillard correlates the Paulin *affaire* with the end of "la grande héroisation des criminels." Baudrillard does not refer to any specific criminals, but merely notes that criminals in earlier times were more likely to achieve a "heroic" stature because of their violent acts. Other writers and journalists, such as Imbrohoris, Bourgeois, and Bonvoisin, refer to the Paulin *affaire* as one that will certainly be remembered; the conservative press likewise hails Paulin as the "assassin of the century." Nonetheless, the apparent coolness of Paulin's acts confirms a change in crime for Baudrillard, and the resulting public indifference to his crimes (which has yet to be proven) testifies to this metamorphosis. As Baudrillard explains, "He had no identity, and was of indeterminate sex and mixed race. He committed his murders without violence or bloodshed. And he recounted them with an odd detachment. Being indifferent to himself, he was eliminating people who were themselves indifferent" (*The Perfect Crime* 146–47). Baudrillard's statement warrants, again, close scrutiny. His understanding of Paulin as lacking an identity and being sexually indeterminate is assumed to be the indirect discourse of the public; by labeling Paulin a "personage," he steps into the public's understanding of Paulin, whose ignorance of his lifestyle as a transvestite might lead them to conclude that he lacks an identity. This said, Baudrillard seems driven to use Paulin to fit his theory that the *fait divers* has become banal. His statement that Paulin accomplished his murders without violence is erroneous and misguided. This conclusion presumably alludes to Paulin's practice of strangling the old women. Although strangling may not be perceived as violent a death as a gunshot (the victim's face is not seen; there is a lack of blood; the victim is relatively quiet), Baudrillard neglects to mention that Paulin brutally tortured his victims. The omission of this evidence (Paulin burned the genitals and feet of several of the elderly women before killing them, poured bleach down one woman's throat, and stabbed another) leads to two assumptions: either Baudrillard has defined violence as an act that must *appear* violent, i.e., bloody; or he believes that for an act to be violent, its perpetrator must commit the act in a violent manner, that is, that the act itself must be caused by some internal violence (*haine*) in the criminal. This latter idea fits with Baudrillard's belief that Paulin was indifferent to himself, and thus capable of committing such heinous crimes. Nonetheless, his manipulation of language and his assumptions about Paulin's state of mind point to a flawed, although provocative and sensational argument.

Baudrillard's comments are enticing in today's society, where crime is perceived as increasing, where people seem numb to violence, and where even the most sensational *fait divers* appears to carry only a fleeting concern. Yet to claim that the public is tired of crime and no longer moved by serial killers is inaccurate. Such a statement not only alleges our lack of interest, but moreover ignores the very reasons for this public indifference. More fundamentally, however, it seems to me impossible to determine whether Paulin has already vanished from the public memory; it is at best infeasible to conclude within two years of Paulin's conviction that he has disappeared. Furthermore, Baudrillard offers no explanation or data for his conjecture. His theory seems to be based on an overall belief that crime today does not carry the same lasting effect on society as it did in earlier periods. And although earlier criminals were not as excessive as Paulin in the number of people they killed, they nonetheless enjoyed "successful" careers; to this date, most French people have heard of Gilles de Rais, Violette Nozières, and Henri Landru. In addition, as evidenced by earlier *affaires*, the notoriety and staying power of a *fait divers* is based as much on its inscription into artistic productions as it is on its actual occurrence. In the Papin *affaire*, for instance, maids and sisters Claire and Solange Papin rose to notoriety after brutally killing their mistresses. Their crimes were made even more famous by the writings of Jacques Lacan, Simone de Beauvoir, and Jean Genet, whose works helped secure a place for the *fait divers* in the public's collective memory. The *affaire* also became the subject of several films, including Nancy Meckler's *Sister My Sister* (1994), Claude Chabrol's *La Cérémonie* (1996), and, most recently, Jean-Pierre Denis's *Les Blessures assassines* (2000), guaranteeing the sisters' everlasting fame. Baudrillard has maintained that the banality of today's crime lies in its inability to produce a spectacle: "we used to be able to make these things literary, but now, it's simply obscene" ("Cool Killers" 143). Again, it appears that Baudrillard has spoken too soon. Claire Denis's release of a film about Paulin's crimes effectively repudiates Baudrillard's claims that "there is nothing left to do." The circulation of such a film indicates that the Paulin *affaire* has, in fact, lingered in the public memory, and furthermore, that it sustains a significant cultural presence. Triumphantly proclaimed as a tour de force, her work again opens the Paulin *affaire* for consideration, providing a site of resistance that contradicts Baudrillard's claims.

Chapter Three

Viewing Crime

From the earliest cinematic endeavors, crime has figured predominantly in French film, and *faits divers* have been frequently the subject of cinematic productions. While this recreation of historical events has been a consistently popular theme in film, adaptations of sensational *faits divers* represent an increasingly significant body of work. The American film industry is particularly replete with examples, many of which have become popular in France. John McNaughton's *Henry: Portrait of a Serial Killer* (1987, based on Henry Lee Lucas), Jonathan Demme's *Silence of the Lambs* (1991, based on Edgar Gein), Eric Till's *To Catch a Killer* (1992, based on John Wayne Gacy), and Spike Lee's *Summer of Sam* (1999, based on David Berkowitz) are examples of successful mainstream films that highlight the growing presence of serial killers in the international psyche. The increasing popularity of these works faithfully coincides with the dramatic rise of documented sensational killings since the 1960s (Black 135). In France, there have been fewer examples of cinematic adaptations of serial killing, if only because there have been relatively few documented cases until very recently. In fact, the growth of this genre seems to directly reflect the increasing number of these crimes committed, a trend that I will return to in the conclusion of this book. The growing number of violent films provides the media with endless fodder for debate, yet rather than examine the reasons audiences enjoy these films, the media instead focuses on whether these images create or reflect violent behavior. This narrow focus characterizes the media's response to both *J'ai pas sommeil* and *Roberto Zucco*, which were works reproached for their potential to incite and sensationalize violence. Instead of examining what these works seek to communicate and why people may be outraged or enlivened by their production, the media centers on the simple fact that these were representations based on real events; as such, these *faits divers* are held to an impossible standard of accurately representing the truth (which cannot be known) without offending their viewers (a hopeless task in that one cannot account for all spectatorial positions).

Claire Denis is a French director who began her career in the apprenticeship of directors Wim Wenders, Jim Jarmusch, and Bertrand Van Effenterre. She has directed documentaries (*Man No Run,* 1988), as well as fictional films (including *Chocolat,* 1988, *S'en fout la mort,* 1990, *US Go Home,* 1994, *Beau Travail,* 2000, *Trouble Every Day,* 2001 and *L'Intrus,* 2004). In 1994, *J'ai pas sommeil* made its much-anticipated appearance at the Cannes Film Festival. While it received minor attention from the Cannes public, critics reviewed it with considerable interest; as may be anticipated, while several reviewers responded favorably to her work, others were repelled by Denis's choice of subject. *J'ai pas sommeil* is not a typical film about a serial killer, and some would say that it is not, in fact, about Paulin, but rather about the state of contemporary France, the concept of belonging and alienation, and the idea that anyone is capable of murder. The plot of *J'ai pas sommeil* establishes three central story lines. In one, a young, attractive Lithuanian actress, Daïga (Katherine Golubeva), arrives in Paris on the empty promises of a theater director with whom she presumably had an affair. Unable to work as an actress and unable to speak French, Daïga finds work as a chambermaid in the same hotel that the two killers occupy. In a second thread of the story, Camille (Richard Courcet) and his lover (Vincent Dupont) party until dawn almost every night, frequenting upscale drag clubs, dining at fine restaurants, and casually murdering old women to sustain their extravagant lifestyles. Camille's older brother, Théo (Alex Descas), provides the third strand. With his young son in tow, the serious Théo works odd jobs in order to save enough money to return to Martinique, despite the protests of the child's indecisive mother, Mona (Béatrice Dalle). Although all the characters reside in the 18th *arrondissement,* their lives barely intersect, and Daïga and Théo never meet at all. Instead, Denis links the characters through the solitude and humanity of their lives, through their desires and personal failures.

Similar to the Succo *affaire,* whose retelling generated public outrage and faced censure for its portrayal of a local killer, the rewriting of the Paulin case was problematic for many spectators, as evidenced through reviews and interviews. Denis does not focus exclusively on Paulin's fictional representation, but centers on several fictional characters. Rather than using these other characters to polarize Camille as a crazed serial killer (as the *fait divers* does), Denis instead shows the foibles of his neighbors: Théo's neighbor abuses his wife, Mona abducts her son, Daïga smuggles goods across the European border, Théo is an illegal immigrant, and Camille's friends use drugs. While these illegal habits do not parallel the serial killer's crimes, they do, on the other hand, serve as important perspective. Denis makes it nearly impossible to entirely "Other" Camille without also judging the other characters of the film. In this way, she decenters readers and critics, who, familiar with the binary presentation of criminal acts, may be unaccustomed to the representation of crime as a continuum. The temporal proximity of Paulin's crimes also invites uneasiness from the victims' families as well as from his own. In advance of these issues, Denis addressed her concern in a published interview: "It was impossible for me to imagine making a film only about this affair: Paulin is dead, but his accomplice is in prison for twenty years, and his mother lives in France. It was not necessary that she relive the horror that she must have gone through at the time of the events for a second time" ("c'était impossible pour moi d'imaginer tourner un film strictement sur cette affaire: Paulin est mort, mais son complice est en prison pour vingt ans et sa mère vit en France. Il n'était pas nécessaire qu'elle subisse une deuxième fois l'horreur qu'elle a dû subir au moment des faits") (qtd. in Jousse 25). Denis's comments reflect a moral concern that allegedly influenced the plot of her film. While her statement is not especially reliable in the context of an interview promoting her film, it may be helpful in pointing to the importance the media places on authorial intention, representing as well a significant incrustation of the film. Centering on authorial intentions rather than outcomes, interviews such as these offer a narrow view of the text as constructed by its author. By retreating to this individualist stance, Denis's comments about the film serve as a unified representation of what the film means, rather than as one of many discourses that create meaning. Had Denis not addressed her "concern," she might have further angered audiences who perceived her as callous; this kind of statement or disclaimer, then, partly excuses her choices. On the other hand, Denis's alleged consideration of Paulin's mother does not necessarily translate to the viewers of the film, some of whom were nonetheless upset—to say nothing of Paulin's mother, who may have been horrified to find out about the film's release. Other comments from the filmmaker display indifference to potential negative audience reaction. In response to criticisms that the film is racist and homophobic, for instance, Denis defiantly dismissed these potential problems. As we saw with *Le Monde*'s minor attention to Paulin subsequent to his capture, Paulin's identity (as an Other) renders him an uncomfortable subject to regard, particularly for many liberal citizens, who spend considerable political energy defending immigration policies and the rights of homosexuals. Despite these potential misunderstandings, however, Denis refuses to acknowledge this problem, stating that the notion of "correctness" does not conform to her film. As she explained in an interview, "I felt it was impossible that we speak to this notion, which was evidently raised with a character that kills more than twenty old women, the most fragile beings in society after children, who is black, homosexual, and vaguely drugged. The complete opposite of what black people in cinema should be, according to 'politically correct' scenarios" ("Je sentais qu'il était impossible qu'on aille vers cette notion, dont la question se posait évidemment avec ce personnage qui tue plus de vingt vieilles dames, les êtres les plus fragiles de la société après les enfants, qui est noir, homosexuel et vaguement drogué. L'inverse absolu de ce que doivent être les personnages noirs au cinéma selon les schémas du 'politiquement correct'") (qtd. in Jousse 28).

Later correlating political correctness with racism ("for me, this notion is nothing but a corollary of racism") ("pour moi, cette notion n'est que le corollaire du racisme") (28), Denis stated that she hoped to remove such notions from her film. It is interesting to note that several (non-French) reviewers allude to the film's potential racism and homophobia before dismissing it; these allusions seem to reflect the reviewers' discomfort as spectators. In the British daily *The Guardian*, for instance, a journalist writes that "eventually the film takes a genuinely shocking turn that is certain to guarantee controversy. It lays itself bare to charges of homophobia, conceivably of racism" (*Guardian* 18). While each of these reviewers notes the problematic and uncomfortable portrayal of gay men in the film, they are nonetheless unable to blame Denis, as the facts validate her representation. Ultimately, despite the possibility of offending the families of victims and of transgressing public tolerance for displays of violence, racism, and homophobia, Denis decided to direct the film. Her manner of portraying the criminal is decidedly uncharacteristic of typical movies about serial killers, which focus on the killer and his crimes to drive the plot. While Denis's film is based on Thierry Paulin's killings, the story revolves around the lives of Camille, Daïga, and Théo, who are equally represented. Rather than focusing on Paulin's acts, then, *J'ai pas sommeil* instead moves in concentric circles, each story a separate plot with the characters' lives just barely intersecting. Although Denis's interest in making this film stems from the *fait divers* itself, she seems keenly interested in problematizing the crimes in a social and political context. This novel treatment of the serial killer refuses a unidimensional understanding of crime. Her depiction of society's problems (illegal immigration, ineffective police, unemployment), its Others (immigrants, old women, gay men), and the stifling nature of the city (conveyed by darkness, lack of private space, tight shots of the city, invading noise) reflect the larger world that the *fait divers* represents. In this way, she reveals how the crime story is representative of contemporary society in presenting current ideological struggles about race, insecurity and the Other. When Denis explains how she categorizes her film, she emphasizes the importance of the *fait divers* to her film as a social reflection. As she stated in an interview with Sonja Benjamin, "The repercussion of this *fait divers*, which calls into question how society functions, led me to reflect. And this film constitutes a trio with *Chocolat* and *No Fear, No Die*. The first speaks of colonization, the second of immigration, and this one of the way people are integrated into a society" ("Le retentissement de ce fait divers, qui met en cause le fonctionnement de la société, m'a amenée à réfléchir. Et ce film constitue un tryptique avec *Chocolat* et *S'en fout la mort*. Le premier parle de la colonisation, le second de l'immigration, et celui-ci de la façon dont les gens sont intégrés à une société") (Benjamin 10).

In another interview, Denis elucidates more clearly her interest in the individual's place in society. When Thierry Jousse prompted that the origin of the film is a *fait divers*, Denis responded: "Yes, but it comes from a really contradictory desire. I never wanted to tell this *fait divers*, but as it happened, a lot of things in my life brought me back to it. I crossed paths with Paulin without knowing it many times . . . this story would come back when I wasn't looking for it, there were a lot of signs" ("Oui, mais c'est parti d'une envie vraiment contradictoire. Je n'ai jamais eu envie de raconter ce fait divers, mais il s'est trouvé que beaucoup de choses dans ma vie m'y ont ramenée. J'ai croisé Paulin sans le savoir plein de fois . . . cette histoire revenait tout le temps alors que je ne la cherchais pas, il y avait beaucoup de signes") (qtd. in Jousse 25). Again, Denis downplays the film's association with the actual events. Explaining how she is perplexed by her own strange affinity for the *fait divers*, she claims to be more interested in Paulin's invisibility. The sense that Paulin is everywhere and yet invisible is central to Denis's film and at the same time typical of the serial killer's erroneous representation in the media. As Tithecott explains, "Contrary to the evidence that the majority of serial killers tend to operate within one city or even one neighborhood is the myth of the increasingly mobile and transient killer who can strike anywhere at any time" (31). Although Denis appears to fall victim to the media's sensational depiction of the killer, her representation of Paulin's invisibility does not focus on his geographical omnipresence. Rather, she stresses the invisibility of "evil" within people, an idea that foregrounds her later film *Trouble Every Day*, which presents all-too-human vampires. Denis states, "for me, the monster cannot be seen. If there's an underlying theme in my work, it's that evil is never the other, all is within and never outside, neither good nor evil. It's the one thing that moves me" ("pour moi, le monstre ne se voit pas. S'il y a un tout petit fil conducteur dans mon travail, c'est que le mal n'est jamais l'autre, tout est dedans et jamais dehors, ni le bien ni le mal. C'est la seule chose qui me meut") (qtd. in Jousse 27). It is this nonbinary vision of the criminal, as one who is not a caricature of pure evil, that has elicited the most response from critics and the media. Before delving into the details of Denis's film, then, I summarize first the critical response to her film, as it mimics the media's relationship to the *fait divers*. Similar to the media's role in shaping the presentation of the *fait divers*, the film critic shapes and encrusts the film with his or her own ideology. As Bennett states, "we know that the reader's response cannot be deduced from an analysis of the formal properties of the text, that there are independent determinations bearing on the ideological and cultural formation of the reader which may be taken into account" (5). Looking at these published critical works about the film, which represent several readers' responses, we see how the film is "activated" or presented in the general media. Moreover, as these reviews are often read in advance of seeing the film, they function as incrustations and thus affect how we read the text; Bennett summarizes that "it is the readings already produced in relation to a text, and not some notional 'text itself,' which bears upon and limit[s] present and possible readings of a text. It is for these historical, and not at all essentialist reasons, that texts are encountered as resistance" (6). In other words, the incrustations of the text, in this case the film reviews, create varied—and therefore resistant—readings of the text. From this standpoint, then, we may use these various readings of the film to show how Denis offers a space to examine the public's role in constructing the criminal and in resisting his mediated representation.

Reviewing the Crime

J'ai pas sommeil made its debut at the 1994 Cannes Film Festival, where it had been chosen to preview under the category "Un Certain Regard." The much-anticipated release of the film contrasted sharply with the minor attention it received from the public at the festival. Like the film reviews, this meager public interest reflects public expectations about criminal representations. The film's clear departure from the media's Manichean depiction of Paulin seemed to unsettle many spectators unaccustomed to a "nonjudgmental" or "cool" depiction of the criminal. We may examine several reasons for the film's mediocre showing at its Cannes début. The reviewer in *Le Monde* hypothesizes that "*J'ai pas sommeil* frightens. How else to interpret the poor score received by Clare Denis's beautiful film? 8000 entries in nine theaters is a disappointment. But was it really necessary to release this fragile film in the middle of the Cannes Festival?" ("*J'ai pas sommeil* fait peur. Comment interpréter autrement, en effet, le score décevant réalisé par le beau film de Claire Denis? 8000 entrées en neuf salles, c'est une déception. Mais fallait-il vraiment sortir ce film fragile en plein Festival de Cannes?") (*Le Monde* 22). When this review concludes that the film is disconcerting or even fear-inspiring, it refers not to the film itself, but rather the *idea* of it; spectators did not leave the theater upset, but instead chose not to attend the film's screening. It is important to note that the Cannes viewing public does not represent the cultural, social, economic, racial, or sexual make-up of the French public, so we should not draw erroneous conclusions as to the interest in Paulin's case. That *J'ai pas sommeil* did not appeal to this particular viewing public is significant, however, in that the paltry response to the film strongly affected reviews and publicity about the film, most likely impacting its further success. Nevertheless, we might consider the possible reasons for its less than spectacular showing. We might speculate as to the public's discomfort in not wanting to see these all-too-recent events portrayed on screen (although the popularity of reality shows and the interest in the *affaire* before Paulin was apprehended demonstrate otherwise). We might simply assert that there were several more interesting films released in 1994, with the result that Denis's film did not fare so well. On the other hand, we might instead concur with Baudrillard and conclude that Paulin is indeed "une banalité absolue." Perhaps, in fact, no one is interested in this *métissage* of a man. Perhaps killing is suddenly and increasingly dull for the contemporary French spectator. Yet film critics report otherwise, and their reviews point to the nonsensational portrayal of Paulin as an important factor in generating public opinion. As film critic Steve Erickson writes in the American film quarterly *Cinéaste*, *J'ai pas sommeil* is "one of the least sensationalistic films ever made about serial killing" (64). This observation is the most common one made about the film, and Denis's manner of filming the murders reportedly appears "cool" to many spectators, hinting at the "disappointing" reception of *J'ai pas sommeil.* This response is significant in marking Denis's departure from the standard representation of the *fait divers* as a sensational story. In a review in the monthly French cinema magazine *Première*, Jean-Jacques Bernard remarks that Camille "goes nightclubbing and eliminates old women with the same detachment that one takes money out of an ATM" ("court les boîtes et supprime des vieilles dames avec le même détachement qu'on retire du fric d'une borne de carte bleue") (64). Lisa Schwarzbaum's review of the film in the American magazine *Entertainment Weekly* states that in this "deceptively languid" film, which is "not your standard portrait of a serial killer," it is "up to the viewer to figure out: *psycho killer, qu'est-ce que c'est?*" (52). Other reviewers also focus on how Denis's treatment of the killer leaves much to the viewer's imagination. In *Variety's Film Reviews* Deborah Young surmises that "Denis chooses to recount these adventures as neutrally and non-judgmentally as if the characters were drinking a cup of coffee, making it strangely difficult to condemn the murderer" (210). In a review of the film in *Le Monde*, Jacques Siclier likewise concludes that "*J'ai pas sommeil* is a strange, troubling, admirable film without any real dramatic construction, without moral or social judgment placed on the protagonists of this reinvented *fait divers*" ("*J'ai pas sommeil* est un film étrange, troublant, admirable, sans véritable construction dramatique, sans jugement moral ou social jeté sur les protagonistes de ce fait divers réinventé") (19). Again, I would hypothesize that Denis's deliberate refusal to make a moral condemnation opens the door for new and frank discussions about crime that include society's role in its production.

While the previous critics noted Denis's detached representation of Paulin with positive interest, other reviewers responded more strongly to Denis's choice of subject. According to Alain Riou, Denis is to blame not for venerating Paulin, but for portraying him in neither a positive nor a negative fashion. Riou writes, "It is not for glorifying a murderer that we reproach you, but for having no kind of clear point of view about him, nor about his victims, nor for that matter about the *fait divers* itself, since the affair takes up little more than one-fifth of your film, which brings together three or four other stories in a complete and utter hodgepodge" ("Ce n'est pas de glorifier un meurtrier qu'on vous reproche, mais de n'avoir aucune espèce de point de vue clair sur lui, ni sur ses victimes, ni d'ailleurs sur le fait divers lui-même puisque l'affaire occupe à peu près un cinquième de votre film qui remue en même temps trois ou quatre autres histoires dans un salmigondis complet") (64). Riou voices further agitation at the film's focus on themes other than the *fait divers* itself. He seems to interpret Denis's film as an affront to the spectator, viewing her choice to not focus exclusively on Paulin as a conscious decision to deemphasize the brutality of the crimes, a reaction that shows how deviations from the static nature of the *fait divers* may be upsetting to readers. While Riou and others criticized the abbreviated version of Paulin in the film, Pascal Merigeau of *Le Monde* applauds how Denis employs Paulin as a signifier for contemporary society. Calling it "a film about fear, a film that embodies fear" ("un film sur la peur, un film de peur," 22), he explains that "*J'ai pas sommeil* is a film without suspense, without inquest, almost without policemen. A film that shows how society's dysfunctions and deficiencies can lead to the edge of a cliff from which some end up falling, who we then qualify as a 'monster' because the definition is both easy and reassuring" ("*J'ai pas sommeil* est un film sans suspense, sans enquête, presque sans policiers. Un film qui montre comment les dysfonctionnements et les manques d'une société peuvent conduire au bord d'un abîme dans lequel certains finissent par sombrer, que l'on qualifie ensuite de 'monstre' parce que la définition est à la fois commode et rassurante") (22). Merigeau points to Denis's keen focus on the murders' symbolic meaning rather than their literal significance. He does not fall into the trap of wanting to know (*la volonté de vérité*), like other readers who search for Denis's judgment of the criminal, but rather recognizes the film's interrogation of the public's desire to categorize Paulin. In acknowledging how society labels and classifies difference, Merigeau highlights that Paulin is a product of contemporary society. His review serves to further rupture the binary opposition that allows society to construct Paulin's acts in an ahistorical and apolitical vacuum.

Law Enforcement and the Media

In the beginning scenes of *J'ai pas sommeil*, Denis presents images of law enforcement and the media that radically contrast how these groups project themselves to the general public. In the film, the police are not fearless crusaders, and the media is not a determiner of public sentiment. In contrast to the traditional representations of these powerful groups (in mainstream film and television, for instance), Denis instead reveals their relative impotence. These groups do not inform the public and control public sentiment; the cynical responses of Denis's characters are more akin to boredom than fear and excitement. Instead, Denis's iconoclastic portrayal of the police subverts their subjectivity. *J'ai pas sommeil* opens to the sound of raucous, uncontrolled laughter. The camera immediately zooms in on two traffic policemen in a helicopter, high above the smog and clouds of Paris, who are presumably surveying the city's traffic patterns. Their side-splitting laughter is almost contagious, except that the spectator has no idea why the men are laughing so hard. This opening sequence is rich in symbolism and texture. On the one hand, Denis introduces us to the Parisian police. This first glimpse at the law enforcement of Paris relieves the spectator of any misconceptions he or she may have about the film. This may be a film about a serial killer, but the opening shot removes all traces of suspense. Similar to Dumont's human portrayal of the police in his low-key thriller *L'Humanité* (1999), Denis will introduce these policemen as no different from anyone else: their humanity, as well as their callousness, is laid out for the spectator to see. In most films depicting crime, the presence of the police is employed to reassure the public and to give order to chaos; as professionals whose jobs ensure public safety, their presence signifies the return of calm and orderliness. In this film, however, Denis does not produce picture-perfect policemen who spend all day searching for clues to the killer. Instead, as the camera follows the helicopter into Paris, the echo of their mad laughter drifts above the city. In her interview with Jousse, Denis explains this representation of the police in the following way: "The police have a concrete function, they regulate traffic, they watch from the helicopter to see if there is a traffic jam, and they're eventually there to stop the killers, but it's more as nice guys. They do not lead the action" ("les policiers ont une fonction concrète, ils règlent la circulation, ils regardent de l'hélicoptère s'il n'y a pas de bouchon, et ils sont éventuellement là pour arrêter les tueurs, mais plutôt d'une façon bonhomme. Ils ne sont pas les moteurs de l'action" (qtd. in Jousse 26). *J'ai pas sommeil* thus subverts popular representations of the police in dailies like *Le Figaro*, which present law enforcement as the ultimate solution in a long and public battle with crime. Denis's film instead presents policemen who seem incapable of maintaining the prototypical panoptic surveillance of the city. In this brief scene, the spectator learns that the traditional mechanisms of surveillance no longer function.

In this opening scene of the film, Paris provides a stark contrast to the bright skies above. From the helicopter, miles outside the city, Paris appears dark and remote. As the camera rolls, tracking the helicopter's viewpoint as it swoops into the capital, a gray smog encrusts the city. Following along the highway, we center in on a small car with foreign license plates; as the camera follows the traffic, the music is kitsch-dramatic, like something from an old spy movie. Through a profile shot, the camera focuses in on a young woman (Daïga), who ejects a tape cassette to tune into a local radio station. The camera is now inside the car, close up on the radio, and the announcer comes on. In an upbeat tone, he proclaims "Don't open your door to just anyone! Be careful! The granny killer's on the prowl. The news proves it to you every day. So, take my advice and keep a sense of humor" ("N'ouvrez pas vos portes à n'importe qui! Soyez prudent! Le tueur des vieilles dames rôde. Les informations vous le prouvent tous les jours. Alors, suivez mon conseil et gardez votre bonne humeur"). The camera zooms out to profile Daïga, who continues to stare blankly at the traffic, seemingly nonplussed about the news that a killer is in her midst. While the spectator will later learn that Daïga does not speak French, at this early point in the film, this information signals the media's minimal effect on her state of mind; she seems not at all interested in or fearful of the killer. The radio announcer's energetic voice utterly contrasts with his morose message, and the song that he selects after his announcement confirms his nonchalance towards the crimes: "Relaxez-vous." This song is as revealing in its lightheartedness as in its lack of profundity. A perfect symbol of France seen by foreigners like Daïga, the song presents the quintessential French attitude as seen from afar: relaxed, suave, and cool. It also points to the influx of American music on French radio, and its retro-cool flavor calls back to an era when "people were happy" and the term serial killer did not exist. Denis thus immediately draws the spectator's attention to the schizophrenic attitude of the media. With on the one hand a warning of brutal killings, and on the other an almost flippant tone and choice of kitschy music, the media sends very different messages. Should the public be alarmed? Daïga, the only person we have "met" up to this point, seems very relaxed. Not unlike the carefree spirit of the police, the media's relaxed attitude conveys a cockeyed assurance; as if aware of their own invisibility (whether high above the city or falling on deaf ears), these powerful people "keep it light." Within the first five minutes of the film, then, Denis has conveyed an unorthodox if not subversive look at some of society's most influential knowledge machines. Throughout the film, Denis's characters continue to interact in a significant way with the media. For example, at the beginning of the film Daïga listens to the radio but she cannot understand it. Later, she will ignore newspapers that the camera will pan to, their headlines escaping her gaze but not the spectator's eyes. Although the front-page headlines proclaim that "France is scared," Daïga is not afraid; she is not even aware of the danger. In another example towards the end of the film, we overhear a television interview coming from an open window, broadcasting Interior Minister Joxe's thoughts about *l'insécurité*. Although the spectators hear the man's voice, the camera does not show anyone watching the television. Similar to Cédric Klapisch's *Chacun cherche son chat* (1996), where characters ignore all forms of media that report the election news, the media sound bites in *J'ai pas sommeil* appear to fall on deaf ears. Denis's depiction of these media clips highlights their omnipresence in society, yet above all it stresses the media's relative insignificance in the lives of ordinary people. Not only are people not paying attention to the media's sensational hype, but the media doesn't seem to exert any influence over the public, which is engaged in its own struggles.

When Daïga arrives in Paris, the camera follows her closely as she enters a café and orders a coffee; her heavy accent reveals her foreignness, and when she attempts to pay her bill, we learn that she neither speaks French nor is familiar with French customs. In what will soon be seen as typical police behavior, two officers follow Daïga to her illegally parked car and badger her, asking her about her foreign license plates and mocking her nationality ("nyet, nyet," they mimic). True to herself, Daïga curses them in her native tongue and drives away without much bother. As she arrives at her aunt's house, the camera cuts to the steps of the apartment building, where her aunt cautiously climbs the stairs. After a brief reunion and a visit to other Lithuanian tenants in an apartment upstairs, Daïga steps outside to smoke a cigarette. Leaving the apartment, she passes the crime scene in the apartment below, where neighbors have gathered to gossip about the death of their elderly neighbor; Daïga takes no notice of the crowd. The policemen appear again, and although they are on the scene of a murder investigation, they seem more interested in pestering (or flirting with) her. "People are beasts" ("Les humains sont des bêtes"), says one of them, echoing the media's labeling of the murderers. In the mouths of these officers, however, the statement seems simplistic and patronizing. Suddenly the police are important authorities, important enough to stop and talk to Daïga, this time questioning her legal status. She again does not react to them, and while it is clear that she does not understand their French, her comportment suggests disdain and dismissal rather than confusion. In later scenes, it is the absence of police that is most remarkable. While the police are readily available to harass immigrants on the streets, their scarcity is notable when Daïga is pursued along a well-lit boulevard and followed down an alley. Similarly, when Théo is awakened by his neighbors' fighting, there are no police to hear the woman's screams. Camille's arrest at the end of the film captures this circumstance exceptionally well, even more so because it reflects the actual events of the *fait divers*. In the film, we see Camille strolling down a street in the evening, and then the camera cuts to a police car that drives by slowly and pulls up next to him. The camera then cuts to a policeman who gazes at Camille, evidently recognizing him from the wanted posters in the station.

The difference between the two men is palpable: a white, overweight, older man in a suit, inside a car watches a young, black man with colored hair and an earring, on foot. The contrast is stark, but its situation is even more startling. By complete hazard, the policeman has come across Camille. After years of searching for him, his identification is made to a lucky instant when dozens of random events have come together to allow this moment. The element of happenstance (*le miracle de l'indice*) that allows Camille to be caught characterizes the role of the police in the criminal investigation. Denis thus uncovers the reality of the dreariness of police work, yet she does not judge this fact any more than she judges Camille. It appears that there is little that the police can do. Despite their efforts, it is impossible to halt crime, and it is likely that many of the most important crimes will go unnoticed. The attention paid to Daïga thus differs little from that paid to Camille; just as she is asked where she is from and whether or not she is legal, the police ask Camille for his papers. An inquiry into identity may uncover nothing at all, or it may provide the key to dozens of unsolved murders. In either case, the method is unpredictable at best.

Looking at the Criminal, Female Spectatorial Desire, and the Gaze

In the previous section, we saw how the characters' gaze, and Daïga's in particular, falls neither on the media's efforts to attract public attention nor on the brave attempts by the police to stalk criminals. Instead, it is drawn to the criminal. Significantly, the women in the film (potential victims of "the monster") turn their attention away from these powerful groups and toward the criminal. Through their interactions with Camille, these female characters contrast with the media's routine depictions of women as crime victims. In her film, Denis imagines a female empowerment that does not negate the criminal's humanity. Although Daïga is similar to the empowered female character of contemporary horror films, she breaks from this depiction by deconstructing the image of the criminal as an evil Other. In this way, Denis creates a space for female spectators to look at the criminal through female characters on-screen.

The term "spectatorial gaze" was introduced by Laura Mulvey in her seminal essay "Visual Pleasure and Narrative Cinema," first published in *Screen* in 1975. Mulvey's psychoanalytic approach defined the cinematic gaze as a male gaze that recreates ego libido and scopophilic instincts, or pleasure in looking at another person as an erotic object. She explains that in order for a female spectator to experience pleasure, she must put herself in the position of the male. Although Mulvey's research has been rigorously challenged by numerous critics, it has nonetheless had a significant impact on feminist cinematic theory and is therefore critical to this study for its analysis of how the spectator's gaze shapes textual meaning. It is particularly significant for us in its illumination of how Denis subverts traditionally male notions of the gaze throughout her film. Unlike Mulvey's work, which focuses on a passive one-way female gaze, E. Ann Kaplan suggests that there also exists a "look" that operates in cinema, which she differentiates from the gaze. Noting that the look implies a relation that is "determined by history, tradition, power hierarchies, politics, economics," Kaplan examines how the female directors she studies imagine their interactions with Others "as a process, a relation, rather than a gaze" (14). In *Looking for the Other: Feminism, Film, and the Imperial Gaze*, Kaplan examines the racialized gaze in an effort to analyze what happens when whites look at nonwhites and vice-versa; studying female-directed films about colonialism, she interprets and defines the visual systems that produce the look. Kaplan specifies that "the gaze is active: the subject bearing the gaze is not interested in the object per se, but consumed with his own anxieties, which are inevitably intermixed with desire" (xviii). Kaplan explains this gaze as neither relation nor process. She writes, "like the consumption of pornography, it is a one-way gaze that seeks to alleviate anxiety in the one gazing through sexual fantasies; it produces a sexual arousal in that subject which is enjoyed alone, not with an Other." She concludes that the gaze "connotes an active subject versus a passive object" (xviii). Furthermore, the object of the gaze is "a threat to the subject's autonomy and security and thus must be placed, rationalized, and, by a circuitous route, denied" (xviii). This one-way gaze characterizes how we typically read (and are presented with) the criminal as a categorical Other who is distanced from the rational public. With the criminal in this position, we may safely gaze at him without fear and without having to interrogate ourselves (our fears, our desires) in any way. In contrast to this idea, Kaplan believes that there exists a very different spectatorial position, which she labels the "looking relation," borrowing Jane Gaines's term. This process of looking at the criminal recalls Todorov's hypothesis of the three dimensions of alterity he outlines in *The Conquest of America* (axiological, praxeological, and epistemic) (186). Eschewing the value judgment of the axiological level, these directors instead create a relationship at a praxeological level, one that is characterized by the identification of oneself with the Other or vice-versa. This notion, which comprises a two-way relationship, connotes a certain curiosity about the Other, as well as a desire to know; as Kaplan remarks, the look is "never innocent" (6). In accordance with Todorov's hypothesis that these axes are neither sequential nor exclusive, we find both the gaze *and* the look at operation in *J'ai pas sommeil.* One of the film's greatest strengths, then, lies in how it *facilitates* a look rather than a gaze at the criminal, a difference that upsets the traditional moral boundaries established by the media and affords the Other a subjectivity denied in the traditional gaze. Deceptively subtle, this distinction is quite radical because it disconcerts many spectators by asking them to engage with someone they find morally offensive.

Women spectators watching the criminal represented on screen deserves special examination. How do they respond to a man who has killed over twenty women? Are they able to put aside their fear and anger at the man who preys exclusively on their gender? What kinds of negotiations might women be making in experiencing this film? Mulvey's discussion of the gaze attempted to show that in traditional film, women were always in a position of inferiority, as the gaze was associated with a man. One of the most strident critiques of Mulvey's theory suggests that women are able to enjoy varied subject positions. In *J'ai pas sommeil*, we may thus explore the possibility that female spectators do not necessarily adopt the direct gender identification of a female victim. As Berenstein writes in relationship to horror films, "fluid subject positions invite spectators to engage in roles similar to those appropriated by actors in the performance of drag" (235). Thus, a female spectator may assume Théo's or even Camille's viewpoint. As a man in drag, Camille's fluid gender performance theoretically allows women to identify with his character all the more. Although they are "victims" of Paulin's crimes, women watching the film are in the unique and potentially empowering position of voyeur; as spectators, they may use this position to gaze at Camille, transforming *him* into an object. (Male spectators may also assume this viewing position, as cinema by no means precludes direct gender identification; in the construction of the criminal, the binary oppositions in place in society oppose the mad and the sane, theoretically allowing men and women to share the same subject positions. Yet men were never victims of Paulin's crimes, so although Camille may threaten their masculinity in his drag or their sense of safety in his "evil," he does not represent a threat in the same manner that he may for female spectators.) More important to this discussion, however, is that Denis also provides characters with whom women may directly identify. As Kaplan asks (in response to Mulvey's assertion that women must adopt a passive spectator's role), "but what happens when the subjects deploying the gaze are ones white women can identify with directly?" (xix). Here, these women would include the director, whose gaze behind the camera guides the spectators, and the female characters in the film, especially Daïga and her aunt, Ninon. In this film, Denis thus succeeds in opening a space for resistant readings of the criminal body.

In contrast to the radio announcer's admonition that women stay inside, *J'ai pas sommeil* presents the spectator with several shots of older women outside. By shooting the majority of scenes outside, Denis captures the feel of Paris and conveys the sense of hazard inherent in the murders. There is a sense that the murderer can be anywhere or anyone: in a café, on the metro, crossing the street, any number of *non-places*. Like Daïga, who crosses Camille several times without knowing who he is, anyone might pass Camille on the street. Yet the older women we see outside are hardly panic-stricken by the *affaire* that has swept the country. Stubbornly refusing to do what they are told, Denis's women are life-affirming and headstrong; as Ninon's mother proclaims when her daughter suggests that she go to bed: "J'ai pas sommeil!" In another example, Ninon, who runs the hotel, teaches a judo class for older women. In a humorous scene, she encourages a student to "Go for his balls!" ("Vise les couilles!"). The sight of some thirty older women punching judo sticks at the crotches of imaginary aggressors does not conjure up a vision of helpless older women; its comic nature instead attests to an adaptive elderly population. In creating these images, Denis's film fractures media stereotypes and contradicts press reports that claim old women are scared to leave their homes. Above all, the film lowers the spectators' expectations that they should feel afraid for this population. This sense is further accentuated by Daïga's character, whose general aloofness and particularly fearless response to Camille empower spectators to *look* at the criminal. By offering a resistant space that further refuses the static gaze, this new relationship alters the traditional reading of crime. This reading of *J'ai pas sommeil* focuses on Daïga as a general way of situating the (female) spectator's gaze, and to show how Denis desensationalizes the criminal of the *fait divers* through this character. While point-of-view shots do not signal a necessary identification with the character (since spectators often assume multiple viewing positions), Denis's choice of a female lead and the scenes in which the camera follows Daïga's gaze *allow* the spectator to experience scenes from her perspective, establishing a preferred reading. As we will see in *Roberto Zucco*, the female character's interaction with the criminal is central to creating a richer understanding of the crime. This relationship ruptures the media's binary Othering, which refuses a look at humanity and remains at what Todorov refers to as an epistemic level of judging the Other. Daïga is particularly interesting, because as a foreigner who struggles to express herself in French, she is positioned outside the societal norm. Although her youth and beauty make her more socially acceptable, she nonetheless sees herself—and is perceived—as an outsider, perhaps more like than unlike Camille. Her difference is thus palpable from the beginning of the film. It gives her a specific perspective on society and later on Camille that likens her to modern horror's "Final Girl," a feminist character that faces the criminal and escapes.

Although *J'ai pas sommeil* is not a "horror film," its subject matter and its use (and subsequent subversion) of elements typical of modern horror films make this a relevant and insightful point of comparison. Carol Clover's research also helps us to decode Daïga's role in the film. As a character that very much resembles the so-called "Final Girl" of horror films, Daïga also departs from this type, a deviation that contributes to creating a new vision of the criminal. Clover's *Men, Women, and Chainsaws: Gender in the Modern Horror Film* (1992) tracks viewer identification in modern horror films. Clover demonstrates that instead of engaging young males in misogynist portrayals, many of these horror films are strident feminist works whose victim-heroes ("Final Girls") prevail. According to Clover, the Final Girl is discernible through several developments in the film. From the very beginning of the film, she will clearly be the main character, and at the end she will be the one who "lives to tell the tale." Daïga is arguably the central character of *J'ai pas sommeil*, since her presence both opens and closes the film. As she drives away in her car at the end of the film, it is she who escapes the tangle Camille has left of everyone's lives. Clover adds that the Final Girl's gender is "compromised from the outset by her masculine interests, her inevitable sexual reluctance, her apartness from other girls" (45–46). Daïga, too, is decidedly masculine in aspect. Although very attractive, she functions as a prototypical male: her appearance is slovenly (she wears pants, no makeup, her hair is dirty, her gestures are not refined), she swears, smokes, and steals, and she deliberately smashes a car without apology. In addition to these masculine characteristics, she rebuffs two men (the theater director who wants to sleep with her, another who chases her), and spends time only with Ninon. Indeed, the most sensual representation of her is when she and Ninon slow-dance to an old song, drunk and giddy. Clover shows how these kinds of elements make the Final Girl a fluid gender reference, allowing both male and females to identify with her. Finally, Clover explains that the Final Girl "is intelligent, watchful, levelheaded; . . . the only one whose perspective approaches our own privileged understanding of the situation" (44). She adds that as spectators "we register her horror as [the Final Girl] stumbles on the corpses of her friends" (44). Indeed, Daïga's watchfulness most approaches what we know of the murders, but it is curiosity rather than horror that characterizes her reactions. Here, Daïga departs from the traditional Final Girl. When she casually notes the dead bodies at her aunt's apartment building, looks past the newspaper headlines that proclaim more murders, and stares at the wanted posters for Camille and Raphaël, Daïga registers these facts with calm detachment rather than abject horror. In this lack of surprise or fear, her reaction (or lack thereof) helps to assuage spectator fears of the killer and, most importantly, replace the derisive gaze with a look.

In classical horror, Clover notes, the viewer's identification shifts with the Final Girl. "If, during the film's course, we've shifted our sympathies back and forth and dealt them out to other characters along the way, we belong in the end to the Final Girl; there is no alternative" (45–46). Like this definition, the perspective of *J'ai pas sommeil* is relatively elastic, as it shifts from character to character, and although the film tracks both Théo and Camille's lives, in the end we return to Daïga. She is indeed the last character to escape, although in a significant departure from the horror film, she does not flee the murderer but rather the city of Paris. Rather than killing Camille (as in a slasher film) or turning him in to the police (which would be this film's equivalent), Daïga uses Camille to further her own needs: stealing all the money from his killings, she packs up her things and leaves the city. This radical action shows how Denis subverts traditionally anticipated plot lines to alter the typical representation of the crime story. Finally, when Camille is jailed at the end of the film, it is not the Final Girl who has devised his capture. Not fearful but vaguely curious and resourceful, Daïga shows this strength and vulnerability in two particular scenes as she redirects the gaze. In a scene towards the middle of the film, we see Daïga standing at a *crêperie* when a man approaches her and begins talking to her. Daïga laughs at his obviously sexual advances and brushes him aside, walking away. As the man follows her into the street and begins to run after her, Daïga breaks into a run, turning down a dark alley. Interestingly, this may be the most suspenseful moment of the film, as we fear her capture. Daïga rushes to the counter of an old movie theater, where she buys a ticket from a seedy-looking woman, glancing worriedly behind her for her pursuer. It is dark inside the theater, and as Daïga's eyes adjust, we hear the music from the film playing: a 1970s romantic track that suggests a pornographic film. As she inches past several men to take her seat, Daïga becomes the focus of the shot, and she gazes intently at the screen, fascinated.

It is interesting here to return to Mulvey, for in the scene in which Daïga enters the dark theater, Denis seems to deliberately overturn Mulvey's theory. Rather than participating in her own objectification by assuming the male spectator's position, Daïga ridicules this space. As spectators caught in a *mise-en-abîme*, we see that Daïga's presence has disconcerted the men; panning back, the camera reveals that there are in fact only men in the theater. Each of the men averts his eyes from the screen and looks at Daïga in disbelief, yet she is oblivious to their stares and begins to laugh at the movie. As her giggle turns into full-blown laughter, the camera pans to the movie, which depicts a stereotypical scenario of a woman taking her clothes off for a man in front of a glowing fire. The brilliance of the scene lies in Daïga's command of it; she has taken over the traditional scenario in which the woman's sexuality is the object of the male gaze. Succeeding not only in eluding her pursuer, she moreover deflects the gaze of a roomful of men. Although the men turn to look at her, their gaze is broken, becoming more akin to a curious look: what is she doing here? Here Denis establishes a two-way visual interchange rather than a one-way exchange. The men's astonishment at Daïga's laughter thus testifies to her triumph and affirms their expulsion from the subject position. By successfully displacing the traditional male gaze, Denis subverts its negative implications and allows Daïga to become a subject in her own right. This scene clearly demonstrates that while women are frequently pursued and even stalked, their fate is not determined by this intimidation. Like the judo-practicing grandmothers who take action in the face of adversity, Daïga is able to turn a distressing situation into a humorous one, showing her to be both courageous and resourceful.

Daïga's courageousness extends well beyond necessity, however, as her fascination with Camille begins to consume her. At the police station following a car accident that she caused, Daïga spots a wanted poster of Camille and Raphaël. She stares at it a moment, recognizing the two men from the hotel where she works; here the camera first watches Daïga notice the pictures and then shifts to her position, from which the spectator views the police sketches. Later that night, Daïga reveals her inquisitiveness as she follows Camille from the hotel. The spectator follows her gaze as she tracks Camille through the busy streets. In this scene, Denis parallels and reverses the dynamic that Daïga experienced with the man at the *crêperie*; instead of being pursued by a man, Daïga is shown pursuing a man. Rather than repeating her negative experience as the object of the gaze, then, Daïga places herself in the subject position, empowering her gaze as she watches Camille. Moreover, since the camera holds her point of view (as spectators we move from watching Daïga watch Camille to watching Camille), the spectator witnesses Daïga's transformation from object to subject. She follows him until he stops at a stand-up café that resembles the *crêperie* stand where she was harassed by the unknown man, a further parallel that solidifies her transformation. According to Clover, in modern horror films, the Final Girl will often seek out the killer in an effort to trap him and put an end to his heinous crimes (e.g., *A Nightmare on Elm Street*, *Friday the Thirteenth*). Again we see a correlation in Daïga's actions, but unlike the Final Girl, whose hunt for the killer stems from fear (like the gaze), Daïga's deliberate pursuit (like the look) derives from a certain dose of curiosity about the Other. In her final act of stealing Camille's money, Daïga secures her triumph as a Final Girl, but her process of doing this remains distinct. While her fascination was piqued by the drag pictures of Camille found in his room, Daïga now wants to know more about him, moving toward an epistemic level where knowledge of the Other is desired. Unlike the man who chased her into the theater, then, Daïga's pursuit of Camille does not constitute a one-way gaze, but rather a look. Seemingly fearless of Camille, her search opens a space for a looking *relation.* She is curious to know more about Camille, and as he smiles at her and pays for her coffee before walking off, they symbolically brush hands. In choosing to film this sequence from Daïga's perspective, Denis removes the spectator from the traditional position of gazing at the Other and allows the audience to establish a relationship with Camille. Far from constructing a sympathetic view of the criminal (he is politely distant), the neutrality with which Denis depicts his character symbolizes a process that we might endeavor to recreate with Camille, viewing him as a neutral character who warrants our minimal bias.

Denis's representation of female characters interacting with the criminal in safe ways collapses the media's depiction of the public, and of women in particular, as victims. This representation not only empowers potential victims, but likewise imagines a process where the public envisions the criminal as a person. Shedding the veils of mystery, monstrosity, and fear that shield the murderer from the public, Denis demonstrates how we may begin to imagine another way of constructing the criminal. Looking, rather than gazing, at Camille, the public is able to examine its own relationship with crime by embracing its own curiosity.

Capturing the Criminal Body on Screen

In the looking relation that Daïga establishes with Camille, Denis points to how we might learn to disempower the criminal and emerge from the binary definitions that imprison both the criminal and the public. She creates this possibility not only through female characters who interact with Camille, but also in her manner of filming Camille's body. Looking at him through the lens of the camera (which we may characterize as a female look, as Denis is a woman), close-up shots of his body undercut the traditional gaze and remove the fascination with his difference. Just as Daïga looks rather than gazes at Camille in several scenes, then, we may speak of the spectator's establishing a looking relation with Camille through Denis's unique manner of filming his body. This warrants particular discussion, because her subject is a black, homosexual, transvestite, male criminal. Rarely is such a body lingered on in cinema, and for this reason Denis's film is noteworthy but equally subject to critique. As I have shown, the a-politically-correct nature of Paulin/Camille's body as a criminal makes some critics (and presumably some audience members) uncomfortable. In examining how Denis films Camille's body, then, I am particularly interested in how she captures and presents his identity on-screen, and, consequently, how this might be read by spectators.

The first time we see Camille is at dawn. A significant part of the film takes place during the hours between darkness and light, and this dim light visually emphasizes the obscurity of characters that are neither completely good nor bad. The camera pans in on two men getting into a car before cutting to a third man, who approaches the car and pulls the second man out of the passenger side, throwing him to the ground and kicking him. The second man (slim, balding, and dressed in black leather) gets back in the new Mercedes and drives away with the first. The camera then closes in and lingers on a group of sanitation workers that passes by the scene in their garbage truck. The men in the Mercedes have clearly just returned from a night out. The camera then cuts to a person lying in bed, focusing on masculine hands that wear black nail polish. As the man pulls the covers from over his head, we see that it is the same person who had kicked the second man. In the next several shots, other strands of the story line unravel. Camille, who has returned from a night out, has gone back to his brother, Théo's, apartment. From their conversation in the bathroom, we learn that Théo's wife, Mona, has again left him, leaving him to care for their young son. Meanwhile, the camera focuses close-ups on Camille as he removes his eye makeup and peels off his fishnet stockings. We watch him as he enters the shower, the camera focusing in on his skin. There is a fatigue in Camille's slow movements that adds to the feeling that we are watching a private moment. Denis's manner of filming the masculine body closely captures both the strength and softness of Camille, seen in the stillness of his movements. Gestures and movements like these are paramount in Denis's films, which are characterized by an infrequent use of dialogue; both *Chocolat* and *Beau Travail* contain several long shots of the male body in performance. Most of all, there is almost a discomfort in the camera's proximity. As with the scene in which Daïga turns away after glimpsing Camille and his lover in a nude embrace in front of their window, the spectator may have the sense that s/he sees too much. There is an implied desire in the camera's lingering gaze, as well as an element of voyeurism in the intimacy of the moment.

This voyeuristic feeling is best captured in the scene in which Camille and his lover are in their hotel room. In contrast to the many scenes of *J'ai pas sommeil* that are filmed outside, the intimacy of this setting is underscored by its interiority. The Hitchcockian filming of the scene through a window hints at the crimes being committed by the pair, placing the spectator in the helpless role of watching the murders without being able to do anything. The scene begins with Camille frightening his partner, menacing to push him out the window. On the bed, with their shirts off, Camille again threatens Raphaël, standing over him and questioning his devotion. As the camera zooms in through the open window to center on the pair, Raphaël timidly utters that he wants to leave, and Camille glowers, repeating "You want to leave?" ("Tu veux partir?") in a hypnotic manner that seems to calm Raphaël's fears while at the same time increasing the level of the men's desire and intimacy. As they embrace, the camera shifts focus to closely follow the grain of Camille's skin, reflecting both its sheer power and simple grace. The camera then abruptly cuts to

Daïga cleaning a hotel room. In this representation of Camille, Denis records the conflicting feelings of desire and loathing that the spectator hypothetically feels for the killer. Rather than denying these feelings, however, Denis is able to capture them within a single scene, best exemplified in her manner of recording Camille's body. With almost perverse interest, the camera follows Camille's body and lingers on it a moment too long, as if fascinated. Filming the body in these long shots, the spectator's gaze is directed on Camille for minutes at a time with no other action taking place. The effect of this restricted focus on Camille transforms his body; no longer grotesque in its difference, it becomes fascinating, and then it passes into invisibility, his difference no longer the focus of our attention. As Deleuze explains, "'To give' a body, to mount a camera on the body, takes on a different sense: it is no longer a matter of following and trailing the everyday body, but of *making it pass through a ceremony*, of introducing it into a glass cage or a crystal, *of imposing a carnival or a masquerade on it which makes it into a grotesque body, but also brings out of it a gracious and glorious body*, until at last the disappearance of the visible body is achieved" (190; my emphasis). Denis's close filming of Camille's body stretches the spectator's gaze to eventually neutralize how it watches Camille. As Deleuze explains, the body "forces us to think, and forces us to think what is concealed from thought, life" (189). Towards the end of this scene, for instance, the spectator is more accustomed to Camille's difference (as a black, as a transvestite, as an HIV-positive man). Denis's focus on his body thus offers a way to transcend the criminal's difference. She does not ignore or erase his Otherness, but instead Denis makes it the focus of the shot; in this way, she gives his difference a subjectivity denied by Baudrillard. Gone, for instance, is the masquerade of Camille's black fingernail polish and fishnet stockings, as these close-ups offset their importance. Denis's shots of Camille getting dressed best illustrate this portrayal. While Camille is often dressed to go out, there are several scenes in which he is either dressing or undressing, or in various stages of undress. In the beginning scene in which he removes his eye makeup and stockings to take a shower, for instance, Denis focuses the camera close upon his skin, centering on his buttocks as he steps into the shower. Later, a tailor tightens Camille's new faux-leather bustier; as she pulls the strings from the back, the camera zooms onto his skin, which pushes out from the tightness of the cheap fabric, resisting its constriction. In both of these scenes, Camille's body springs from the clothes that confine him, a "grotesque body" that cannot be held, and that is foreign to these female garments.

In a later scene that takes place in a drag club, Camille slow dances and lip-syncs a torch song before the men in the dark club. His tight dress and long gloves outline his muscular body, and the slow sensuality of his movements commands the erotic scene. At the same time, while decidedly masculine in strength, Camille's body is delicate; his bare feet and exposed nipple convey his fragility before the men who gaze at him. This partial drag that Denis creates distinguishes the fictional Camille from the real Paulin, who always appeared in complete drag at his performances. Denis explains that she deliberately chose not to show Camille in complete drag. Clarifying that in the nightclub where Paulin had worked, drag was no longer fashionable, and since her film was not a period piece, she says she went looking for a "place that would be both male and female" (Lippy 87). This scene thus includes Camille with long nails but no falsies, "so he was very male, with his wide shoulders, and this worked as something that was in-between." In making Camille distinctly more masculine, Denis also disassociates him from the typical cross-dresser found in horror films, who disguises himself as a woman to distance himself from his hated maleness (*Dressed to Kill*, *Psycho*, *Silence of the Lambs*, *Friday the Thirteenth*). Aroused by women who remind him of his mother, this archetype then murders women. But unlike Bobbi of *Dressed to Kill*, Camille does not dress in drag to commit his murders, nor are his homicidal tendencies explained by a frustrated sense of sexual confusion, as in *Silence of the Lambs*. Camille's homosexuality—rather than transsexuality—negates this clichéd scenario, making him at once more vulnerable and his motives less clear. As the camera lingers on Camille's body for several moments while he slowly dances to the song, what begins as a gender parody in a drag club is transformed, and Camille emerges as a Deleuzian gracious body. Although the men in the club gaze at Camille, the spectator's ability to take in the whole scene (the scene is shot not from a particular viewpoint but instead pans from one man's gaze to another) works to establish a looking relation with Camille. The audience watches him being objectified (he looks down for much of the song, not meeting the men's eyes), but also witnesses his control of the club (all the men's attention is turned toward him), and in this way, we are able to absorb Camille more fully. In this scene, then, we see an example of Deleuze's description of the masqueraded body in ceremony, as Camille commands the sexual gaze of the men in the club. Deleuze calls what emerges from this kind of ceremony "the third body," or the "protagonist that passes through all the other bodies" (*Cinema 2* 190). Thus, from the two poles of the everyday body (Camille in the hotel with Ninon, with his friends) and the ceremonial body (Camille in drag, Camille killing elderly women) emerges the third body, which is arguably the most problematic for most viewers, for it replaces the binary (gracious/grotesque) body with a single being.

Denis's emphasis on Camille's physique seems to reflect his own interest in his body; Paulin was a model and a drag performer, and police found numerous photos of him in various ensembles. In the film, as Daïga cleans Camille's room, she finds black-and-white pictures of him strewn about the floor. Her reaction to these photos represents the familiar dynamic of fascination and repulsion, yet here it is in relation to the intimacy of Camille's sexuality rather than the brutality of his crimes. We see her look at each picture intently with a kind of shock and then turn away. The pictures are erotically suggestive: a close-up of Camille's buttock and leg, his handcuffed hand, his head sporting devil's horns. In each of these photos, as in the earlier scenes, Camille is in a state of transformation. Again, this representation of the killer distances him from the traditional horror genre. According to Clover, the *victim* is usually depicted as dressing or undressing (*Psycho*, *Halloween*), revealing her vulnerability. In depicting Camille in this same manner, Denis reverses the spectator's expectations, aligning Camille with the victim rather than the conventional predator. (In *Dressed to Kill*, we do see the killer getting dressed, and in *Silence of the Lambs* we see Buffalo Bill sewing his suit of real women's skins, but in neither case do we see his face.) Camille's identity is never hidden in this conventional way, making his portrayal more like a victim than a murderer. Neither dressed nor undressed, he is in between, in a state that might be described as "becoming," to use Deleuze's term. This notion of "becoming" suggests a state neither undone nor finished: the person is in transformation. Deleuze discusses this idea in relation to contemporary cinema's use of movement-image and time-image, explaining that because the movement-image is characterized by its adherence to chronology, it never attempts to fool the spectator. Conversely, the time-image is identified by gaps in narration and false cuts, opening the door from the real to the virtual. Denis's montage sequences illustrate this practice: shots that cut from one character to another allow for clear blanks in the narration where the spectator does not know what happens in between. As Deleuze explains, "time has always put the truth in crisis" (130), and this film is no exception. While *J'ai pas sommeil* is not groundbreaking in this kind of montage, these temporal distortions are central to contesting the media's reports about the killer. By deliberately showing parts of Camille's life ignored by the media, for instance, Denis emphasizes the one-sided nature of their reports. Cuts to newspaper headlines and television broadcasts about the murders show that while these gaps may allow us to perceive traces of what might be true, we will never know exactly what happened in the actual crimes. Just as the press almost entirely neglects Paulin's humanity, so Denis neglects Camille's sheer brutality, pointing to the one-sidedness of her own representation of the criminal. In the case of the criminal body, then, Camille is not represented as containing one single truth or identity. Rather, Denis shows him in a variety of situations behaving in a variety of different ways: dancing at his mother's birthday party, killing old women, singing in clubs, taking drugs, embracing his partner, buying Daïga a coffee. He is in black leather, in street wear, or in a dress, but mostly he is undressed. There is not one simple truth of Camille, making it difficult to distinguish fact from fiction.

The impossibility of representing a "truth" leads Deleuze to the conclusion that there is not a true world that may be trusted, prompting him to ask, "what is there left to believe in?" (139). He concludes that bodies, in their expression of a "will to power," are forces that cannot lie: "What remains? There remain bodies, which are forces, nothing but forces" (139). Denis captures this "will to power" in the intimate and visceral shots of Camille's body. There is truth in his body, although his constant transformations may convey that he does not know what to do with this truth. In other words, in his various stages of undress, as his identity changes from lover to brother to son to killer, there remains the one truth underneath the many masks that are his body. Thus, while Camille's actions are unreliable, in a perpetual movement of "becoming" where the truth is false and falsehood may be true, his body cannot lie. Looking at Camille, the truth of his body is most apparent in his health: despite his physical prowess, Camille is HIV-positive, suggesting that his strength is temporary and thus false. His power can therefore not disguise his fragility. The duality that Denis represents in the figure of Camille exemplifies the spectator's anxiety in viewing him. In this way, Denis succeeds in demonstrating that the fascination with Paulin is imbued with discomfort not only because of his crimes, but also and especially because of his physical body. The notion of the spectator's gaze/look on the body, in particular on the criminal body, is central to the study of this *fait divers* rewritten as film. As I have explained in the introduction, the allure of the *fait divers* extends beyond the morbid curiosity of human nature; rather, the desire for knowledge forms its fundamental appeal. Through both the event and its representation, society learns what constitutes acceptable behavior, how to function in crisis, and what characteristics are associated with criminals. We have to ask, therefore, what knowledge is being presented in the rewriting of a *fait divers*, in particular where the criminal is a black, homosexual, HIV-positive serial killer. Here we might turn to the spectator's unfamiliarity with Denis's technique of close-ups of Camille's body. Just as there are not many films that celebrate the beauty and strength of the male body, there are a scant few that record the black male body in this manner; fewer still portray the sensuality of homosexual relationships, even fewer the complexity of transvestism, and so on. Thus, on the one hand, the spectator's desire for and fascination with Camille's body may be due to a lack of familiarity; this unfamiliarity resides in Camille's difference, which might be experienced as exciting. As Judith Mayne writes of sexual viewing points, "one of the distinct pleasures of the cinema may well be a safe zone in which homosexual as well as heterosexual fantasies can be fantasized and acted" (qtd. in Berenstein 235). Thus, spectators may experience pleasure in assuming different viewpoints.

On the other hand, there may exist a parallel sensation of fear or repulsion in the face of this representation. Camille's transvestism prevents a rigid one-to-one pattern with either female or male viewers. As Marjorie Garber writes, "the transvestite is both terrifying and seductive precisely because s/he incarnates and emblematizes the disruptive elements that intervene, signaling not just another category crisis, but a category of crisis itself" (qtd. in Berenstein 234). The public's complex fascination/repulsion with the criminal is thus echoed in watching Camille's gender performance. Yet while this subversive drag may signal a category crisis for many viewers, it does not, as Baudrillard claims, signal the banality of an identity that escapes categorization. As a society, we have not yet arrived at a place where transvestitism may be considered banal; while the shock of the difference may have worn off among the public, this familiarity does not indicate a level of saturation or acceptance of the difference. There is nothing everyday or banal about Camille's identity, and in his particular *métissage* he represents a uniqueness on-screen that confers upon him a subjectivity denied in traditional film. For this reason, Denis's representation of Camille's identity may prove problematic for some. If this is one of the few looks at a black gay transvestite, for example, Denis's choice of subject may be construed as racist or homophobic, particularly given the violent and psychotic nature of the characters' relationship; this reading has been echoed by reviewers. Despite her similar portrayals of other characters in the film, who likewise experience dysfunctional relationships, Denis cannot avoid society's racism and homophobia, or its fears of their politically incorrect representations. Moreover, as I have shown in the liberal press's retreat from the issue of Paulin's race and reviewers' comments about his nonjudgmental treatment, Camille's difference makes many spectators uncomfortable. Certainly attuned to this response, Denis uses this discomfort to her advantage by not shying away from the subject. Indeed, she forces the spectator to confront his or her discomfort by directing the camera on Camille's body, and in this way, she opens the *fait divers* to alternative readings.

Filming the Murders

Unlike Scorsese, De Palma, or filmmakers of the slasher genre, Denis does not manipulate the fantasies and fears of her audience. She instead depicts the murderer's crimes in a cool and nonjudgmental manner that parallels how she films Camille's body. The scenes that enact these crimes are filmed back-to-back more than halfway through the film. Furthermore, there are no clues or dramatic music announcing these scenes, omitting commonly used suspense mechanisms; at the same time, she does not dismiss them. Significantly, Denis chose to film just two murders to evoke the whole series. If *J'ai pas sommeil* asks that the spectator *look* rather than *gaze* at Camille, then the murder scenes most acutely challenge these efforts; the sheer discomfort of watching them discourages anything other than a one-way objectifying gaze. Nevertheless, the film manages to achieve this perspective. The placement of the murders at the center of *J'ai pas sommeil* marks their importance, yet also diminishes any suspense that spectators might feel. It is not until the middle of the film that the spectator learns that Camille is the killer. This nontraditional sequence strongly differs from how the criminal appears in the media; in a *fait divers* the criminal is immediately associated with his killings. In contrast, Denis explains, this "first murder scene, we felt, really had to be after the first act. That way, there would be no opportunity for the audience to look at him differently" (Lippy 87). If the murders had occurred at the opening of the movie, Denis stresses, "Camille would never have had a chance to be looked at as a human being, just as a killer" (87). She explains that "Just as one can't escape these scenes, nor can one hide the murders behind a door, under a table, in a corner, they need to be filmed on screen. At the same time, these scenes prohibit editing, you have to film them in one shot. If not, it's disgusting or it's not very moral, one embellishes the crime" ("Comme on ne peut pas échapper à ces scènes, on ne peut pas non plus masquer les meurtres derrière une porte, sous une table, dans un coin, il faut qu'ils soient filmés plein champ. En même temps, ces scènes interdisent le montage, il faut les filmer en un seul plan. Sinon, ou c'est dégueulasse ou ce n'est pas très moral, on embellit le crime") (qtd. in Jousse 26).

Significantly, Denis's film contains no shortage of elderly women: Daïga's aunt, Ninon, Ninon's mother, the women in the karate class, Camille's mother, and several nameless women whom we see on the street. While this relatively large number of older women increases the fear that any one of them could die at any given moment in the film, not a single one of these characters does. In this way Denis's film contrasts with the traditional horror film, where a main character is pursued and killed by the murderer. That Camille's victims are unknown to the spectator is thus significant in reducing the sense of drama and identification. Without a relationship to the women who are killed, the crimes seem even more random and senseless. Indeed, Camille and Raphaël's choice of victims seems haphazard and strange. We do not understand why they are killing these women, as the women do not appear to be particularly wealthy. The mystery surrounding the motive may be intriguing, but without any explanation, the spectator does not have any way to comprehend the murders, somewhat reducing his/her desire to know. Significantly, Denis does not try to assign a motive. Camille's manner of murdering the women further obscures comprehension of the crimes. His approach is calm and methodical, absolutely cool. At the beginning of the first murder scene, Camille and his lover slip past a locked gate after an older woman has entered the courtyard. Following the woman's slow walk to her apartment, the spectator maintains Camille and Raphaël's perspective, and once at her door, we see the woman's shocked face as Camille pushes her over the threshold and onto the floor. At this point the shot shifts perspective, allowing us the full view of Camille strangling the woman, a character we have not yet seen. This more neutral manner of filming the murders differs from the contemporary horror genre, which shows killing exclusively from the point of view of the victim. Rather than positioning the spectator with the victim and thus choosing an angle that theoretically heightens audience fear, Denis selects a less sensational shot that desensationalizes the crime. As the woman is pushed to the floor, Raphaël keeps his hand over her mouth while Camille takes off his belt. Once he places it around the woman's neck and begins to tighten it, his partner is freed of his task, and Raphaël goes into the kitchen, evidently uncomfortable with the scene. Camille tightens the belt around the woman's neck until she collapses. Her face turned away from the camera, the woman appears dead, and Camille casually removes her earrings, sorts through her wallet, and, finally satisfied, he tosses her jacket over her head in a gesture that may be read either as dignity or as disgust. In either interpretation, he is methodical and calm in his actions. Raphaël, on the other hand, rummages noisily through the kitchen drawers, presumably looking for silver; we hear a woman's scream from the open window of another apartment building, a loud contrast to Camille's silent victim; this scream seems to stand for all the other crimes being committed against women and diminishes the novelty of Camille's murders. The next frame shows Camille in the woman's bedroom. Musing over her jewelry and listening to her music boxes, his slowness is in stark contrast to Raphaël's hurried movements. As the door to the apartment shuts, and Camille and Raphaël exit casually onto the stairwell, the camera lingers on the old woman's body, which begins to move. When we see a deliveryman ringing the bell to her apartment, we imagine that she will be saved.

The following sequence cuts to a spunky older woman letting Raphaël into her apartment, chattering steadily and thanking him for his help. Now that the spectator has seen one murder, the likelihood of another seems probable, and this scene introduces elements of what might be termed suspense. The naïve and spunky woman, who resembles Daïga's aunt, invites Raphaël inside, offers him milk, and then coffee, never questioning his motives for a moment. As she stands in the kitchen, turned away from him, she asks him to hang a curtain rod that had fallen. Her careless chatter is as nerve-wracking as it is endearing; this is the closest that Denis will allow us to feel to one of the victims. At this moment Camille appears through the entranceway, and we hear the woman's muffled exclamation of surprise as a hand goes over her mouth. The camera then drops to her feet, which are lifted off the floor as she is presumably being strangled. The scene is over, and the next sequence returns us to Théo's apartment. For spectators familiar with the actual events—and we may assume that the majority of French spectators know at least some details of the *affaire*—Camille's murders may prove troublesome in their relative neutrality. Out of twenty killings that she had to choose from, Denis selects two, one in which the victim does not die, and another that fails to portray the prolonged violence of the act. Paulin also committed several of the murders alone, but Raphaël's participation in the murders on-screen leads one to believe that Mathurin was Paulin's faithful co-conspirator. Looked at together, this alteration of the *fait divers* is significant, if not problematic for some viewers.

The nontraditional look at the serial killer in *J'ai pas sommeil* sharply contrasts with the media's typical profile. Camille's neutrality is not constructed solely through the depiction of the murders but rather germinates and grows in the vast majority of scenes that depict him in the context of his larger life. In Denis's depiction of the mediated diffusion of the *affaire* throughout the city, in her emphasis on Camille's life beyond his killing, and through female characters who refuse to live in fear, she subverts popular representations of the criminal spectacle. Moreover, it is nearly impossible to completely dismiss Camille's humanity. By showing him "becoming" through his masqueraded body, Denis blurs the binary categorizations that define the Other, and she allows a third body to emerge. As a three-dimensional character, the criminal significantly departs from the media's inhuman representation of Paulin, making it difficult to dismiss him as an Other. Denis thus creates a *looking relation,* where the spectator encounters points of view that challenge those promoted by media reports of the *fait divers*. This provocative film opens a resistant space for imagining the criminal in a way that may make us uncomfortable. It is out of this discomfort that a new way of reading the criminal emerges, made possible by resisting the media's sensational representation of crime that encourages reaction over reflection.

Chapter Four

Sensation and Censorship

In February of 1988, wanted posters publicizing four pictures of "the crazed killer" ("le tueur fou") were plastered throughout Parisian metro stations, announcing the police's progress in putting a face to the man who had murdered a policeman in Toulon and at least two civilians near Annecy. Almost immediately following the issuance of the wanted poster, the killer was identified, and one month later, Roberto Succo was arrested near Venice and placed in a high-security state prison. Within less than 24 hours of his capture, however, Succo escaped from his cell, climbing to the roof of the prison to capture the attention of the international media. Hurling tiles at the journalists below, Succo stripped to his underwear and spoke wildly to the gathering crowd for over an hour. When he eventually fell from the roof and emerged unhurt, *Le Figaro* called him a "hero" and a "madman" ("héros," "fou") (Léridon, "L'Insupportable"). Succo rapidly became a figure of fluid significance. Representing both evil and purity at once, he encapsulated both the fascination and the repulsion characteristic of so many *faits divers*. Despite his deadly actions, Succo's affable personality and highly mediated body afforded him a heroic status, and the testimonies of several young women who called him "nice," "good-looking," and "sweet" firmly contrasted with the actions of this cold-blooded killer. As Pascale Froment writes in her detailed journalistic account of the crimes, *Je te tue: Histoire vraie de Roberto Succo, assassin sans raison*, "the 'crazed killer' did not have the mug for the job" ("'le tueur fou' n'avait pas la sale gueule de l'emploi") (221). The wanted photos of Succo, revealing four identities so distinct as to have warranted their simultaneous distribution, further added to this image of a mysterious, slippery identity. In the media's hurry to grasp this indefinable personage, however, its dogged sensationalization of the criminal reflected considerable impudence. Eager to announce his capture and immediately determine his identity, journalists erroneously attributed Succo's deeds to another man, misspelled his name as Zucco, and prematurely released his identity to the public, placing his accuser at considerable risk. In another example of journalistic irresponsibility, the discovery of syringes in Succo's apartment quickly became proof that he was a drug user ("il se drogue"), although this was not the case. News that police had found a single cassette with his voice likewise became *several* cassettes with a cold and unpredictable voice ("une voix métallique, désaxée") (d'Arrigo 17); journalists ignored that the importance of the tape lay in its ability to assure Succo's guilt in a battery charge, instead using this information to try to construct the image of a cold-blooded and detached monster. This journalistic exuberance reflects the shoddy reporting consistent with the contemporary media's penchant for sensationalism.

In this chapter, I analyze the media's representation of "le tueur de Toulon." Through a presentation of the historical facts of the *fait divers* (Succo's crimes and escapes), an examination of the marketers and producers of the *affaire* (the media's efforts to sensationalize the story and to classify Succo), and an understanding of the public that responded to Succo (the labels of "hero" and the noteworthy female attraction to the criminal), it is clear how the media shapes our reading of the criminal. Interrogating the media's discourse of immediacy, I demonstrate how it guided the public's fascination with Succo by creating a simplified view of the criminal. In this way, the media obscured the possibility of understanding either his motivations or our parallel fascination.

"The Full-Moon Assassin" on the Lam

Succo committed his string of crimes in 1987 and 1988, during the time he lived in "Le Petit Chicago," a sordid area of Toulon. In April of 1987, Succo shot and killed policeman André Castillo in Chambéry, and several weeks later he abducted France Vu-Dinh, whose body was never found, from Sévrier, near Lake Annecy. Succo then shot Michel Astoul, a young doctor living near Sisteron. Again near Lake Annecy, he killed Claudine Duchosal, and finally, during a showdown in a Toulon hotel in early 1988, Succo shot and killed a second policeman, Michel Morandin. Added to this list are several aggressions, rapes, and robberies, most notably that of Nicole Veillet, who was taken hostage from Aix-les-Bains with her fifteen-year-old son, Damien; this episode would later become a part of Koltès's play. Due to the high concentration of Succo's crimes in the Savoie region, the trauma felt there was especially palpable, making the area ripe for the protests that would occur several years later. Yet while the enormity of Succo's acts made his crimes fitting for front-page coverage, it was his fluid personage that constituted the principal draw of the *affaire*. Witnesses described Succo in radically different ways (as having various foreign accents and distinct physical characteristics), making it hard to form a composite picture of the killer. As in the Paulin case, police had considerable difficulty apprehending Succo, and it took several months and another *miracle de l'indice* before he was turned in by an ex-lover. Throughout this search and seizure, the media portrayed Succo as a man of multiple identities who could be anywhere at any time. By heightening public fear through its unbroken, detailed coverage of the *affaire*, the media capitalized on Succo's multifarious character to create an exciting *fait divers* sure to captivate the public's attention.

After Morandin was killed in January, police launched a full-blown search for Succo, posting his photo in police stations and public spaces alike throughout Italy, Switzerland, and France. No name was attached to the pictures, as Succo had managed to survive in France on invented first names Kurt, Pol, Fred, and André; still, the media dubbed him otherwise: "l'assassin de la pleine lune" ("the full-moon assassin"), "le tueur polyglotte" ("the polyglot killer"), and "l'homme au treillis" ("the man in military fatigues," as the killer was seen in military garb). On 6 February 1988, the police issued three additional photos on a second wanted poster, which was plastered throughout Parisian metro stations and in the pages of *Le Figaro* (8 Feb. 1988). So different was Succo in each photo that police could not come up with a composite sketch of the killer. Succo seemed to resist definition in his physicality as in his actions, his slippery representation mirroring his schizophrenic personality and lending itself to a portrait that matched his motiveless crimes. Nevertheless, the day the new poster was circulated, a 16-year-old young woman named Sabrina recognized the young man as someone she had known as a brother, a friend, and a father ("un frère, un ami, un père") (Salino, "Mais qui a peur" 101). Alerting the police, she explained that he had said that his real name was Roberto Juce, and that he was born near Venice, where he had killed his parents and spent five subsequent years in a psychiatric ward, from which he later escaped. This testimony allowed the police to embark on a full-fledged international search for the man, whom they erroneously identified as "Roberto *Z*ucco." The mini-drama was thus reignited as the discovery of Succo's identity provided new fodder for journalists weary of the same details and allowed them to resensationalize the simmering *affaire*. Interviews with acquaintances of the criminal lent authenticity to the case, the accumulation of details gave the illusion of accurate reporting, and quotes from Succo joined the violence of his actions with his remorseless attitude to create a perfect monster.

Succo was revealed to be the only child of a policeman and homemaker from Mestre, Italy. In April of 1981, just after turning nineteen, he stabbed both of his parents to death. According to reports, Succo said that his father would never let him use the car because he drove too fast, and that his mother marginalized him and excluded him from his family (Duplouich, "Maman ne m'aimait pas" 8). What many journalists failed to detail in their sensational reports of Succo's brutal acts were the circumstances of his childhood. Although described as "normal" by neighbors, Succo's mother physically abused her son; Succo's cruelty to animals might also have been seen as a warning sign of later violence. Instead, his crimes were publicized as occurring without warning, emphasizing the motiveless nature of the murders.

After being diagnosed with schizophrenia, Succo was placed in a low-security home for the criminally insane. Like an absurdist moralist living without consequence of his error, he reportedly explained to the commissariat: "I don't regret a thing. If I had to do it all over again, I would do it in exactly the same way" ("Je ne regrette rien. Si c'était à refaire, je le referais exactement de la même manière") (Duplouich, "Le Tueur fou" 42). Despite several statements in which he claimed that his actions were justified, including one to his priest, Succo's good behavior allowed him to join an academic release program and finish his baccalaureate degree. He was then allowed to attend university courses, during which time he escaped from the ward and fled to the south of France, where he lived without incident until 1987. According to police inspector Francisco Zonno, "it was only by sheer luck that there weren't any more victims" ("seul le hasard a permis qu'il ne fasse pas d'autres victimes") (Duplouich, "Le Tueur fou" 42). This last statement demonstrates the skillful way the media uses fear to instruct the public about crime. Able to rely solely on "le hasard" for their safety, the public was once again coached that crime surrounded them; at any minute they could be the victims of Succo, who was still on the loose. The information the media chose to provide about Succo's upbringing likewise gives considerable insight into how the media constructed its vision of the criminal as a cold-blooded killer.

Weeks later, the police were still searching furiously in the Swiss Alps and near the Franco-Swiss and Italian borders and were becoming desperate. Succo seemed to have disappeared, and the *affaire* began to die down in the media. Finally, on 28 February, Italian police captured Succo near Venice. Afterwards, Succo would explain that he had tried to not return to Venice, but that it was stronger than he ("J'ai essayé de me dire de ne pas y aller mais c'était plus fort que moi") (Froment 395). As Koltès would later highlight in his play, Succo's destiny was stronger than his identity, adding to his image as a mythic hero driven by his fate. Following his questioning, Succo was escorted into a police car to be further detained. Outside a crowd of journalists and photographers awaited his appearance, and when he arrived, Succo beguiled the media. Letting out a long whistle, he shouted out "Forza ragazzi" ("Good luck, boys") with a wink and a big grin. In a matter of seconds, journalists captured the adolescent face that they would liken to a young Rimbaud. While *Le Monde* did not cover the event until a full two days later, with the *affaire* receiving a small anonymous column on page 12 detailing the arrest ("Roberto Succo pourrait être jugé en Italie" 12), *Le Figaro* pounced on the news with a front-page headline that Succo had been arrested in Italy ("Roberto Succo arrêté en Italie" 1). The media blitz had begun.

The Spectacle of the "Tueur fou"

While Succo's sensational arrest made headlines throughout Italy, France, and Switzerland, the newspapers barely had time to give coverage to the *affaire* before Succo's next stunt elicited their awe and undivided attention. Having been jailed at Trévisa prison, Succo tried to escape a mere twenty-four hours later, a near-breakout that assured his renown in the pages of the *faits divers*. But it was his deliberate orchestration of the media during his escape that speaks to the power of the *fait divers* to attract and influence public opinion. Having jumped onto a small roof and then onto a rain shelter, Succo grasped window bars to pull himself onto the roof of the prison. Powerless to prevent his escape, the men in the guard towers looked on helplessly in a significant reversal of the panoptic tower. As Foucault explains, the panoptic schema may be used "wherever one is dealing with a multiplicity of individuals on whom a task or a particular form of behavior must be imposed" (*Discipline and Punish* 205). In the panoptic tower, and the prison tower is one example, the guard watches but cannot be seen, thus effectively surveying and controlling his subjects. Succo, in climbing higher than the tower, dethrones the guards from their superior position, an action that Koltès will use to frame his play. While his actions do not reposition him in the role of surveyor (since he wishes to be seen), they nevertheless demonstrate an upset of the symbolic power from its hidden locale in the tower. As Foucault confirms, "it does not matter who exercises the power. Any individual, taken almost at random, can operate the machine" (*Discipline and Punish* 202). As word got out that Succo had escaped onto the roof, police, local press, and regional television representatives gathered at the site, where Succo walked along the edge of the roof, balancing himself. Succo took off his shirt and shouted down to the crowd, "Hey you with the camera! Come here, I need to talk to you!" ("Hé, la caméra! Approche, il faut que je te parle!") (Froment 408). A crowd of over one hundred people had gathered, amongst them the Italian television station Antenna Tre, journalists from *La Tribuna* and *Le Dauphiné libéré*, and even a helicopter. According to Froment's recounting of the *affaire*, "they had all understood that Roberto's demonstration wasn't really an attempt to escape. There was something gratuitous in it, a cry without precise revindication or premeditation. An opportunity to show himself, to make himself into a spectacle. Pure theater" ("tous avaient compris que la démonstration de Roberto n'était pas une tentative d'évasion. C'était quelque chose de gratuit, un cri sans revendication précise ni préméditation. L'occasion de se montrer, de se donner en spectacle. Du théâtre pur") (409). Succo's deliberate manipulation of the media affirms the importance of the *fait divers* in contemporary society; aware of the media's preoccupation with sensationalism, he performed the perfect show, invigorated by their presence. Shaking his fist and pacing on the roof in his underwear, he was a vision of insanity. He seemed to know that his attractive body would make a great story, and he posed and paced for the crowd below, asking whether there were any journalists there ("Il y a de la presse?") (Froment 409); television reporters were overheard muttering that it was getting worse and worse ("c'est de pire en pire") (410). Although conscious of Succo's charade and deliberate orchestration of the scene, the media recognized that Succo's theatricality would perfectly translate into sensational headlines, and they remained to watch him. At last Succo put his clothes back on and walked over to an electric cable; grabbing onto the cord and suspending himself from his hands and ankles, he shimmied across the wire over the empty prison yard. Suddenly, Succo dropped his feet, swinging as if from a trapeze. As the crowd below held its collective breath, Succo fell eight meters into the yard below. Many people were unable to determine whether or not he was alive, and Froment reports that people wiped away tears; Succo's show was clearly a success. Police crept toward him cautiously, the criminal still inspiring fear in his injured state. One onlooker declared,

"He was right. He was like a bird. He should have flown away" ("Il avait raison. Il était comme un oiseau. Il aurait dû s'envoler") (Froment 415). Even the prison officials were dumbfounded: "We haven't had an escape in eleven years" ("Nous n'avons pas eu d'évasion depuis onze ans") (Froment 416).

The 8:00 p.m. television news in France, Switzerland, and Italy began with the *affaire* for the second night in a row, broadcasting Succo's charade on the roof of the prison. According to Froment, many spectators found him handsome, sincere, and nice, even though his actions made him despicable (417). A "real star," according to an embittered Toulon judge, Succo's audacious stunt on the roof was making a mockery of the case, and the press was not letting up. Succo's escape elicited a full-page article from *Le Figaro*, with a sensational headline announcing that the crazed killer had fallen from the prison roof ("Le tueur fou tombe du toit"). The article was accompanied by three large photos of Succo: one of him looking deranged as he stood in his underwear waving his hands above his head, a second of him picking his way across the roof, and a third of him shimmying across the electric wire. Superhuman, deranged, and with what amounted to nine lives, Succo provided a visual treat to the readers of *Le Figaro*. In comparison to this sensational coverage, *Le Monde*'s response was again comparatively minor. On 13 March 1988 they printed a small article whose headlines read "Roberto Succo hurts himself while attempting to escape" ("Roberto Succo se blesse au cours d'une tentative d'évasion" 12).

Just before his twenty-sixth birthday, Succo met with psychiatrists in Italy for two lengthy interviews. Excerpts of Succo's comments were publicized on television and in newspaper articles, many of which Koltès later included in his play. Finally, the Italian psychiatrists diagnosed that Succo was "paranoid schizophrenic" and therefore judged him "not responsible" for his crimes. French and Italian authorities had been in profound conflict about how Roberto Succo should be sentenced, since he was an Italian citizen who had committed his crimes in France. To the ire of the French, Succo was judged in Italy, and the leniency of his sentence only served to fuel the sense of injustice. When the French judge Bernard was alerted of the diagnosis, he exploded to the cameras, "C'est une comédie!" effectively confirming the theatricality of the *affaire*. Outrage seethed through Annecy and Chambéry, where, according to Froment, "the mediatization of this story only profited one person, Succo-the madman" ("la médiatisation de cette histoire ne profitait qu'à un seul, Succo-le-fou") (448). Succo's deliberate manipulation of the press during his escape made him an instant star of the media. His poetry, his fearlessness, and his beauty combined with his dangerous lunacy to make him the perfect object of fascination. Able to distance themselves from Succo physically (by watching him on television, where he was safely captured by cameras and police) and psychically (by referencing the media's labels of his "madness"), the public could indulge its fascination at a comfortable distance. Although people were reportedly concerned throughout his escape, Succo's eventual capture was reassuring for the public, whose faith was at least temporarily restored in the criminal justice system.

Six weeks later, "le tueur fou" made the front pages one last time. Succo was found dead in his prison cell, where he had suffocated himself. He had placed a plastic bag around his head, as he had done to his father after he killed him, a detail that was not lost on the press; journalists ascribed his repetitive use of the plastic bag as "Hitchcockian," again highlighting the performative nature of the *affaire*. Justice had been served for many, but for others there remained questions surrounding Succo's death. No one had seen Succo's face after the discovery of his body, and the four Polaroids taken of his body did not reveal any distinguishing features. Rumors flew that he was not really dead, that he had again escaped, and that the police had hired someone to kill him. These stories served to add to the sensation of Succo, likening him to the cult figures of Hitler and Jim Morrison, whose bodies were also never seen. Several days later, however, Succo was buried quietly, putting to rest the stories of his disappearance. While Succo's highly sensationalized capture and escape remain engraved in the minds of many French citizens, the controversy surrounding Roberto Succo did not fully reach its apex until four years later with the dramatic rewriting of his story by Bernard-Marie Koltès, *Roberto Zucco*.

Controversy and Censorship

At thirty-nine, Bernard-Marie Koltès was at the height of his literary career when he saw the pictures of Succo in the Parisian metro. A playwright, novelist, and director, Koltès had already received critical acclaim for his work both in France and abroad. After considerable struggles to get his early works produced, Koltès began to achieve renown in theater circles in the 1980s, when he was at last able to make a living on his writing. In 1983, Patrice Chéreau premiered *Combat de nègre et de chiens* (*Black Battles with Dogs*) in France at the Théâtre des Amandiers in Nanterre, outside of Paris, where critics were "enthusiastic." As Bradby confirms, from this moment until the end of his life, "Koltès was widely accepted as the most important new voice in French theater" (73). In 1985 *Quai ouest* (published by Minuit in 1988) received its worldwide premiere in Dutch at the Fublikestheater in Amsterdam, and the following year Chéreau premiered it in France at the Théâtre des Amandiers. In 1987, Chéreau premiered *Dans la solitude des champs de coton* (*In the Solitude of the Cotton Fields*) (Minuit, 1986) at Nanterre, and in 1988, he debuted Koltès's play *Le Retour au désert* (*Return to the Desert*) (Minuit, 1988) for the first time in the center of Paris (Théâtre Rond-Point). Later that year, Koltès's translation of Shakespeare's *A Winter's Tale, Le Conte d'hiver* (Minuit, 1988), was directed by Luc Bondy at Nanterre. *Roberto Zucco* is Koltès's last complete work, which he finished just before his death in April of 1989. Peter Stein premiered *Roberto Zucco* at the Berlin Schaubühne in 1990 (German translation by Simon Werle), and the play was later premiered in France in 1991 at the Théâtre Nationale de Paris de Villeurbanne by Bruno Boëglin. Subsequent productions include the following: Denis Marleau (Festival de Théâtre des Amériques, Montréal: 1993), Lluis Pasqual (Barcelona: 1993; Théâtre de l'Odéon, Paris: 1994; St. Petersburg: 1995; Madrid:

2004); Jean-Louis Martinelli (Théâtre National de Strasbourg: 1995; Théâtre des Amandiers, Nanterre: 1996); Travis Preston (La Cucaracha Theater, New York: 1995); Krzysztof Warlikowski (Poznan, Poland: 1995), James MacDonald (The Other Place, Stratford-upon-Avon: 1997); Royal Shakespeare Company (London: 1999); Oskaras Korsunovas (Festival de Dijon: 1999). In 2004, *Roberto Zucco* saw its Los Angeles premiere (Russell Milton's Open Fist Theater Company), and the United States premiere of the French version was staged by the University of California at Berkeley's Drama Department. *Roberto Zucco* has been performed in over 30 countries, including Argentina, Australia, Belgium, Brazil, the former Czechoslovakia, Chili, Estonia, Greece, Italy, Japan, Mexico, New Zealand, Poland, Portugal, Romania, Russia, Slovenia, South Africa, Spain, and Sweden. Most recently, the play was censored in Shanghai (Bedarida 17). Koltès's final play continues to be staged around the world, where it fascinates spectators and critics alike.

Until *Roberto Zucco*, Koltès's plays had been directed exclusively by Chéreau in France, but following Koltès death in 1989, Chéreau chose not to direct *Roberto Zucco*. Bruno Boëglin instead agreed to direct the play, and on 7 November 1991, he opened *Roberto Zucco* at the Théâtre National de Paris to four sold-out weeks. Subsequent productions were to be held in Nice, Valence, Chambéry, Brussels, and Toulouse, before returning to the Théâtre de la Ville in February of 1992. While the Valence, Brussels, and Toulouse representations were performed without objection, the Nice playhouse received bomb threats, although the press ignored this in their reports. Instead, attention focused on the highly dramatic 8 and 9 January productions at Chambéry, which were met with protests and calls for censorship. In a polemic rivaling the great literary battles of Molière's *Tartuffe* (Paris 1654), Victor Hugo's *Hernani* (Paris 1802), and Jean Genet's *Les Paravents* (Marseilles 1991), the Chambéry productions of *Roberto Zucco* were cancelled a day prior to their planned production in what the author's brother François Koltès called a "political-moral polemic" (qtd. in "La Polémique" 13).

The controversy surrounding *Roberto Zucco* points to contemporary society's complex relationship with crime and violence. While realistic violent images doggedly fill television and film without a great deal of public resistance, the staging of a play about a fictionalized killer waged a citywide dispute and national debate. Interestingly, the play contains relatively little violence compared to the considerable gratuitous screen violence characteristic of contemporary television and cinema. While the emotions of a wounded community are clearly at play in the calls for censorship, the controversy in other cities around France (bomb threats, letters of complaint) indicates that the polemic represents a deeper malaise. Under the public's tangled relationship to violence seems to lie a fundamental anxiety about death and violent impulses. If, for instance, the *fait divers* allows the public to vicariously act out its violent impulses without the consequences of actually behaving in a violent manner, the reader may only achieve this fantasy within a clear-cut binary conception of violence (where the criminal is evil and the victim represents purity). In other words, the catharsis achieved by this fantasy is only made possible within the context of explicit moral judgment. Removing the moral judgment on the crime leaves an uncomfortable gap where meaning is not predetermined. Violence becomes neutralized and open to interpretation outside the media's clear classifications and in the hands of the playwright. In this way, the criminal's violence becomes a fluid signifier that appears to reveal shifting—and therefore potentially threatening—attitudes about crime.

Claims that Succo was a "hero" only served to enliven and sensationalize these debates, which fed the fear-inspired decision to opt for censorship. Although Succo does not adhere to the characteristics of a hero (see Kooistra), he has nevertheless been labeled as such by several persons central to constructing his media image, such as Froment, Koltès, and numerous journalists. Labels like these create controversy, which further sensationalizes violent acts. Returning to Hyatt's provocative questions raised in the introduction of this project ("Is the definition of 'hero' significantly changing before our very eyes? Will historians in the next millennium pinpoint the word's altered meaning to this century?" 36), we must address the possibility that Succo's "heroism" signals a broader shift in society. While Hyatt's impassioned rhetoric is reminiscent of the play's detractors in their conservative consensus, his decision to view this fascination in the context of an ever-public society is important in understanding how the heroization of a man like Succo is not so incongruent with current social mores. Like Baudrillard's exaggerated hypotheses about the Paulin *affaire*, comments like these show how the *fait divers* is used to incite controversy by echoing public debates that society is undergoing dramatic changes, thus augmenting public fear and insecurity. The controversy surrounding *Roberto Zucco* reflects not only these fears of an increasingly violent society, but also deeper political struggles for power. As Ferrell explains, "this broader epistemic domain of knowledge, meaning, and interpretation . . . is actually at stake in battles over obscenity, pornography, and the criminalization and control of popular culture" (77). In other words, the polemic also reflects the government's efforts to control public access to and interpretation of knowledge. The threat of an impartial or nonjudgmental portrayal of the criminal is therefore twofold: to law enforcement who strongly opposed the play, it threatens their very existence as purveyors of binary law, and to a public unaccustomed to grappling with its own criminal impulses, the play's reflection of the public's gaze is fundamentally threatening by refusing meaning.

The dispute, which would take a significant place in the annals of French drama, began rather simply. In October of 1991, the widow of slain policeman André Castillo saw a poster advertising *Roberto Zucco*. After discovering that the Maison de la culture was funding the program, she read a copy of the play and promptly addressed a letter to the mayor of Chambéry, Louis Besson, asking him to intervene in the play's production. A debate about the integrity of the play's production quickly ensued, and in early November of 1991, two months before the play's projected opening in Chambéry, the polemic reached the front pages of the newspapers. Officials at the Maison de la culture set out to explain the importance of performing the play. Director Dominique Jambon emphasized that a constructive dialogue was underway, and called the polemic an important ethical debate. Stating that his first duty was to respect the families' pain, he added that the play did not glorify the assassin, and that in any case, it was not up to the Maison de la culture to censor itself (Belleret, "Z comme Succo" 17). Rather than developing into a healthy debate, however, the discussion of the play's production quickly deteriorated into an emotionally fused polemic between the play's backers (represented primarily by the Maison de la culture and theater patrons) and its opponents (most notably the mayor of Chambéry and the police force). Protestors distributed copies of the play throughout Chambéry in an effort not to educate the public but to heighten emotional response. A petition demanding its prohibition gathered 1,700 signatures (out of 55,000 inhabitants), and anonymous threats were made on members of the administrative council of the Maison de la culture, including one man's children. Clearly, Jambon's efforts at public reconciliation had failed. At its most basic level, then, the controversy surrounding the play stemmed from its temporal and spatial proximity to the crimes. As Daniel Brard, the regional president of the Union of Police (USCP), summarizes, "this play could be put on anywhere but Chambéry" ("cette pièce peut être jouée partout ailleurs mais pas à Chambéry") (qtd. in Léridon 22). Opponents of *Roberto Zucco*'s Chambéry production protested that the events were simply too recent and too painful. As Jean-Marc Lantéri wrote, Succo is "someone who is dead from the beginning of the play, but who doesn't manage to die before the play ends" ("l'être qui est mort dès que la pièce commence, mais qui n'arrive pas à mourir avant que la pièce s'achève") (Lantéri 67). Indeed, the polemic surrounding Succo/Zucco seems to hinge on this very fact. Succo is dead, but the staging of *Roberto Zucco* resurrects rather than buries his memory. Because Koltès refuses to explain or condemn Zucco, the play (like *J'ai pas sommeil*) lacks the sense of resolution central to the *fait divers*.

Yet, the mere knowledge that the text was even loosely based on Succo provided sufficient motive to cancel the production. Headlines proclaimed that Succo's crimes were too near ("Trop près, trop frais") ("Too near, too fresh") (Belleret, "Z, comme Succo" 17). While this headline implies that the text is based on the *fait divers*, and Zucco on Succo, this kind of shallow critique can be made without having seen or even read the play, and for many of the play's opponents, including Besson, it was simply unnecessary to read the text. Rather than staging a "healthy debate" about the nature of violence, its victims, and the freedom of expression (as Boëglin, Planchon, and Jambon advocated), the controversy instead remained at a rudimentary level, dissolving into a polarizing debate between conservative policemen and liberal representatives of the art community. For the two months preceding the play's début, little was published about the debate that seethed through the Maison de la culture. On 7 January, however, in an apparent effort to avoid any further controversy, a sudden decision was made to withdraw the play. Radical and well-orchestrated demonstrations by police and victims' rights advocates had succeeded in intimidating the mayor, and insinuations, bomb threats, and death threats eventually took their toll. In addition, police made clear that they would not defend the play against impending riots, declaring that they would oppose the staging by all means necessary ("nous nous opposerons par tous les moyens à ces représentations") (Planchon 12). As the production and consumption of culture increasingly determines contemporary social life, controversies such as this one habitually involve politicians and law enforcement. Ferrell explains that "these controversies consistently incorporate conflicts over popular morality, mass media influence, and the boundaries between art and obscenity. They also regularly include attempts by politicians, legal authorities, religious leaders and others to criminalize popular culture—that is, to recast popular culture activities and identities as criminal and to define the social effects of art, music, and media as criminogenic" (71). Indeed, the police syndicate was almost unanimously opposed to the play's representation. While Brigadier-chief Lucien Lefebvre stated that the play read like a defense of the crimes, Daniel Brard was more virulent, declaring that the director was trying to make Succo into a hero ("on cherche à donner une image héroïque de Succo") (Belleret, "Z comme Succo" 17). Brard called for the immediate and total censorship of the play. At the center of of these conflicts, *Roberto Zucco* threatened the status quo. As a result, rather than submitting to police protests and contesting their threats to obstruct access to the theater, Besson (who had been hostile to the city's staging of the play) effectively censored the play prior to its staging. Exhausted and embittered by the highly public battle, the mayor complained that he had been placed in a difficult position and manipulated by the events; the cultural ministers, he insinuated, could not have been blind to the potential problems that such a performance could have engendered. Besson explained that given his options (stopping the protests and asking the police to intercede and thereby inflict a painful spectacle or canceling the play), he didn't have a choice ("où [sic] bien j'interdisais la manifestation de protestation et je demandais l'intervention de la force publique afin d'imposer un spectacle blessant pour de nombreuses sensibilités, ou bien j'interdisais les représentations. En fait je n'avais pas le choix") (Belleret, "*Roberto Zucco* déprogrammé" 19). A rigorous socialist, Besson further explained that in the context of a politically progressive penal system, it was more important to respect the victims. Supporters of the play abhorred this view of the mayor as a purveyor of victims' rights, particularly one that excluded dialogue about freedom of expression and democratic ideals. In fact, the ultimate decision to censor the play was made by the Maison de la culture of Chambéry, whose final statement declared, "before a unique and exceptional local situation, we do not wish to expose our public, personnel or actors to the risk of direct confrontation with uncontrolled elements" ("devant une situation locale unique et exceptionnelle, nous ne souhaitons pas exposer notre public, le personnel, les interprètes, à un risque majeur d'affrontement directs avec des éléments incontrôlés") (Belleret, "*Roberto Zucco* déprogrammé" 19). This kind of cowering to public pressure not only shows how a small number of demonstrators can affect political action, but above all it points to the weakness of cultural organizations in the face of public opposition. Without the backing of the local government, which controls their funding (and which is primarily concerned with its own tarnished image), organizations such as the Maison de la culture, which typically advocate freedom of speech, are forced to abandon the principles on which they stand.

As a result of the decision to cancel the play, artists and directors defiantly voiced their contention. Actor Michel Piccoli and directors Patrice Chéreau and Ariane Mnouchkine wrote a letter endorsing the play's defenders. "White angel, black angel. All of these cries are within us, hangmen, assassins and victims all at once. . . . Koltès, parched of life, dying, wanted to be reborn through *Zucco* and die at his side. Don't assassinate Koltès!" ("Ange blanc, Ange noir. Tous ces cris sont en nous, toujours, bourreaux, assassins et victimes tout à la fois. . . . Koltès assoiffé de vie, mourant, a voulu renaître à travers *Zucco* et mourir à ses côtés. N'assassinez pas Koltès!") (Belleret, "*Roberto Zucco* déprogrammé" 19). This poetic outcry recalls Denis's film in its avowal that anyone can be an assassin. At the same time, the plea clearly asserts that the play is a metaphor for the author's death. In associating Koltès with Zucco, Piccoli and his co-authors distance Zucco from Succo, effectively dismantling the opponent's arguments. Yet the use of Koltès's death to elicit emotional reaction from the public demonstrates the desperate measures of the play's defenders, who deliberately manipulate Koltès's biography to encrust the text and incite an emotional response from readers.

Koltès and Succo: "I Was Fascinated, I Don't Know Why"

Koltès's fascination with the Succo *affaire* has provided a similar, if not greater, fascination for critics. Like Piccoli, most critics who write about *Roberto Zucco* inevitably cite the playwright's interest in the *fait divers*, recounting the story in which Koltès sees Succo's pictures in the metro station. The story has been recycled and restated so often that the anecdote itself has become a cliché. On the one hand, its importance speaks to the tradition of using an author's life as a key to his or her work; literary criticism prior to the 1960s often consisted of using the literary text as a guide to discover more about the author, or conversely, of using biographical details to unlock keys in the text. On the other hand, the themes of *Roberto Zucco* do not significantly differ from Koltès's other works, which may also be related to Koltès's personal life. Instead, the use of Koltès's struggle with death has been used to *separate* Zucco from Succo: by likening Zucco to Koltès, critics refocus their analysis on thematic rather than realistic representations of the play. Moreover, the author's memory of the *affaire* mirrors the experience of the thousands of viewers who watched Succo's spectacular swan dive from the roof of the prison. Thus, when journalists recount Koltès's fascination with Succo, they attempt to align the author with the public, many of whom were also fascinated by Succo's televised stunt. The anticipated result is that the author becomes less remote and his story less seditious. My belief is that these reviewers—by citing this similarity and by evoking Koltès's personal struggle with death—manipulate fragments of the *fait divers* to curtail public protest of the play. Just as Denis's comments about her film do not represent a preferred reading, but rather an additional encrusted text through which we may read her film, so must we qualify Koltès's comments. Since his intentions have become so mediated and because his biography has been so tightly woven into readings of the text, this mediation provides an excellent backdrop for a discussion of the play's controversy and its relationship to the *fait divers*.

In interviews about the play, Koltès has interpreted his curiosity with Succo as a kind of inexplicable and intrinsic understanding of the criminal. In one example, Koltès stated, "The source is the wanted poster. I saw it in the metro, and I stayed there in front of it, I was fascinated, I don't know why. Some time later, I, who never watch television, I turn it on for the news, and I come across this absolutely incredible scene where Roberto Succo is on the roof of the prison. Afterwards, I found articles in *Libé*, and I started working on this story, which I find exemplary" ("Le point de départ, c'est l'affiche de l'avis de recherche. Je l'ai vue dans le métro, et je suis resté devant, j'étais fasciné, je ne sais pas pourquoi. Quelque temps après, moi qui ne regarde jamais la télé, je l'allume pour les informations, et je tombe sur cette scène absolument incroyable où l'on voyait Roberto Succo sur les toits de la prison. Après j'ai récupéré des articles de *Libé*, et j'ai commencé à travailler cette histoire, que je trouve exemplaire") (Klausner and Salino 85). Highlighting the "incredible" and "exemplary" nature of Succo's story, Koltès also references his fate-like sense of chance in seeing Succo on television. Like the public, he appears awe-struck by Succo's spectacle. In the same interview, Koltès clarifies his fascination with the killer. When he cites how Succo killed his parents without motivation and that at twenty-four years old he killed again without reason, Koltès states, "Succo has an incredibly pure trajectory. Unlike potential killers—and there are many—he doesn't have repugnant motivations for murder, which has no meaning for him. It only takes a small derailment, one thing, which is a little like Dostoyevsky's epilepsy: a little trigger and Wham! It's all over. That's what fascinates me" ("Succo a une trajectoire d'une pureté incroyable. Contrairement aux tueurs en puissance—et il y en a beaucoup—il n'a pas de motivations répugnantes pour le meurtre, qui chez lui est un non-sens. Il suffit d'un petit déraillement, d'une chose qui est un peu comme l'épilepsie chez Dostoïevski: un petit déclenchement et hop! C'est fini. C'est ça qui me fascine") (85). This remark recalls Baudrillard's comments about Paulin's crimes not having any meaning. Yet rather than concluding, like Baudrillard, that because Succo's crimes are nonclassifiable, they represent the end of the criminal-hero, Koltès instead testifies to Succo's power to captivate our fascination. (Here, I would again like to emphasize that in quoting Koltès, I do not intend to grant him a greater authority than a given spectator of the play. Instead, his remarks serve to show how reviewers *do* grant the author this status. The insistence on his personal interest in Succo is given a preferred status as a way of devaluing negative public response to the play. In other words, reviewers cite Koltès's fascination in an effort to deflect public criticism and thereby neutralize the play's polemic.)

In a variety of reviews and articles, writers cite Koltès's interest in the Succo case as a catalyst for the play. Articles in *Le Monde* (Godard), *American Theatre* (Nash-Siedlecki 6), and *New Theatre Quarterly* (Bradby 74) testify to the widespread commingling of Koltès's personal fascination with the *fait divers*. Koltès's interest in Succo has also been taken by writers to parallel the author's biography with the criminal's trajectory. Olivier Schmitt, for instance, embellishes the narrative by writing that "It's another young man, handsome, with an energy that AIDS hadn't yet cannibalized, that took the metro one day and saw in Succo's face the reflection of his own. Bernard-Marie Koltès liked his face, loved this face, even said that he instantly fell in love with it" ("C'est un autre jeune homme, beau, d'une énergie que le sida n'avait pas encore cannibalisée, qui prit un jour le métro et vit dans le visage de Succo le reflet du sien propre. Bernard-Marie Koltès aimait son visage, aima ce visage, dit même qu'il l'aima d'amour, instantanément") ("*Roberto Zucco* à Barcelone" 11). Schmitt's jump from recounting Koltès's interest in the killer to paralleling Koltès's life with the killer's trajectory marks a clear departure from the author's own admission, a course echoed by several other journalists and critics.

Like the *fait divers*, the literary work that takes its inspiration from crime quickly becomes a struggle for meaning. Drawing on Koltès's bout with AIDS at the time he wrote the play in an attempt to explain his affinity for Succo, reviewers explain that Koltès sympathized with the wanted man, whose youth and beauty made his crimes seem all the more tragic. This hypothesis, although entirely unsubstantiated, is supported by a range of critics. Literary critic Sven Åke Heed writes that Koltès's life as a gay man mirrored Zucco's double condemnation as madman and criminal (58), playwright Jean-Pierre Sarrazac explains that Koltès had a tendency to identify with the suffering of his quasi-heroes (144), and director Bruno Boëgin, whose staging was in considerable jeopardy of being cancelled, affirms that it is Koltès's identity that is transmitted through the play (Jurgenson 25), a view also confirmed by journalists Godard and Macabru. By establishing a connection between the two men's struggles with death, this reasoning provides a seductive (and somewhat troubling) argument that correlates Koltès's life with the criminal's. In this juxtaposition, Succo's violent acts are completely disassociated from the original *fait divers*, becoming part of a moral struggle that likens him to a hero rather than a murderer. The critical manipulation of *Roberto Zucco* is relevant especially here, because the writers who cite the similarity between the author and the criminal share the common interest of supporting the play in the face of its controversy: not one protester of the play cited Koltès's likeness with Succo. This collective effort to support the play's production points to the need to create a meaning for Zucco's crimes. Although an author's life is bound to influence his artistic works in some ways, Koltès's works have consistently drawn on themes of solitude and nothingness, making *Roberto Zucco*'s themes no more remarkable than those of *Quai ouest* or *Combat de nègre et de chiens;* both texts deal with questions of life and death. The inextricable linkage of Koltès's biography with Roberto Succo's life thus appears to be an oversimplified psychological explanation that is as intangible and complicated as the public's interest in the young killer. Specific parallels between the two men beyond the author's own musings are mere conjecture, and while they may feed the public's interest in the *fait divers*, they are not helpful in a literary analysis. The ways in which these resemblances have been employed by the media do, however, bear on the cultural significance of a work, even posthumously. In the case of *Roberto Zucco*, the similar issues facing both author and killer enter into the dialogue about the play's realistic depiction of the criminal, strengthening the arguments of the play's supporters. The link established between Koltès and Succo not only serves to explain his reason for writing the play, but also promotes a metaphorical view of the play that distances Zucco from Succo.

When Koltès himself was interviewed about why he wrote the play, he eschewed personal motivations. Stating that *Roberto Zucco* was his most beautiful play ("ma plus belle pièce"), Koltès called Succo's exemplary trajectory "Sublime, forcément sublime," recalling Marguerite Duras's article in *Libération* about the Gregory *affaire*, another highly mediated and encrusted *fait divers*. Significantly, Koltès denied the influence of his life on his work, stating, "It has nothing to do with it. It's the most banal life there is, apart from my profession" ("Elle n'a aucun intérêt. C'est la vie la plus banale qui soit, à part ma profession") (Klausner and Salino 84). As if anticipating the controversy that would follow his death, Koltès explained: "When they tell me that I'm a glorifying a murderer or something like that, because that's what they'll tell me, I would say that he's an exemplary killer in the way that I think he resembles everyone. . . . I think it's an incredible and mythic trajectory. That he killed his father and then himself is mythical, it's a classic course, Greek. There's something aesthetic, more than that, tragic, a tragedy without motive like all tragedies, destiny" ("Quand on me dira que je fais l'éloge du meurtrier ou des choses comme ça, parce qu'on va me le dire, je dirais que c'est un tueur exemplaire dans la mesure où je pense qu'il ressemble à tout le monde. . . . Je trouve que c'est une trajectoire incroyable, mythique. Le fait de tuer son père et de se suicider, c'est mythique, c'est un trajet 'classique,' grec. Il y a un truc esthétique, plus que ça, tragique, une tragédie sans motif comme toutes les tragédies, le destin") (Attoun 24). By addressing the controversy before the fact, Koltès acknowledged the similarities between Succo and Zucco. More importantly, however, is that in situating his work in the larger genre of tragedy, Koltès removed it from the *fait divers* and located it within the more universal space of theater. His foresight in linking Zucco to a Greek tragedy indicates not only his understanding of the contemporary public's resistance to a non-Manichaen view of the criminal, but also his own clarity in seeing that the criminal occupies a larger place in literary and cultural history. In addition, Koltès's avowal of Succo's mythical nature helps to distance him from the actual person, making his play difficult to condemn. More effective than the reviewers, whose tactics include hypothetical juxtapositions between the author and criminal, Koltès's explanation does not attempt to remove Succo from Zucco but rather to move Succo the criminal into the broader realm of the past.

A Polemic Turned Political

On the day following the play's cancellation, *Le Monde* printed three articles pertaining to the *affaire*, including an extensive response from Roger Planchon, co-director of the Théâtre National de Paris and co-producer of the play. Planchon's article, like the critics previously cited, attempts to distance the literary text from the *fait divers* and thus from the danger of censure. Unlike the writers who invoked Koltès's interest in Succo, Planchon and others such as Pascale Froment focus on the misguided criminalization of culture. Calling attention to how the protestors erroneously assign blame to the text that succeeded the *fait divers* rather than condemning the acts themselves, Planchon endeavors to redirect the discussion of crime away from the play and back to the criminal who originally performed it. Planchon's article immediately calls into question the reasoning of the protestors. "Whom will we have believe that poets arm assassins? That the author of *Macbeth* is responsible for all regicides? How many criminals can we cite who found their inspiration in a theatrical performance or in a book?" ("A qui fera-t-on croire que les poètes arment les assassins? Que l'auteur de Macbeth est responsable de tous les régicides? Combien peut-on citer de criminels qui ont puisé leur inspiration dans une représentation théâtrale ou dans un livre?") (12). These questions are central to the works in this study. The idea that society's artistic endeavors, so often dismissed as inconsequential, might cause such deliberate actions is hypocritical at best. Underlining the ridiculousness of this approach, Planchon cites several examples of threats to council members and to Besson's career. He then references the avowal by the police to oppose the play "by all means possible," asking, "How to interpret that since, here, it references illegal measures? As far as I know, the play hasn't been censored by the courts. If the officers overlook laws and copy the actions and procedures of wrongdoing associations, the world will soon be turned upside down" ("Comment entendre cela puisque, ici, il s'agit de moyens illégaux? La pièce n'a pas été interdite par les tribunaux, que je sache? Si les policiers oublient les lois et copient les actions et procédés des associations de malfaiteurs, le monde, bientôt, marchera sur la tête"). Planchon ends his letter with an ironic plea to the mayor of Paris, Jacques Chirac, asking him to refrain from yielding to mafia politics ("M. Chirac, vous n'allez pas interdire Koltès à Paris? Vous n'allez pas céder à des mafiosi politiques?"). He queries, "Must we ask everyone who believes in freedom of expression, and in the first place policemen who feel solidarity with those close to the victims of assassins and who hate political exploitation and the suffering of poor people, and all those who are shocked by the idea that Paris can censor a dead poet to write you to encourage you to resist?" ("Faut-il demander à tous ceux qui sont attachés à la liberté d'expression, et en premier lieu aux policiers qui se sentent solidaires des proches des victimes des assassins et qui répugnent à l'exploitation politicienne et la douleur des pauvres gens, et à tous ceux que choque l'idée que Paris puisse censurer un poète mort de vous écrire pour vous encourager à résister?") (12).

Replies to Planchon's letter were plentiful, attesting to literature's sustained ability to provoke controversy and discussion in larger society, and *Le Monde* opted to print excerpts of several letters. As we saw in the efforts to associate Koltès's and Succo's lives, these journalists and critics maintain their focus on the literary nature of the play; as the actors of *Roberto Zucco* wrote in a letter, "this is about a play, not a reality show" ("il s'agit d'une pièce de théâtre, pas d'un reality show") ("*Roberto Zucco* sera joué à Paris" 13). Indignant responses to the censorship of the play came from the Théâtre de la Commune Pandora d'Aubervilliers ("that a play, in other words, a testimony of the soul, chose as its subject the life and death of a criminal, even a declared killer, has been one of its most enduring rights since its origins") ("qu'une pièce de théâtre, autrement dit une preuve de l'esprit, ait choisi pour sujet de peindre la vie et la mort d'un criminel, voire d'un 'tueur' déclaré, est un de ces droits les plus imprescriptibles depuis ses origines") ("Roberto Zucco sera joué à Paris" 13), the Société des auteurs dramatiques (previously cited), and from Gilles Costaz, president of the Syndicat national de la critique dramatique ("the critics read and saw the play") ("les critiques ont lu et vu la piece"). The actors and technicians of *Roberto Zucco* also responded with a show of solidarity and consternation. They clearly state their disappointment: "We find ourselves brutally summoned to not act, to not practice our work and our art. The reality is serious. The artists of this performance did nothing other than give form to the words of one of the most essential dramatic poets of our century, one who questions our mysteries and brings to light our hypocrisies. This is why it is scandalously painful that to our conscientious quest be opposed the pain of those men and women who see in this work a direct relation with their suffering or worse, a being that was objectively the cause of their pain and that has been punished by society" ("Nous nous trouvons brutalement mis en demeure de ne pas jouer, de ne pas exercer notre travail et notre art. Le fait est grave. Les artisans de ce spectacle n'ont rien fait d'autre que de donner forme au verbe d'un des poètes dramatiques les plus essentiels de notre siècle, l'un de ceux qui questionnent nos mystères et lèvent les lièvres de nos hypocrisies. C'est pourquoi il est scandaleusement douloureux qu'à notre consciencieuse recherche soit opposée la douleur de celles et ceux qui croient voir dans cet ouvrage une relation directe de leur malheur ou, pis, l'apologie d'un être qui fut objectivement la cause de leur peine et que la société a puni" ("*Roberto Zucco* sera joué à Paris" 13). In other words, the play's protesters wrongly correlate their own suffering (in regards to the *fait divers*) with the play's objectives (which are distinct from the crimes).

Other replies demonstrate soundly the highly political nature of these debates. In particular, three responses to Planchon's article appeared in their entirety in a separate column on the same page: a brief interview with Chirac, and two letters: one from Théâtre de la ville director Gérard Violette and another from Chambéry Mayor Besson. The spokesperson for Chirac is quoted as saying that "Mr. Chirac, who never intervened in any way in the programming of any municipal cultural establishment, is astonished that one would organize proceedings against him without the least foundation" ("M. Chirac, qui n'est jamais intervenu de quelque manière que ce soit dans la programmation d'aucun établissement culturel municipal, s'étonne qu'il lui soit ainsi fait des procès d'intention sans le moindre fondement") ("La Déclaration de la Mairie de Paris" 13). Equally incensed was Gérard Violette, who explained that while he and Planchon led the same fight, Planchon was misguided in his criticisms of Chirac; Chirac, he wrote, was very dedicated to freedom of expression, and the play was hardly in danger of being cancelled in Paris; and in fact, Chirac did allow the performances of Boëglin's *Roberto Zucco* in Paris in February of 1992. Besson's response displayed even more indignation, as he categorically denied Planchon's interpretation of the events in Paris. Defending his choice to stand with the victims of the play, Besson explained that "in Chambéry, it wasn't possible to ignore a local, human situation, and the Maison de la culture, understanding this, protected, at its initiative—and therefore at its honor—the cultural life from an unavoidable, grave incident that would have surely been unworthy of it" ("à Chambéry il n'était pas possible de ne pas tenir compte d'une situation humaine locale particulière et la Maison de la culture, en le comprenant, a préservé à son initiative—et donc à son honneur—la vie culturelle d'un inévitable incident lourd qui aurait été assurément indigne d'elle") (Besson 13). Besson and Violette pointed to the political wavering that characterized the play's representation, and combined with the excessive defense of Chirac's policies, they dramatically stressed how political this decision became. In an apparent show of support for the play's production, *Le Monde* distanced itself from Chambéry's conservative choice of censorship. It published several articles that maintained that Koltès's play raises much larger questions than the *fait divers* itself. Olivier Schmitt, for instance, interviewed director Boëglin, who he says had never imagined the storm that would surround the play's staging. The director stated that "we can't say that Bernard-Marie Koltès wanted to respond to these questions people ask themselves when they're children, or when they're a little naïve: why is a killer a killer? This isn't the question of the play, not at all" ("on ne peut pas dire que Bernard-Marie Koltès ait voulu répondre à ces questions que l'on se pose quand on est enfant, ou un peu naïf: pourquoi un tueur est-il un tueur? Ce n'est pas la question de la pièce, pas du tout") ("Rencontre avec Bruno Boëglin" 19). Boëglin's condescending response to the play's opponents displays his anger and disappointment at the censors, who have grasped the play at only its most infantile level of meaning.

Other writers attested with equal conviction to the play's thematically varied and weighty issues. As the controversy raged even after the play's staging in Paris, Pascale Froment, the author of the book about the Succo *affaire*, wrote an article for the *Nouvel Observateur* unequivocally condemning the play's censorship in Chambéry. Her article strikes at the political strong-arming behind the censorship that had previously only been implied. Blaming the controversy on a handful of "Ayatollah cops," Froment asked, "Who's afraid of Roberto Zucco?" ("Qui a peur de Roberto Zucco?") ("Zucco contre Succo" 65). Recalling both the controversy and content of Albee's 1962 play *Who's Afraid of Virginia Woolf*, Froment castigates the protesters of the play, pointing to the political maneuvering of the Right. She explains that rather than protest at the opening of the play, for instance, Castillo's widow and the policemen attacked the play as a defense of the murderer. Froment accuses, "Frustration at not being able to catch the killer? Hatred for the supposedly disdainful intellectuals? Contempt of culture? A scandal dear to a certain Right wing?" ("Frustration de n'avoir pu arrêter le coupable? Haine pour les intellos supposés méprisants? Mépris de la culture? Tapage cher à une certaine droite?"). She concludes that there isn't a real Succo and a false Zucco, but simply a man and a play. Clearly separating the real from the fictive, Froment removes the possibility of correlating the *fait divers* with the play. Proof that this controversy had lasting significance is manifest in the international response to the play. While *Roberto Zucco* ceased to draw calls for censorship or even public outrage in France following the play's initial controversy and censoring in Chambéry, the scars from the decision nonetheless remained for years to come. In most announcements and reviews of the play's international performances, writers alluded to the censorship in an apparent effort to stir public interest in the production. The majority of reviews contain references to the Chambéry polemic (see Caplan, Bommer, Curtiss). Kahn's film about Succo was also met with protests by the same group of policemen at its 2001 Cannes release. Ironically, the protests and censoring of the *affaire*'s incrustations have done more to ensure the knowledge of the crimes themselves, for Succo's crimes were not well-known outside of central Western Europe prior to the play's international release and performance.

Chapter Five

Performing Murder

Koltès began writing his play in 1988, just prior to Succo's suicide. As I have shown, Koltès's interest in Succo, fueled by the media's images of the killer, has been consistently cited in reference to the play, encrusting it with layers of meaning. Used by both proponents and opponents of the play to defend their opinions of *Roberto Zucco*'s representational validity, Koltès's interest in the killer represents a fluid signifier that can be manipulated by opposing parties. Yet as Pascale Froment suggests, this information is completely insignificant relative to the text. She explains that "Koltès knew few details. Four photos of a changing face, on a wanted poster seen in the metro. Three newspaper clippings recounting the journey of the 'crazed killer,' who didn't have the ugly mug of the profession. Just a few televised minutes of a temporary escape on the rooftops of an Italian prison. He understood, seeing this film, that the criminal was at the end of his rope. And that had something theatrical" ("Koltès connaissait peu de choses. Quatre photos d'un visage changeant, sur un avis de recherche aperçu dans le métro. Trois coupures de journaux contant la cavale d'un 'tueur fou' qui n'avait pas la sale gueule de l'emploi. A peine quelques minutes télévisées d'une évasion provisoire sur les toits d'une prison italienne. Il a compris, en voyant ce film, que le criminel était au bout de chemin. Et ça avait quelque chose de théâtral") ("Zucco contre Succo" 65). In this understanding of the events, Koltès's experience of Succo, although pivotal in sparking his interest, merely serves as a catalyst for the play's genesis and should therefore be absent from any serious discussion of the play. Froment's statement is written in clear defense of the play, but her comments nevertheless resonate with the play's partisans and return us to the important questions the play's controversy raises to allow us to examine the particular causes of the polemic. The debate as read in the press, for instance, seems to ask whether it is the incorporation of factual elements into the fiction or rather the fictionalization of the facts that is more disturbing. While the polemic hovered around these questions, there is little interest in focusing on them alone; discussions of "real" and "fictional" have bearing on the argument only in that they arouse an emotional response from both protesters and supporters. On closer examination, the polemic alludes to deeper questions that transcend the details of the *fait divers* and cross into more fundamental queries about how the criminal is portrayed. Like Denis's depiction of Camille, Koltès's *look* at the criminal shatters binary criminal portraitures that are used to reassure the public of their normality. Zucco does not equal evil nor does he inspire fear; rather, his thoughts and actions are open to interpretation, leaving his significance debatable and thus potentially problematic. An analysis of how Koltès portrays the cool killer and the characters that interact with him uncovers a mirror of contemporary society's fears and fascination with the murderer. By closely examining Zucco's relationships with the other characters in the play, we see how *Roberto Zucco* (and the controversy surrounding it) reflects current thought about violence, reality, and artistic freedom.

Combining historical events with imagined scenarios, Koltès mixes direct citations from Succo with fictional and mythological characters in his play, wholly fusing the real and the fake. That Roberto Succo forms the root of the Zucco character there is no doubt, but the *extent* to which this real-life killer is superimposed on the stage-Zucco seems to represent the core of the deeper controversy: Zucco is subversive as much for his deviation from Succo as for his resemblance to him. As evidenced from the debates surrounding the representation of the *fait divers* onstage, this subversion (which challenges the very structure of the traditional *fait divers*) lies in its refusal to judge the crimes, as well as the addition of another dimension of Zucco not seen before. The elimination of a determining judgment is thus twofold. Spatially, the *fait divers* is removed from its placement in a specific newspaper section on crime, where judgment is clear, and the journalistic style leans toward a condemnation of Succo's acts. Thematically, the removal of judgment is evidenced by Koltès's neutral depiction of the criminal, notable in how Zucco interacts with the other characters on stage. In contrast to a *fait divers* that tells of completed actions, this theatrical production shows Zucco in the process of committing murderous acts, interacting with other characters, and displaying characteristics such as kindness and humanity that sharply contrast the ways criminals are commonly portrayed. Like Denis's depiction of Paulin in *J'ai pas sommeil*, Koltès's Succo seems to commit a deliberately subversive act that disconcerts many readers and spectators. Yet as Judith Butler has stated, "there is no easy way to know whether something is subversive. Subversiveness is not something that can be gauged or calculated. In fact what I mean by subversion are those effects that are incalculable" (84). While Butler makes this statement in the context of gender and heterosexual hegemony, her central idea (that the notion of subversion is difficult to locate) pertains to the difficulty with which we might determine *Roberto Zucco*'s challenge to criminal depictions. The subversiveness of *Roberto Zucco* is incalculable primarily because its effect on the public is difficult to both situate and monitor. Koltès's unique manner of questioning Zucco's acts is fundamental to generating this unease.

In *Un Hangar, à l'ouest* (1990) a series of reflections that appears in the Editions de Minuit edition of *Roberto Zucco*, Koltès warns that "we too often have the tendency, when someone tells us a story, to ask the question 'why?' when I think that the only question to ask oneself is 'how'" ("on a trop souvent tendance, lorsqu'on vous raconte une histoire, à poser la question 'pourquoi?' alors que je pense que la seule question à se poser est 'comment?'") (115). Here Koltès provides a hint as to how we may begin to determine Zucco's subversiveness, as this is precisely the nerve that Koltès touches in steering the audience away from asking *why* Zucco killed. If we apply Koltès's statement to our current exploration of the play's subversion, it is clearly not enough to ask *why Roberto Zucco* caused such controversy and outrage, but rather *how* Koltès effected this outcome. Through a close reading of the text itself, an exercise that many of the play's deterrents opted to eschew, we will better be able to assess where this subversion lies, as well as what the play communicates. In other words, we must continue to ask how the theatrical text subverts history, and, accordingly, in what ways it breaks new ground.

From Succo to Zucco

Many opponents of *Roberto Zucco* contested the play's representation based on a cursory reading of the text, and in some cases on the mere existence of it as text, as several protesters opted not to read it. It seems that the very idea that a play had been based on Roberto Succo was enough to stir up resistance. Because the controversy did not stem from the performances themselves but rather from the possibility of their representation, it is more revealing to analyze the text of the play rather than its various representations, which succeeded the controversy. *Roberto Zucco* is made up of fifteen scenes of varying length, ranging from one page of text to fourteen. The play contains nineteen almost archetypal characters, as well as several nameless figures ("men," "prostitutes"). The characters are listed vertically on the page, grouped and set apart by spaces. In a significant reversal of the *fait divers*, where the perpetrator remains nameless, Zucco is the only character with a name. Following Zucco's name, and separated by a space, is his mother ("sa mère"). Separated by another space are the girl, her sister, her brother, her father, and her mother ("la gamine," "sa sœur," "son frère," "son père," and "sa mère"). The use of possessive pronouns rather than indefinite articles (*sa/son* versus *la/le*) highlights the importance of the characters' ties to one another; rather than possessing separate identities, the family members are defined by their ancestral association, an important detail, since Succo had no family, having murdered his parents. Following the family, after an additional space, are the old gentleman ("le vieux monsieur") and the elegant lady ("la dame élégante"), and, set off by another space, a list of ten auxiliary characters: the fat guy, the impatient pimp, the panic-stricken prostitute, the melancholy detective, an inspector, a police chief, first guard, second guard, first policeman, and second policeman ("le balèze," "le mac impatient," "la pute affolée," "l'inspecteur mélancholique," "un inspecteur," "un commissaire," "premier gardien," "deuxième gardien," "premier policier" and "deuxième policier"). At the bottom of the page are listed "Men. Women. Whores. Pimps. Voices of prisoners and guards" ("Hommes. Femmes. Putes. Macs. Voix de prisonniers et de gardiens"). The characters are not listed in the order in which they appear, but in what is presumed to be their order of importance. The articles that define the characters descend from possessive (his mother/"sa mère") to definite (the old gentleman/"le vieux monsieur") to indefinite (a detective/"un inspecteur"). The final characters listed are sufficiently indistinct as to warrant no defining articles, reflecting their marginalized location in the play. Koltès's characters represent a broad cross-section of society, emphasizing that everyone interacts with the killer.

While the majority of Denis's characters are entirely fictitious, the characters in *Roberto Zucco* are a skillful mix of fiction and reality, loosely resembling persons in the actual *affaire*. For those readers/spectators familiar with the *fait divers*, the similarities are quite obvious. The character of "his mother" is a clear signifier for Succo's murdered mother. Although Succo's father is not present onstage, his mother alludes to his murder, making him an authentic stage presence we might label a character. Other characters are disguised under thinly veiled titles, such as "the girl," who closely resembles Sabina (who fell in love with and turned in Succo), and "the melancholy inspector," who represents the slain policeman Morandin. Other identities are less apparent to those who are not as familiar with the details of the *affaire*. "The elegant lady" parallels the hostage that Succo released, although in a change from the *fait divers*, Zucco kills "the child," who was actually freed with his mother; it is noteworthy that the murdered boy of the play does not appear in the list of characters, although he speaks onstage. Other characters blend fact with fiction by quoting statements from the *fait divers*. Likewise, several of Zucco's lines are taken from the actual story, as are those of the policemen and the girl. Furthermore, several scenes of the play take place in Little Chicago ("Le Petit Chicago"), where Succo committed many of his crimes. However, Zucco commits only three murders during the course of the play, one of which is offstage, whereas Succo committed at least six.

As I have shown, many critics prefer to compare Zucco with Koltès rather than Zucco with Succo, denying the numerous parallels between the *fait divers* and the play. If instead we choose to explore the play's intertextual references to the Succo affair—an approach I advocate because it allows us to examine *how* rather than *why* Koltès adapted his text to the affair—we may better grasp how the play challenges the media's representation of crime, as well as the public's reaction to it. Most revealing is Koltès's choice to transform Succo into Zucco, a slight modification that invokes the killer without naming him. Unlike Denis, who transforms Thierry Paulin into "Camille," or Kahn, who elects to use Succo's real name in his film, Koltès chooses a tiny, yet significant gesture. As Barthes writes, "all subversion, or all novelistic romantic submission, thus begins with the Proper Name" (*S/Z* 95). In this slight fictionalization, Koltès makes a deliberate allusion to the police and media's error in misspelling Succo's name. While Koltès may be mocking their overzealous attempts to label Succo, several critics have attempted to assign this change a deeper significance. Froment writes that for Koltès, the name evokes at once sugar ("zucchero" in Italian), the candor of an adolescent who had known Succo, and the youthful romanticism of a Zorro ("Zucco contre Succo" 65). Jean-Pierre Sarrazac sees in Zucco the same sugar, one that he calls "the desire to disappear, for Zucco to literally melt like a sugar cube, liquefy himself in the rain" ("le désir de disparaître, pour Zucco de fondre littéralement comme un sucre, se liquéfier sous la pluie") ("Résurgences de l'expressionisme" 144). Referencing Succo's diagnosed schizophrenia, journalist Olivier Schmitt likens the "z" to the one in "schizo" ("*Roberto Zucco* à Barcelone" 11). While the change in name carries a potential multiplicity of layers of meaning, the reversal of letters also suggests a much broader intertext. The slide from "S" to "Z" recalls Barthes's work *S/Z*, which is a reading of Balzac's work "Sarrazine;" Balzac is another writer who used *faits divers* as inspiration for his work. In explaining Balzac's modification of the word *sarrasin* to *sarrazine*, Barthes writes that "Z is the letter of mutilation: phonetically, Z stings like a chastising lash, an avenging insect; graphically, cast slantwise by the hand across the blank regularity of the page, amid the curves of the alphabet, like an oblique and illicit blade, it cuts, slashes, or, as we say in French, *zebras*; from a Balzacian viewpoint, this Z (which appears in Balzac's name) is the letter of deviation" (106). Z, declares Barthes, is the letter of deviance. Because Succo is defined by his deviant acts, examining Barthes's explanation of this letter allows us to locate the criminal in a larger literary context that further removes him from Succo. The "Z" speaks to Zucco's difference, not only from society (he is "crazy"), but also from Succo the real murderer. Branded by this letter that speaks of mutilation and madness, Zucco is linked to a history that seals his fate; the letter itself is determining, as Barthes's statement suggests; the definitive present tense of *être* ("to be" and omission of qualifiers (often, usually, sometimes) determine the prophetic role of the letter "Z." Yet the "Z" in itself is not as consequential as its transformation. In relating the metamorphosis of S to Z, Barthes writes that "S and Z are in relation of graphological inversion: the same letter seen from the other side of the mirror: Sarrasine contemplates in Zambinella his own castration. Hence the slash (/) confronting the S of SarraSine and the Z of Zambinella has a panic function: it is the slash of censure, the surface of the mirror, the wall of hallucination, the verge of antithesis, the abstraction of limit, the obliquity of the signifier, the index of the paradigm, hence of meaning" (107).

In the suggestion that the "Z" provides an inverse and deviant manner of understanding "S," Barthes's statement points to the significance of Koltès's decision to change Zucco's name. The playwright's choice of the name *Zucco* thus provides a distinct perspective of the criminal that allows us to examine how his deviance is provocative to the public. On the one hand, in changing Succo into Zucco, Koltès furnishes the criminal with his other half ("the other side of the mirror"), the mythological figure of flight he wanted to become in life. Barthes's statement about this

"Z" thus suggests a key to Koltès's enigmatic portrayal of Zucco. On the other hand, in creating an "imaginary" Zucco who consists of elements of the real Succo, Koltès blurs the boundary between fiction and fact. Essentially erasing this "slash of censure" between the real and the imaginary criminal, he shatters the binary representation of the criminal. We can see proof of this subversion in critics' efforts to keep Succo separate from Zucco; aware of Koltès's audacious move, they focus on fortifying the slash of censure in order to (ironically) save the play from censure. Koltès's fusion of real and fictive elements in Zucco's character is threatening because it metaphorically blends "S" with "Z," not merely fusing fact and fiction but furthermore erasing the distinction between good and evil.

Structured Ambiguity

In contrast to Koltès's earlier plays, which followed a more classical model of three acts, *Roberto Zucco*'s characters occupy fifteen separate scenes. This Brechtian structure perfectly echoes Zucco's flight and race against time. Gone, too, are the heady monologues that characterized his earlier works; *Roberto Zucco* is composed primarily of shorter replies that, coupled with the short sketches, lend the text a rapidity and vivacity that reflect the criminal's Faustian pact with time. Looking at the organization of the diverse sketches, as well as their titles, the patterns of place and time suggest predominant themes of the play I will return to throughout this chapter. For this reason, it is helpful to summarize the narrative of the play in the context of its structure. In the following synopsis, the title of each scene is in quotes, followed by the location.

> 1: "The Escape" ("L'Évasion"), prison rooftops. The play opens like *Hamlet*, with the first and second guards discussing whether or not they see or hear a prisoner escaping. Zucco appears, but the guards still cannot agree whether or not they see him; the scene is farcical, suggesting that Koltès mocks the watchmen, and at the end of the sketch, Zucco escapes. Like *J'ai pas sommeil*, the initial presentation of law enforcement is critical, if not comical.
>
> 2: "The Mother's Murder" ("Meurtre de la mère"), mother's house. Zucco returns home to fetch his military fatigues ("son treillis"), and his mother refuses him this Lacanian *petite boîte*, telling him she won't forget that he killed his father. When she finally divulges that his clothes are in the hamper, Zucco "goes up to her, strokes her, kisses her, grips her" ("s'approche, la caresse, l'embrasse, la serre") (18). The mother falls to the ground, strangled. The sensuality of the murder, present in the almost imperceptible slip from embrace to suffocation, likens the murder to an act of beauty rather than brutal violence.
>
> 3: "Under the table" ("Sous la table"), kitchen. The sister scolds the girl for staying out late and reminds her that she must remain a virgin: "What matters

is that you don't get stolen from you that thing that shouldn't be stolen from you before the time comes" ("L'essentiel est que tu ne te fasses pas voler ce qui ne doit pas t'être volé avant l'heure") (20–21). When the father enters, the girl hides under the table at her sister's urging; as he retreats, the brother storms in, worried that the girl had earlier escaped him. He leaves, the father enters and leaves with the sister, and the girl lets Zucco in the window. She asks him his name, and after much discussion ("I won't ever tell you my name"; "it's a secret"; "I can't remember") ("jamais je ne te dirai mon nom"; "c'est un secret"; "je l'ai oublié"), he tells her (25, 26). The mother enters, and Zucco hides, with the girl joining him under the table. The girl's voice closes the scene: "you've taken my virginity, and it's yours to keep. I've marked you like a scar after a fight" ("tu m'as pris mon pucelage . . . tu es marqué par moi comme par une cicatrice après une bagarre") (28).

4: "The Detective's Melancholy" ("La Mélancholie de l'inspecteur"), brothel lobby in Little Chicago. The detective tells the madam that "without knowing where the evil comes from" ("sans savoir d'où vient le mal") (29), he feels sad. Zucco's violent impulses are diffused here, suggesting that the evil emanates not from him, but rather from his environment. The inspector leaves, and Zucco follows him out of the room. The prostitute then rushes in to the reception to exclaim that "this boy with the sweet look, this beautiful boy" has just stabbed the inspector to death ("ce garçon au regard si doux; ce beau garçon") (30).

5: "The Brother" ("Le Frangin"), kitchen. The brother lectures at the girl, who is clearly terrorized by him. He tells her that now that she is a female ("une femelle"), "there's no reason to be modest for even one more second . . . just like that, everything's screwed up: marriage, family, your dad, your mom, your sister, and me, I don't give a shit" ("ça ne sert à rien d'être modeste une seconde de plus . . . en un seul coup, comme cela, tout est fichu: le mariage, la famille, ton père, ta mère, ta frangine; et moi je m'en fous") (33).

6: "Metro" ("Métro"), on a bench under the unnamed wanted poster of Zucco. The old gentleman tells Zucco how after years of taking the metro, today he has gotten lost and is now scared, as if victim of an existential *nausée*. Zucco reassures the man and tells him that he is "a normal guy . . . discrete and invisible" ("un garçon normal . . . discret et invisible") (37). The old gentleman reminds him that "you can always get off the tracks, young man, yes, now I know that anyone can derail, at any time" ("on peut toujours dérailler, jeune homme, oui, maintenant je sais que n'importe qui peut dérailler, n'importe quand") (38). Zucco leads the man out of the subway into the light. The old man's wise words contrast with Zucco's disingenuous remark and emphasize what the *fait divers* very superficially reflects, that no one is immune to violence.

7: "Two Sisters" ("Deux Sœurs"), kitchen. The sister tries to discourage the girl, who is holding her bag, from leaving. Calling her sister an old maid ("une vierge prolongée"), the girl says that she wants to find him ("je veux le retrouver" 40), which we understand to mean Zucco. The father enters and exits (looking for his beer), then the mother enters and threatens the girls before leaving ("if you weren't so old, I'd beat the two of you") ("si vous aviez encore l'âge je vous battrais toutes les deux") (44). The sister swears that she will die if abandoned, but the girl leaves anyway.

8: "Just before dying" ("Juste avant de mourir"), outside a nightclub, near a telephone booth. Zucco is thrown through a bar window, after which he quotes Hugo ("and thus I was created like the statue of an athlete") ("c'est ainsi que je fus créé comme un athlète" 45); this poetry likens him to a romantic figure rather than a violent criminal, and the spectators glimpse Zucco's charm. Drunk, he fights with the fat guy, then in a delirium, he quotes the real Succo: "sooner or later, we all have to die, all of us. And that, that makes the birds sing, that makes them laugh" ("tôt ou tard, on doit tous mourir, tous. Et ça, ça fait chanter les oiseaux, ça fait rire les oiseaux") (49). He passes out at the end of the sketch.

9: "Delilah" ("Dalila"), police station. The girl, followed by her brother, enters the police station and declares "I know him" ("Je le connais") (51). For several minutes she tries to remember Zucco's name, finally remembering it as something sweet. The police direct her to give her deposition without her brother ("what do you need with a brother? We're here") ("qu'as-tu besoin d'un frère? Nous sommes là") (56).

10. "The Hostage" ("L'Otage"), public garden. In the longest scene of the play, Zucco sits down on a park bench next to the elegant lady. After talking with her about her irritating son ("un petit morveux") and her stingy husband ("un radin"), Zucco demands her car keys. He takes out a gun, and her fourteen-year-old son runs over. As Zucco warns the child to stay away, the gathering crowd's comments dominate the scene. Creating a theater within the theater, the crowd interacts with Zucco, the elegant lady, and the child ("Give him the key, imbecile") ("Donnez-lui la clé, imbécile") (65). Eventually, the police come, they deliver a Porsche to Zucco, and, like a Girardian sacrificial act, Zucco shoots the child and takes the woman hostage. This scene is central in portraying Zucco's allure to the woman despite his gruffness with her. Most importantly, Koltès keenly portrays how society appropriates and recycles the media's discourse on crime.

11. "The Deal" ("Le Deal"), Little Chicago: the reception area of the same hotel. The girl is complaining to the madam that she is overweight when the brother comes in with the pimp. Agreeing on a price, the brother sells his sister

into prostitution. Confused, she leaves with the pimp, and the brother defends his actions to the madam ("she's the one who wanted to come to this area to find work") ("c'est elle qui a voulu venir dans ce quartier et faire le travail") (75).

12. "The Train Station" ("La Gare"), train station. Zucco repeats his name several times, and when the elegant lady asks why, he responds, "because I'm scared I'll forget it" ("parce que j'ai peur de l'oublier") (76). She swears she will remember it for him. Zucco reproduces some of his former monologue to the old gentleman ("you have to be transparent") ("il faut être transparent") (79) and explains that he had no choice but to kill her son ("I didn't want to kill him, but one thing led to another because of the whole Porsche story") ("je ne voulais pas le tuer, mais tout s'est enchaîné tout seul à cause de cette histoire de Porsche") (80). When he gets up to leave, the elegant woman cries and begs to go with him ("you're going to leave without your memory") ("vous allez partir sans votre mémoire") (82). The woman's desire attests to Zucco's magnetism, but even more to her own confused attraction. Titillated by his violent and "outlaw" nature, she reflects the complicated relationship to crime in which the villain is turned into a kind of hero.

13. "Ophelia" ("Ophélie"), same train station at night. In the empty station, the sister is alone and frets about the girl, alternating between self-admiration ("I kept her as white as a dove") ("je l'ai gardée blanche comme une colombe") and self-blame ("I should have killed him, I should have put barbed wire around my love's cage") ("J'aurais dû le tuer, j'aurais dû mettre des barbelés autour de la cage de mon amour") (84).

14. "The Arrest" ("L'Arrestation"), area of Little Chicago. In a reprise of the first sketch, suggesting the circular movement of the play, the first and second officers discuss whether or not they see Zucco, and whether or not he is crazy. Zucco enters, and they debate his identity ("it looks like him," "impossible") ("on dirait que c'est lui," "impossible") (88). When the girl enters calling "Roberto," they declare, "it's him" ("c'est lui"). While she proclaims her love for Zucco, another policeman asks him who he is ("Qui êtes-vous?"). Citing the *fait divers*, he responds "I'm a killer" ("Je suis un tueur") (89). Again, as in Denis's film, the law is shown to be ineffective, a depiction that was undoubtedly not lost on the Chambéry police force, which so vehemently protested the play.

15. "Zucco in the Sun" ("Zucco au soleil"), prison rooftops, midday. Only Zucco is visible to the spectators during this scene, although the voices of guards and prisoners are heard. Voices proclaim that Zucco has escaped, while others assure this impossibility ("it's a modern prison") ("c'est une prison moderne") (91). Zucco appears on the summit of a rooftop as he did in the first scene, although this time barefoot and bare-chested. Asked

> how he got there, he explains, "You have to escape by the rooftops, toward the sun" ("Il faut échapper par les toits, vers le soleil") (92). Voices from the gathering crowd call him a hero, as in the *fait divers*. As the sun becomes increasingly bright, Zucco commands the perplexed crowd to watch. Finally, a hurricane force wind rises, Zucco falters, and voices announce that he's crazy and that he will fall ("il est fou," "il va tomber") (95). The sun rises higher and becomes blinding, "*like an atomic bomb. Nothing else can be seen*" ("*comme une bombe atomique. On ne voit plus rien*") (95). Finally, a voice cries, "He's falling" ("Il tombe") (95).

As is evident from this brief plot summary, *Roberto Zucco* raises several key issues central to the *fait divers:* the allure of the criminal (evidenced by the varied women who are attracted to him: a teenager, a prostitute, an upper-class middle-aged woman); the public's fascination with the spectacle of crime (in both the park and the prison yard); and the sense of legend and history that surrounds the criminal (in his poetics and in his likeness to mythological figures). Ending as it begins with Zucco perched on a roof, gazed at in both awe and admiration, the play has an obvious circular structure that, like Ionesco's circular theatre, reflects the absurdity of life. Like a Racinian tragedy, the play begins with Succo dead, but it ends before Zucco's death, immortalizing him in a heroic mythology. This circularity is echoed by a quote from Jung (the liturgy of Mithra) that precedes the play and becomes Zucco's final words before he falls in the last scene (the lithurgy of Mithra). As Sarrazac writes, this is a "dramatic art of pure circularity, of the vain quest, of the lost quest, that turns in circles and where Man, who had thought to have found his path, only manages to dig his own grave" ("une dramaturgie de la pure circularité, de la quête vaine, de la quête dévoyée, qui tourne en rond et où l'Homme, qui croyait tracer son sillon, ne fait en définitive que creuser sa tombe") (147–48). Interpreting the end as tragic, Sarrazac hypothesizes the futility of Zucco's trajectory. While Zucco's movement is circular, there arguably exists an evolution within this circular structure that suggests a transformation of the character that critics have overlooked. Although Zucco returns to the rooftops of the prison in the end, for instance, he is now nearly naked beneath a bright sun, suggesting purification from the darkness that shrouded him at the beginning of the play. Looking at not only the location of the scenes, then, but also at the time of day that each scene takes place, another structure emerges. As the play begins in the dead of night and ends in midday, *Roberto Zucco* suggests an evolving rather than static circular pattern, a rising spiral transit from darkness and obscurity to light and clarity. The play opens at night, with two sentries who are oblivious to Zucco's escape, unable to perceive him in the darkness. Scenes numbered 2, 3, 4, 6, 7, 8, and 13 also take place at night, whereas 9, 10, 12, and 15 occur in broad daylight (scenes numbered 5, 11, and 14 are not designated as either day or night). This progressive brightness suggests a clarity often associated with light, but in the final illumination, the audience is blinded; a voice calls out, "we can't see anything anymore" ("on ne voit plus rien")

(95). Only the invisible bodies, whose voices the audience hears, can see Zucco fall from the roof. We are left to wonder if Zucco *does* fall, or if he simply evaporates into the sun, as suggested by his disappearance. Koltès deliberately omits the denouement and leaves the reader to speculate what happens. In the amalgam of light and darkness, Koltès breaks down the dialectic of opposites and makes it difficult to determine whether Zucco falls or ascends. In this final explosion of light, the criminal vanishes into an eternity that is void of determinism. Zucco remains impenetrable. In offering an unresolved ending that does not stage Zucco's death, Koltès refuses to create a sense of closure in the play. This indeterminate ending, coupled with the movement and circularity of the play, form a structure that reflects Koltès's nonjudgmental and nondefinitive portrayal of the criminal. Just as Zucco is neither simply criminal nor hero but one and the same, the play's structure cannot be captured in a simple summary. Brechtian in its episodic organization, absurdist in its seemingly endless circularity, Koltès's play resists definition and decenters the reader/spectator accustomed to closure and clearly defined symbolism.

The titles of the fifteen different scenes of the play function with the overall structure of *Roberto Zucco* to project a clearer understanding of Zucco as a fluid figure. We may thematically divide the locations in the following manner: three of the titles suggest a place (3: Under the table, 6: Metro, 12: The Train Station), four an action (1: The Escape, 2: The Mother's Murder, 11: The Deal, 14: The Arrest), six specify a person (5: The Brother, 7: Two Sisters, 9: Delilah, 10: The Hostage, 13: Ophelia, 15: Zucco in the Sun), and two suggest a nebulous feeling or time (4: The Detective's Melancholy, 8: Just before Dying). Of the titles in which characters figure, only Zucco's name is employed; the girl is invoked in the seventh scene as one of two sisters, and "le frangin" refers to the brother, but neither character is named outright. This choice seems ironic given Zucco's desire to be invisible and his propensity to forget his name, and yet his name is not used by any character until the last scene. Zucco's predilection for *and* fear of losing his identity are commensurate with his struggle for selfhood. His desire to blend in (to be transparent) sharply contrasts with his need to be seen and known, a theme that traverses the play. While the titles assigned to each scene convey Zucco's trajectory, the location of each one is instrumental in creating a cold, increasingly detached world where people merely pass through their surroundings. In *Roberto Zucco*, the sites do not function in harmony with the people who occupy them. Koltès's characters do not interact with their surroundings, but rather are betrayed by them: the old gentleman gets lost in the metro (6), Zucco gets drunk in the bar (8), the child gets shot in the park (10), and Zucco falls from the roof (15). In the absurdist tradition, each of these highly public spaces is therefore treacherous despite its familiarity, suggesting a harshness of the world that is commensurate with a violent and emotionless society.

It is noteworthy that the majority of *Roberto Zucco*'s scenes take place in public arenas, many of which may be categorized as non-places (*non-lieux*), as termed by Marc Augé in his book of the same title. Augé writes that non-places are indefinable in their non-specificity and traversed by a wide variety of people. He explains that "If a place can be defined as relational, historical, and concerned with identity, then a space which cannot be defined as relational, historical, or concerned with identity will be a non-place" (78). In the play, scenes 1, 4, 6, and 8 through 15 meet this definition; metros, train stations, hotels, and police stations characterize the second half of the play. In this way, the play reflects an increasingly cold, ahistorical view of contemporary society. Another one of Augé's mandates is that non-places do not integrate ancient spaces through content and dialogue, and certainly Koltès's train stations and public parks do not hark back to ancient locales. On the other hand, they *do* recall culturally historical ancient spaces, highlighting how *Roberto Zucco* fuses the ancient with the contemporary. In other words, although several scenes take place in generic public spaces or non-places (the metro, train station, and garden), the actions within these public spaces recall traces of the past. In the first scene, for example, Shakespeare's *Hamlet* is recalled as the guards argue about seeing Zucco; this literary intertext subverts the contemporaneity of the *fait divers*. Similarly, in the final scene of the play, the mythical Icarus is invoked as Zucco talks of flying to the sun. Other scene titles in *Roberto Zucco* conjure up literary and biblical parables although they occur in non-places; "Ophelia" (of *Hamlet*) takes place in a train station, and "Delilah" (of Samson and Delilah) occurs in a police station. Blending ancient intertexts with non-places, Koltès structures scenes that deviate from Augé's definition of the non-place as an ahistorical locale. In this combination of non-places with ancient stories, Koltès creates a new space where the cool killer is awash in mythology, symbolically transitioning the *fait divers* from ahistorical news item to a relevant meditation on society. The steady movement from past to present, from non-places to ancient spaces, combines with the constant, almost abrupt changes of locale to lend the play a fragmented quality that discourages the spectator from forming a conclusive judgment of the criminal. This disjointed structure is inconsistent with classical theater and certainly with Koltès's earlier plays, and it echoes the rapidity and immediacy of today's media-influenced society. Swiftly moving between past and present, between non-places and mythological locales, *Robert Zucco* thus straddles the centuries.

Another way of categorizing *Roberto Zucco*'s scenes is by their movement from inside to outside, or from private to public space. The progressively strong presence of the non-place in the play is important, particularly as it contrasts with the two private spaces in the play, the mother's house and the family's kitchen. In *Roberto Zucco*, the existence of these non-places does not completely eclipse the familial domain, yet their increased presence manages to obscure the primacy and safety of the private space. Augé explains that "place and non-place are rather like opposed polarities: the first is never completely erased, the second never totally completed; they are like palimpsests on which the scrambled game of identity and relations is ceaselessly rewritten" (79). In other words, the presence of non-places indicates that the outside world is gradually infringing on personal space, resulting in a shift in the private space, which must now accommodate the public arena. In the rewriting of the *fait divers*, then, the crime is no longer separate from the individual, but now enters into his or her personal domain, where the individual is compelled to interact with the violence.

Looking at the play as a whole, the kitchen, a site that *Roberto Zucco* director Lluis Pasqual calls an "espace cœur" (100), dominates the space. Its scenes outnumber all others (three of fifteen), and after the mother's murder in the second scene, all interior scenes take place in the kitchen. The beginning scenes of the play alternate between the kitchen and the public space of a hotel, the metro, and a bar; this oscillation of locale from kitchen to non-place fractures the sense of space and gives the play a staggered quality that parallels Zucco's fragmented identity. Yet while the kitchen dominates the play in both its number of pages and amount of scenes, its presence occupies only the first half of the play; the final eight scenes take place in public spaces, suggesting the increasing importance of these locales. As the non-places progressively invade the scenic space, the reader/spectator's attention is shifted outward. Like the girl who leaves her home in search of Zucco, like Zucco's own nameless search, the public also flounders in search of an understanding of the criminal. Functioning as a labyrinth, these places "are designed to disorder the senses by merging the real and the hallucinatory, thereby making the familiar strange" (Brustein 29–30). Koltès thus effectively decenters the reader accustomed to making quick judgments based on scanty information provided by the *fait divers*.

The Inscrutable Criminal: Deconstructing Zucco

One of the most subversive elements of *Roberto Zucco* is its nonjudgmental portrayal of the criminal. Unlike predecessors Duras and Genet, whose treatment of *faits divers* sympathized with or even glorified the murderer, Koltès does not moralize about his characters, but rather presents them for the reader/spectator's consideration. As he explains, "the psychological personage doesn't interest me—no more than does the 'reasonable' personage, for that matter" ("le personnage psychologique ne m'intéresse pas—pas plus d'ailleurs que le personnage 'raisonnable'") (Martinelli 14). Here again, Koltès makes a clear break with authors like André Gide, whose novel *Les Caves du Vatican* (1914) presents a motiveless murder with the goal of examining the criminal's psychology. This lack of interest in entering into character psychology reaches its pinnacle in *Roberto Zucco*. By refusing to explain or moralize Zucco's crimes, Koltès, like Denis, effectively subverts the media's binary representation of the criminal, disconcerting a public accustomed to cursory conclusions about crime. Upsetting dominant knowledge systems, Koltès removes the boundaries that separate good and evil, allowing that anyone can commit a crime; as the old gentleman states in scene 10, "one can always derail" ("on peut toujours dérailler") (38). More disturbing than the notion that anyone is capable of murder, however, is that the crime has no motive. In the Succo affair, physicians labeled Succo schizophrenic in order to classify him and assign motive to his actions; as a result, he received a lighter criminal sentence. This manner of categorizing the criminal hails from a long history of classification systems. As Foucault's work has shown, dominant discourses label and classify difference, a practice that is upheld through a variety of institutions, including education, law, and medicine. In *Discipline and Punish*, Foucault details how the prison is constructed as a system of exclusion and surveillance that labels the criminal in a dichotomy of mad/sane. Tracing the evolution of punishment in Europe, he notes a general shift, not towards a humanitarian, less cruel system, but rather a movement from the body to the soul. In this shift, the once transparent power systems began to manifest themselves in a far less conspicuous manner, represented by an omnipresent but diffuse system of discipline. It is this system, dubbed the Panopticon, that now permeates society and facilitates the diffusion of power. Foucault maintains that the panoptic machine has penetrated contemporary society at a macro level: in schools, workshops, prisons, factories, and hospitals, and that this practice stems from *la volonté de vérité* or the "will to truth." In other words, the desire to label and thus "know" is so compelling that society has constructed an entire framework with which to categorize people and events. More importantly, Foucault writes that this will to truth "is probably even more profoundly accompanied by the manner in which knowledge is employed in a society, the way in which it is exploited, divided and, in some ways, attributed" (*Archaelogy of Knowledge* 219). In the *fait divers*, then, Succo's classification as "schizophrenic" valorizes the medical establishment and thereby the judicial and political systems that uphold it: psychiatrists label Succo schizophrenic, police then close the case, and, accordingly, judges shorten his sentence. This "knowledge" of Succo's motivations will be redistributed and circulated in the media as well, as is most clearly illustrated by the consistent journalistic references to Succo as "le tueur fou." Interestingly, this label of "fou" was applied even before Succo's identity and schizophrenia were known, proving the media's vested interest in this classification. Just as the psychiatrist's job is validated by Succo's classification and the police is valorized for its ability to catch the madman, so will the media's purposes be served: sensationalism sells more papers and secures the status quo. In endeavoring to reassure the public and maintain its position as purveyor of knowledge, the media's premature classification of Succo exemplifies the diffuse expansiveness of this system of exclusion.

By classifying the criminal as an Other in this *partage de la folie* (separation of madness), the public is reassured of its own normality. Despite the individual's relief ("he is mentally unstable and thus unlike me") and the police's satisfaction ("he did it because he was mad"), this label does not actually reveal anything about Succo or his crimes: Succo did not kill because he had schizophrenia. Nevertheless, as this information is included in reports related to his crimes and his sentence is accordingly reduced, the disease is linked to his behavior, perpetuating myths about mental health issues that associate mental illness with violence. Just as Paulin's race and sexuality became associated with his crimes, so then does Succo's schizophrenia become inseparable from his killing spree.

The idea that a person considered within the norms of society can one day commit an act that defies society's most fundamental laws is a source of constant fascination for the public. Reflecting a darker side of humanity, or "evil" as it is commonly called, the public is struck by the sudden shift in personality, which is further underlined by the testimonies of witnesses attesting to the murderer's normality. While in the *fait divers* journalists often include a statement by a neighbor expressing shock that "such a nice boy" could have committed "such a heinous crime," the statement is often quickly brushed aside and covered up with additional bloody details of the crime (Kellerman 40). Both Denis and Koltès reflect these positive comments in their works through individual characters that attest to the murderer's fine character. In *J'ai pas sommeil*, Ninon marvels at how Camille and Raphaël are "so nice" ("si gentils") and in *Roberto Zucco*, the prostitute (30), old man (36), and Zucco's mother (17) wonder at his pleasant nature. Unlike the media's sole fixation on the suddenness (and immediacy) of Succo's eruptions, then, Koltès seems awestruck by how Succo's volatility functioned *alongside* his so-called normality. Removing the "slash of censure," Koltès's depiction of Zucco thus reflects the coexistence of his madness and his sanity, a duality that threatens to destabilize the binary classification of the criminal. Although Zucco's schizophrenia does not enter into the actual dramatic scenario, the question of his sanity threads through the play like a leitmotif. Words indicating insanity appear throughout the text: *fou*, *dingue*, and *cinglé* appear thirteen times in the play, referring to Zucco in almost all examples; in one exception, the girl's mother refers to her husband as "fou" (43). The other references all refer to Zucco: his mother calls him "sick, crazy" ("malade, cinglé") (14), a prostitute refers to him as mad ("he's insane, that's all") ("il est cinglé, c'est tout") (45), and the elegant lady likewise labels him crazy ("you're insane") ("vous êtes cinglé") (59). Other examples appear on pages 15, 63, 67, and 95. Interestingly, it is (in all cases but one) the female characters that classify him as mad; in the sole exception, a presumably male voice calls from the prison yard, "he's mad" ("il est fou") (95), but here he represents more the anonymous crowd than his masculinity. The female voices that label him are at the same time drawn to or attracted to Zucco, epitomizing the fascination/repulsion of society's relationship with the criminal. While these numerous references reflect how society reproduces the media's discourse of classification, *Roberto Zucco* does not judge Zucco's acts. Society may prefer its murderers to be ugly, evil, and consistently violent, but the playwright projects a man who defies these characteristics. In depicting the fictional Zucco, Koltès instead shows how his madness exists purely as a label rather than a medical diagnosis. Like the media, police, and the courts, the characters label Zucco in an effort to understand him; once understood in this *système d'exclusion* he can be grasped and then released. Yet despite the efforts of these institutions and the reactions of these characters, Zucco resists this tag, and his actions reveal a man who cannot fit into the institutionalized boundaries of mad/sane. He appears to be both one and the same.

In Zucco's interactions with the other characters, Koltès shows how the public traditionally defines evil, how inadequately this definition serves us, and how its upheaval exposes our basest desires and fears. Charmed and reverent despite their repugnance toward his crimes, the characters of *Roberto Zucco* place Zucco on a pedestal, where he becomes the object of their affection. This veneration of the killer is manifest in today's free market, which circulates serial killer trading cards, popular songs and video games about assassins, and even John Wayne Gacey's paintings, which have sold for enormous sums of money. *Roberto Zucco*'s exploration and challenge of the boundaries of mad/sane and evil/good thus reflect society's complicated relationship to the criminal. Through characters like the elegant lady, the girl, and the old gentleman who attempt to use Zucco as a catalyst for their personal transformation, Koltès unveils how we create the criminal-hero to satisfy our need for self-definition. In the beginning of the play, Zucco's mother strives to account for her son's startling violence. Like Thierry Paulin's mother, who implores an explanation for her son's terrible actions, the mother of the murderer often wishes she had killed her son. Whereas Paulin's mother laments not having killed him during her pregnancy ("I should have killed him when he was in my womb"), Zucco's purely fictional mother regrets not having done away with him as an infant. She says, "You're mad, Roberto. We should have known that when you were still in your crib and thrown you in the trash" ("Tu es fou, Roberto. On aurait dû comprendre cela quand tu étais au berceau et te foutre à la poubelle") (15). She furthermore disowns him ("you're no longer my son") ("tu n'es plus mon fils") (14) and later wonders how she could be his mother. "Did I really give birth to you? Did you come from inside of me?" ("Est-ce moi qui t'ai accouché? Est-ce de moi que tu es sorti?") (17). She is confused, both that he could be a product of her body and that he has so suddenly changed. She asks, "Why did this child, who was so good for twenty-four years, become so mad all the sudden? How did you derail again, Roberto? Who put a tree on that straight and narrow track to make you fall off the edge?" ("Pourquoi cet enfant, si sage pendant vingt-quatre ans, est-il devenu fou brusquement? Comment as-tu quitté les rails, Roberto? Qui a posé un tronc d'arbre sur ce chemin si droit pour te faire tomber dans l'abîme?") (17). This series of questions indicates her complete disavowal of his actions. Distancing herself from him ("this child") and exonerating herself from any responsibility ("Who put"), the mother reflects society's renunciation of its role in creating the criminal. Her confusion at his sudden change reflects one of the most frequently discussed enigmas surrounding today's more mediated criminals, like Succo and Paulin: that their "evil" is invisible or undetectable. Her response moreover strongly echoes the public's response to the criminal. Appalled by their murderous actions, the public turns its back on the Other and completely disassociates itself from him, refusing to return the gaze.

In the fourth scene of the play, another woman is dumbfounded by Zucco's crimes. A prostitute rushes into the hotel reception with the news that Zucco killed the inspector and exclaims, "Madam, you have sheltered *the devil* in your house" ("Madame, vous avez abrité *le démon* dans votre maison") (my emphasis 30). She seems particularly unsettled by the fact that Zucco did not look like a killer: "This boy, though, the one with such a sweet look; this beautiful boy, actually, and we've talked a lot about him among us ladies—here he is, following the detective out. We're watching him, us ladies, we're giggling, speculating. He's walking behind the detective, who seems like he's lost in some profound reflection; he's walking behind him like his shadow." ("Ce garçon, pourtant, au regard si doux; ce beau garçon, décidément, et on en a beaucoup parlé, entre dames,—le voici qui sort derrière l'inspecteur. On l'observe bien, nous, les dames, on rigole, on fait des suppositions. Il marche derrière l'inspecteur qui semble plongé dans une réflexion profonde; il marche derrière lui comme son ombre") (30). In continuing to oppose Zucco's good looks with his horrible act, the woman echoes society's perception of criminals as physical monsters. Her surprise and fascination are likewise reflected by the crowd that watched Zucco leave the scene of the crime, "because no one moved, everyone, frozen, watched him leave" ("car personne n'a bougé, tout le monde, immobilisé, l'a regardé partir") (31). The cool killer figuratively and literally immobilizes the public, which is unable to place Zucco's rage and therefore incapable of defining his act.

In the following scene 5, Koltès further obscures Zucco's "evil" by juxtaposing him to the girl's brother. Portrayed as a far more threatening figure, the character of the brother reverses the dichotomy of evil/good, thus calling Zucco's "evil" into question. The stage directions at the beginning of the scene read: *"the girl is against the wall, terrorized"* (*"la gamine est contre le mur, terrorisée"*) (32). The girl's fearful reaction to her brother sharply contrasts her warm response to Zucco in scene 3, showing the brother to be more sinister than Zucco. This reaction is later confirmed in a monologue that composes the thirteenth scene, where the sister blames the brother (rather than Zucco) for having corrupted his sister. She laments, "And it's her brother, this rat among rats, this stinking pig, this corrupted male who dirtied her and dragged her through the mud by her hair into his pile of shit. I should have killed him, I should have poisoned him, I should have stopped him from stalking my turtledove's cage" ("Et c'est son frère, ce rat parmi les rats, ce cochon puant, ce mâle corrompu qui l'a salie et traînée dans la boue et tirée par les cheveux jusqu'à son fumier. J'aurais dû le tuer, j'aurais dû l'empoisonner, j'aurais dû l'empêcher de tourner autour de la cage de ma tourterelle") (84). Unlike her brother, the sister does not blame Zucco for her sister's "demise," instead placing the blame where it rightfully belongs: on the brother who sold the girl into prostitution. Again the brother's actions are contrasted with Zucco's, and the sister represents yet another female character who does not see Zucco as a dangerous figure. Koltès's depiction thus differs from the *fait divers* in that he does not contradict or attempt to explain Zucco's agreeable personality; nor does this affability appear to be in contrast with

Zucco's deeds. Instead, it seems entirely possible that a murderer could have positive qualities. Absolved of guilt by the sister, Zucco may be seen as freeing the girl from her family, which is clearly dysfunctional. Thus, when the girl falls in love with Zucco, although he is a killer, this choice seems somewhat preferable to being sold into prostitution. Once the girl has lost her virginity to Zucco and can no longer play the role of the virgin in her family, she is ready to leave the family cell; having been with Zucco, the girl now has the strength to leave despite her sister's threats ("I'll die if you abandon me") ("je vais mourir si tu m'abandonnes") (44). Moreover, Zucco's fluid identity allows the girl to role-play her fantasies. When she asks him his name, for instance, he responds, "Call me what you want" ("Appelle-moi comme tu veux") (24). As Zucco invents himself as a secret agent, the girl imagines him taking her away: "I want to see the snow in Africa. I'd like to go ice skating on frozen lakes" ("Je voudrais aller voir la neige en Afrique. Je voudrais faire du patin à glace sur les lacs gelés") (25). Here the criminal becomes her desire and is both catalyst (for the girl's departure) and emancipator (in allowing her to fantasize an escape). An unsettling vision of a murderer, Zucco may be read as a positive figure who functions to liberate the girl; that she is later sold into prostitution only confirms her brother's baseness, but does not further condemn Zucco, who has never harmed her. The juxtaposition of Zucco with the brother echoes a similar scene in *J'ai pas sommeil* in which Daïga is chased by an unknown man before (symbolically) taking refuge in a theater. By providing a character whose actions are perceived as more threatening than the criminal's, both Denis and Koltès show that the criminal does not function as a polar opposite of the public. In both of these works, actions, rather than individuals, are judged as evil.

Far from representing evil, then, Zucco seems to symbolize a positive force. More subversive, however, is that in each of these situations, the character expresses an interest in the killer that contrasts with the repulsiveness of his acts: the mother wants to keep Zucco home, the prostitute finds him attractive, the young girl is enamored. The (female) characters' muddled and fascinated reactions to Zucco seem to mirror our own as we watch him. In addition to blurring the categories of mad/sane and evil/good, then, Koltès reveals how the characters' fascination with the criminal mirrors their deeper desires, reflecting the relationship between the *fait divers* and its public. But rather than vicariously experiencing the criminal or fantasizing about these desires, as in a *fait divers*, Koltès's characters, like Denis's Daïga, go a step further in actually *interacting* with Zucco. The relationship that Koltès establishes between the characters and the criminal recalls the *looking relation* that Denis creates between Daïga and Camille. Although theater is distinct from film, making it difficult to discuss the way a spectator gazes or looks at a character onstage, Koltès essentially achieves the same result. In interacting with Zucco, characters in the play are able to look (relate) rather than gaze (judge) the criminal. Knowledgeable about his actions for the most part, these characters choose Zucco's company, engaging in dangerous games that reward them with their freedom. Both the girl and the elegant lady, for instance, continue to pine after Zucco even after they learn of his dangerous crimes. Zucco's ability to mold himself to these individual desires makes him even more remarkable, and likewise speaks to the fluidness of the *fait divers* as a signifier. By emphasizing the public's ability to read its own meaning into the *fait divers* (e.g., a personal definition of the criminal), Koltès subverts the media's authority by empowering the individual character and, by association, the reader. Like the photos on the aptly named "wanted poster" displaying the real Succo, Koltès's Zucco appears different in each scene of the play, depending on both who looks at him and why he is regarded. As the characters reflect their desires onto him, he projects back the vision they want to see. In this role, Zucco reveals how the public constructs the criminal's identity through its particular personal experiences and needs, demonstrating that the criminal functions as a figure of the individual's (and the public's collective) imagination.

By the sixth scene of the play, Zucco has already killed two people. When he meets the old gentleman in the metro, the spectator awaits the inevitable violence, but is surprised to find that Zucco helps, rather than butchers, the old man. In the moment of connection between the two men, Koltès shows us Zucco's humanity. This scene takes place in a metro station after closing. Zucco sits on a bench next to the old man, who has lost his way in the metro; above the bench is a wanted poster with Zucco's picture. The scene opens with a monologue by the elderly man, who explains that he got lost in the metro and became afraid; in referring to the metro as a space as familiar as his kitchen (36), the man juxtaposes his home with a sterile public place, highlighting the increasing replacement of private spaces with non-places. He tells Zucco that a young man like himself is reassuring to him: "But you, young man, your legs seem agile and your mind clear, yes, I can see that your gaze is clear and not troubled and foolish like that of the old man I am" ("Mais vous, jeune homme, dont les jambes me semblent bien agiles, et l'esprit bien clair, oui, je vois bien votre regard clair et non pas troublé et sot comme celui du vieil homme que je suis") (36). When the man says to Zucco, "tell me about yourself, it will reassure me" ("parlez-moi de vous, cela me rassurera"), Zucco assures him that "I'm a normal and reasonable boy, sir. I've never done anything to stand out. Would you have even noticed me if I wasn't sitting next to you?" ("Je suis un garçon normal et raisonnable, monsieur. Je ne me suis jamais fait remarqué. M'auriez-vous remarqué si je n'étais pas assis à côté de vous?") (36). Ironically seated beneath the wanted poster bearing his likeness, Zucco at once references the old man's statement and his own invisibility. Attentive to the old man's fears of being lost (a fear he shares), Zucco reinvents himself as an innocent young man for the old gentleman, who feels bewildered in his unfamiliar surroundings. His attempts to soothe the old man by swearing that he could never be dangerous do not fool him, however. This scene is similar to one in Mathieu Kassovitz's acclaimed film *La Haine* (1992), which explores the juvenile delinquency that consumed the media's attention during the 1990s. In the film, a chance meeting with an older man in the bathroom leaves the three young protagonists dumbfounded; rather than displaying fear towards the seemingly aggressive youths (who represent the prototypical violent offenders), the old man engages them in a puzzling story that leaves the youngest character speechless for the first time in the film. In both *La Haine* and *Roberto Zucco*, the old men are models of how dialogue may dissolve boundaries of mad/sane and old/young and in turn de-escalate crime and violence.

When Zucco explains that he is like "a train that's calmly crossing a prairie and that nothing could derail" ("un train qui traverse tranquillement une prairie et que rien ne pourrait faire dérailler"), the old gentleman reminds him that "you can always derail, young man, yes, now I know that anyone can derail, at any time" ("on peut toujours dérailler, jeune homme, oui, maintenant je sais que n'importe qui peut dérailler, n'importe quand") (38). Like a caricature of a wise man, the old gentleman suggests that anyone can become a criminal, issuing a Brechtian call to the audience to avoid an abstract judgment of Zucco. At the end of the scene, as Zucco leads the old gentleman out of the metro, the man tells him, "You stutter a bit; I like that a lot. It puts me at ease" ("Vous bégayez, très légèrement; j'aime beaucoup cela. Cela me rassure") (39). In this line, Koltès pinpoints how Zucco's fluidness stems from an ability to recognize people's need for reassurance. Able to become what they want (if only temporarily), Zucco is able to fool the public, which, it is revealed, is only fooling itself.

In the tenth scene, Zucco meets the elegant lady, who also seeks Zucco's affirmation and reassurance. The woman, browbeaten and ill-esteemed by her family ("my husband takes me for an idiot, my son takes me for an idiot, the maid takes me for an idiot") ("mon mari me prend pour une idiote, mon fils me prend pour une idiote, la bonne me prend pour une idiote") (59), searches for a man who will respect her: "LADY—You must like these eighteen year-old girls. / ZUCCO—I love all women. / LADY—Oh, that's really good. Have you ever been mean to a woman? / ZUCCO—Never. / LADY—But have you ever wanted to be? You must have already had the desire to be violent with a woman, no? That desire, all men have it some day, all of them. / ZUCCO—Not me. I'm sweet and peaceful. / LADY—You're a strange guy" ("LA DAME.—Vous devez aimer ces espèces de gamines de dix-huit ans. / ZUCCO. – J'aime toutes les femmes. / LA DAME.—Ça, c'est très bien. Avez-vous déjà été dur avec une femme? / ZUCCO.—Jamais. / LA DAME.—Mais l'envie? Vous avez déjà dû avoir l'envie d'être violent avec une femme, n'est-ce pas? Cette envie-là, tous les hommes l'ont eu un jour; tous. / ZUCCO.—Pas moi. Je suis doux et pacifique. / LA DAME.—Vous êtes un drôle de type") (57). Zucco's responses to the woman's questions demonstrate his deftness at recognizing her need to believe in him. Having murdered his mother, his lies are of course outrageous, but they accentuate his desire to fulfill this woman's wishes. Her own desperation is painfully clear when she continues to follow Zucco even after he has murdered her child at the end of this scene. Later, in scene 12, the lady tells Zucco that she wants to get on the train with him: "I have no reason to not take the train with you. I liked you from the moment I saw you" ("Je n'ai aucune raison de ne pas le prendre avec vous. Vous ne m'avez pas déplu dès que je vous ai vu") (77). Despite his violence (or perhaps because of it), she finds Zucco attractive. Zucco's adeptness at imagining other people's desires extends to the police as well. In scene 14, two officers try to determine if the man in front of them is Zucco. Recalling Jenny's betrayal of Macheath in Brecht's *Threepenny Opera*, the girl calls him by his name, and the first officer approaches him. Still unsure of Zucco's identity, he asks: "Who are you?" Zucco responds that he's a killer ("Je suis un tueur") (89). In his answer, Zucco becomes precisely what the officer wants him to be; this response also echoes Succo's reply upon arrest, when he exclaimed to his arresting officers, "Profession? Killer!" (Duplouich, "Le Tueur fou" 42). In conjunction with the critical portrayal of the guards at the beginning of the play, this exchange demonstrates the simple-mindedness of the police, who are unable to identify the killer themselves. Moreover, this retort infers that the police, like the other characters, are content with the simple portrait Zucco furnishes them.

In his fluidness, Zucco exists only as others envision him. His ability to walk the line of the criminal and the sane is reflected in his interactions with characters who make Zucco into whom they wish, thereby suggesting that he exists in our imagination. This interaction with the criminal emphasizes our collective discomfort with (and often overt denial of) the terribleness of Zucco's crimes. For these characters, it appears to be easier to look past or ignore his crimes than to imagine that someone could commit them. In Koltès's portrayal of the characters' interactions with each other and in how they use Zucco to reflect their own desires, he unveils a society that functions on the level of pure exchange, where every human interaction is characterized by a deal: people express love for each other as a way to get something, seeing in Zucco a way to escape their doleful existences. As Zucco explains to a prostitute in the eighth scene, people do not actually interest each other, they merely use them for what they need: "anyway, no one's interested in anyone else. No one. Men need women and women need men. But love, that doesn't exist" ("de toute façon, personne ne s'intéresse à personne. Personne. Les hommes ont besoin des femmes et les femmes ont besoin des hommes. Mais de l'amour, il n'y en a pas") (48). A common theme in Koltès's work as a whole, "the deal" reflects a detached need that drives interpersonal relationships; the eleventh scene, where the brother sells his sister, for instance, is aptly entitled "Le Deal." This view of society understands every exchange between people as one of commerce. In this reading of the play, every exchange between the characters may be reduced to a deal: Zucco's mother gives him his military fatigues hoping that he will return, the girl gives him her virginity in the hopes that he will carry her off, the brother exchanges the girl for money, and the girl tells Zucco's name to the police expecting to find him. Interpreting the end of the play as a negation of itself, Regnault writes that by the last scene, "everything is exchanged" ("tout s'est echangé") (329). While Regnault's statement accurately applies to Koltès's other plays, in *Roberto Zucco* the exchanges are not always realized. When the mother yields to Zucco his fatigues, he instead kills her; although the lady begs Zucco to stay with her, he leaves; when the girl gives up her virginity, Zucco abandons her; and when she offers his name to the police, he is imprisoned and forever lost to her.

Again, the female characters are those who most clearly suffer from the exchange; the brother and old man, for instance, get what they want from their exchanges: money and a way out of the subway maze. Zucco, on the other hand, is arguably the only character that escapes the deal. Turned off by humanity's loveless need for others and unwilling to compromise, he is most rebellious in his absolute refusal to take part in society's game. Most radical is that he escapes the transaction only by the means of crime. Rather than surrender to this level of exchange, disguised as love from the women he encounters, Zucco commits violent crimes that render him visible. As he explains to the old gentleman, he is entirely unremarkable; only his crimes reveal him (36). As in *Quai ouest* and *Combat de nègre et de chiens*, the only remedy for violence seems to be speech, or "l'échange parlée," a metaphor for how society might deal with the Other. The notion of Zucco's transparency is central not only to how the public constructs the criminal, but also to how the criminal constructs himself. As Zucco struggles to find his place in the world, he vacillates between alternating desires that leave him feeling frightened. These alternatives of death and escape haunted the real Succo as well. Succo's last letter to don Franco, a priest with whom he kept in contact while serving his prison sentence, was entitled "to escape or to kill myself" (Froment, *Je te tue* 467). For Zucco, there is nowhere to hide from the world, and when he cannot blend into his environment, the result is a vertiginous emptiness that frightens him. Here we are returned to Zucco's conversation with the old man, where he states, "There is a reason to be afraid" ("Il y a de quoi avoir peur") (39). Zucco's fear is palpable throughout the play. In the tenth scene, when he takes the woman and her child hostage, a man watching from the crowd comments, "Look how he's trembling" ("Regardez comme il tremble"), and in the final scene, a voice explains that the hidden Zucco "must be curled up in a hole, and he's trembling" ("doit être recroquevillé dans un cagibi, et il tremble") (91). Although rarely mentioned in *faits divers*, fear is often a catalyst in murder cases. As Victor Seidler has shown, fear and vulnerability lead to anger, whose auto-transformative state stems from the good/bad dichotomy created by Western Christian thought. Without being able to register fear, which threatens the male identity, this emotion may be transformed into violent behavior. Peter Stein, the German director of *Roberto Zucco*, explains this fear as paramount to the text. He writes that "Koltès allows us to see in Zucco something 'normal,' to know fear. Something that everyone knows very well, that originates in the fact that we all feel too visible. . . . To be noticed is very dangerous because every other being is a potential criminal. It is an archaic idea, an almost animalistic understanding of human behavior" ("Koltès donne à voir chez Zucco quelque chose de 'normal,' à savoir la peur. Celle que tout le monde connaît très bien, qui trouve son origine dans le fait qu'on se sent trop visible. . . . Se faire remarquer est très dangereux car tout être autre est un criminel en puissance. C'est une idée archaïque, une compréhension presque animale du comportement humain") (146). This desire to vanish stems primarily from a kind of metaphysical anguish brought on by the dangerous nature of the world, which Zucco views as a wild and brutal place. Zucco sees humans driven by their most animalistic impulses; as he explains to the crowd in scene 15, "I crush other animals not out of cruelty but because I did not see them" ("J'écrase les autres animaux non pas par méchanceté mais parce que je ne les ai pas vus") (93). Zucco's frequent comparison of himself with animals shows how he constructs the world in an absurd, even primitive manner. Comparing himself to a hippopotamus (38) and stating his desire to be a white rhinoceros (25, 92), a slug (49), or a stray dog (48), Zucco's worldview reduces humans to mere animals, incapable of love or reflection. His reason for killing animals demonstrates that not only are we all capable of committing crimes, but that the crimes themselves are not motivated by anger. He instead sees them as natural accidents, a view that strongly contradicts the media-driven view of crime. Unlike the *fait divers*, which endeavors to show that anyone can be the victim of a crime, Zucco (like Camille) shows that anyone can be a killer. In presenting this view, Koltès blurs the boundaries that separate "normal" society from "mad" criminals, confirming society's greatest fears that it is not safe. Haunted by this feeling of danger, Zucco explains the ubiquity of killers to the elegant lady in scene 12:

> ZUCCO—Look at all these crazy people. See how mean they look. They're killers. I've never seen so many killers at the same time. At the slightest signal in their head, they'll all start killing each other. I wonder why the signal doesn't go off, there, now, in their head. Because they're all ready to kill. They're like rats in laboratory cages. They want to kill, you can see it on their faces, in their steps; I see their fists clenched in their pockets. Me, I can recognize a killer at first glance; their clothes are covered in blood. Here, they're everywhere; you have to keep calm and not move; you can't look them in the eye. They can't see us; you have to be transparent. Because if not, if you look at them in the eye, if they see that we're watching them, they'll start looking at us and they'll see us, the signal will go off in their head and they'll kill, they'll kill. And if even one starts, everyone here will kill everyone. Everyone is only waiting for the signal in their head.
>
> LADY—Stop. Don't have a hissy fit. I'm going to go get the tickets.

> ZUCCO.—Regardez tous ces fous. Regardez comme ils ont l'air méchant. Ce sont des tueurs. Je n'ai jamais vu autant de tueurs en même temps. Au moindre signal dans leur tête, ils se mettraient à se tuer entre eux. Je me demande pourquoi le signal ne se déclenche pas, là, maintenant, dans leur tête. Parce qu'ils sont tous prêts à tuer. Ils sont comme des rats dans les cages des

> laboratoires. Ils ont envie de tuer, ça se voit à leur visage, ça se voit à leur démarche ; je vois leurs poings serrés dans leurs poches. Moi, je reconnais un tueur au premier coup d'oeil; ils ont les habits pleins de sang. Ici, il y en a partout; il faut se tenir tranquille, sans bouger; il ne faut pas les regarder dans les yeux. Il ne faut pas qu'ils nous voient; il faut être transparent. Parce que sinon, si on les regarde dans les yeux, s'ils s'aperçoivent qu'on les regarde, s'ils se mettent à nous regarder et à nous voir, le signal se déclenche dans leur tête et ils tuent, ils tuent. Et s'il y en a un qui commence, tout le monde ici va tuer tout le monde. Tout le monde n'attend que le signal dans la tête.
>
> LA DAME.—Arrêtez. Ne commencez pas une crise de nerfs. Je vais chercher les deux billets. (79–80)

In the lady's rather vacant reply, Koltès mocks the public's response to crime. Just as she *wants* to believe that Zucco is a nice man who doesn't hurt women, her flippant response and disregard for his thoughts in this scene show how she does *not want* to believe his dim view of humanity. In this scene, Koltès exposes how the public sees what it wishes and how, in its preference for the simplistic media-driven understanding of criminality, it is unprepared to deal with Zucco's theory that we are all potential criminals. In blending in and becoming a fluid signifier for the other characters' desires, however, Zucco also risks losing his identity. As Sarrazac notes, Zucco never stops feeling that he's becoming transparent (145). Fearful of relinquishing his identity, he struggles considerably with his name. When the girl asks him what he calls himself, for instance, he tells her that her request is "Impossible. Something bad could happen to me" ("Impossible. Il pouvait m'arriver un malheur") (26). Indeed, the eventual disclosure of his name secures his capture: in the Succo *affaire*, Sabina (the girl) gave Succo's name to the police, facilitating his capture. Likewise, in scene 14, Zucco walks securely past the police when the girl calls out to him, signaling his presence to the uncertain police. After having killed the child at the end of scene 10, Zucco finds that he is slowly losing his identity, and this fear leads him to try to retain his name. Repeating his name to the elegant lady in scene 12, he explains why he must remember it: "ZUCCO—Roberto Zucco. / LADY—Why do you keep repeating this name all the time? / ZUCCO—Because I'm scared of forgetting it. / LADY—People never forget their name. That's got to be the last thing you'd forget. / ZUCCO—No, I'm actually forgetting it. I see it written in my head, and less and less well written, less and less clearly, as if it's erasing itself, I have to look closer and closer to be able to read it. I'm scared I'm going to end up not knowing my name" ("ZUCCO.—Roberto Zucco. / LA DAME.—Pourquoi vous répétez-vous tout le temps ce nom? / ZUCCO.—Parce que j'ai peur de l'oublier. / LA DAME.—On n'oublie jamais son nom. Ce doit être la dernière chose que l'on oublie. / ZUCCO.—Non, non; moi, je l'oublie. Je le vois écrit dans mon cerveau, et de moins en moins bien écrit, de moins en moins clairement, comme s'il s'effaçait; il faut que je regarde de plus en plus près pour arriver à le lire. J'ai peur de me retrouver sans savoir mon nom") (76). In this exchange, Zucco explains his fear as a progressive dissolution of his identity. In the sixth scene, Zucco articulates the same vertiginous feeling to the old gentleman: "I always thought that the best way to live calmly was to be as transparent as a window pane, like a chameleon on a rock, walking through walls, not having any color or smell; that the gaze of others would go right through you and see the people behind you, as if you weren't there" ("J'ai toujours pensé que la meilleure manière de vivre tranquille était d'être aussi transparent qu'une vitre, comme un caméléon sur la pierre, passer à travers les murs, n'avoir ni couleur ni odeur; que le regard des gens vous traverse et voie les gens derrière vous, comme si vous n'étiez pas là") (36). In this statement, we remember that when Zucco killed the police inspector (30), the crowd watched him as he walked away, unable to avert their eyes. Having killed, Zucco at once became visible. This description thus articulates the delicate balance of existing without being noticed, or of being able to blend into society without ever actually losing one's identity. With the girl, the lady, and the old gentleman, Zucco borders on achieving this transparency by becoming what they wish: a secret agent, a nonviolent man, a conscientious student. His identity is never revealed to them, enabling his assimilation. It would appear that the public's desire to believe what it wants, in conjunction with its fascination with the criminal's refusal to partake in society's game, overrides the reality of his crimes. This rationale reminds us of the characters of *J'ai pas sommeil* who ignore the media's warnings about "le tueur des vieilles dames." Regardless of the fear and *insécurité* that the media attempts to generate, the characters of these works ignore these warnings and continue with their lives, choosing to interact with the criminal. Like Denis, Koltès depicts a less-than-perfect world that is attracted to the criminal's abjection. In this way, these artists show how the criminal is useful to the public. By using him to work through their individual struggles (the old gentleman's fear) or reproduce their desires (the girl, the lady), Zucco serves as a beneficial tool to these individual characters. Departing from *faits divers*, which show how the "insane criminal" interacts with "ordinary people," Koltès and Denis reveal the emptiness of these labels. Zucco is fascinating because the struggle he embodies is universal. In reality, the criminal is not so different from the public, as his struggles illustrate his very human fears: death, visibility, and invisibility.

Despite Zucco's desire to become transparent, his actions betray his wishes. Each time he approaches a sense of transparency, Zucco kills someone and is covered in blood, which renders him visible. As he explains to the old man: "It is a tough job to be transparent; it is a calling, it is an ancient dream to be invisible. I am not a hero. Heroes are criminals. There is not a hero whose clothes are not drenched in blood, and blood is the only thing that cannot go unnoticed. It is the most visible thing in the world" ("C'est une rude tâche d'être transparent; c'est un métier; c'est un ancien très ancien rêve d'être invisible. Je ne suis pas un héros. Les héros sont des criminels. Il n'y a pas de héros dont les habits ne soient trempés de sang, et le sang est la seule chose au monde qui ne puisse pas passer inaperçue. C'est la chose la plus visible au monde") (36–37). In describing what resembles an age-old problem, Zucco calls his dream of clarity an ancient one. Indeed, Zucco's destiny seems inescapable, his trajectory more like that of a Greek hero than a twentieth-century killer. His statement is itself somewhat enigmatic, however, similar to other absurdist statements he makes throughout the play: "It's normal to kill your parents" ("Il est normal de tuer ses parents") (92), "I'm a rhinoceros" ("Je suis un rhinocéros") (92), "You have to close the schools and make the cemeteries bigger" ("Il faut fermer les écoles et agrandir les cimetières") (49). In endeavoring to decode his complicated speech, we are able to see how Zucco constructs himself. His statement to the old man reads like a tautology, which we may decipher in the following manner: If Zucco is not a hero, and if criminals are heroes, then Zucco is not a criminal. In this manner, the criminal absolves himself of his crimes. In this reverse logic, Zucco is innocent *not* because he is not a criminal, but because he is not a hero. Moreover, if heros are covered in blood, if blood cannot go unnoticed, and if Zucco is not covered in blood, then Zucco is not a hero. Zucco thus proves to the old man that he is neither a criminal *nor* a hero, constructing himself as an invisible and therefore innocent man. Yet despite Zucco's construction of himself as untainted, his tangled logic contradicts his actions. Similar to when he tells the lady to "look at all these madmen" ("regardez tous ces fous") (79), Zucco unsuccessfully attempts to distance himself from society's criminals. For the reader of the text or for the audience, who has seen Zucco commit several murders, this prattle may be fascinating, but it is not convincing. In fact, if we apply Zucco's crimes to his own logic, he *is* a hero (because we know he is a criminal); his words thus reveal rather than conceal him. This interpretation presents a disturbing look at how the criminal, in his peculiar dialectic, "unknowingly" constructs himself as a hero for the public, which in turn readily accepts this image. Rather than reading this determination of Zucco's heroism as proof that Koltès saw Zucco as a hero (as many of the play's protesters did), then, we may instead return to *how* Zucco's "heroism" and struggle within himself are read by the play's characters.

Although Succo was labeled a hero by the press at the time of the affair, only *Koltès's* portrayal of him as a hero generated negative commentary in the media; Koltès likened Succo to a mythic hero like Samson or Goliath. Yet as I have shown, the image of the criminal-hero is hardly a recent phenomenon. Kooistra's research shows that these criminal-heroes are glamorized because they act as social outlaws, representing society's underlying desires to subvert social codes. While Succo's murders of the two policemen may be popular acts with anti-establishment groups and the like, they are not murders in self-defense or for a higher justice; because his acts do not appear to have any meaning, he cannot correspond to this definition of a hero, even a postmodern hero. Moreover, the fictional Zucco's crimes do not carry any clear significance to the characters of the play, who instead express their surprise at the senselessness of his acts. According to Baudrillard, the inability to assign meaning to Zucco's acts would move him into obscurity, which has not happened. Rather, the random and senseless nature of the killings drew and continues to draw considerable attention to the affair. Zucco's "senseless" crimes represent contemporary society's greatest *insécurité*, while at the same time touching at the very core of society's taboos, patricide and matricide. His crimes are at once ancient and modern. While Zucco's actions do not make him a heroic figure in Kooistra's terms, his early death adds a tragic element that aligns his acts with this definition. More importantly, Koltès weaves Zucco into a web of history and legend that allows us to imagine his heroism. As Nash-Stedlicki writes, "Koltès is creating Roberto Zucco who fits the paradigm of the god who does not (yet) know he is a god" (7). Mythical and legendary, Zucco's identity is embedded in a chronicle of history that removes him from a purely contemporary context, safely placing him beyond the realm of the play's critics.

Imagining History: "A Mythic Character"

Roberto Zucco opens with a scene recalling Shakespeare's *Hamlet.* It is nearly impossible not to draw parallels between the openings of these two plays, whose first scenes share undeniable similarities. Koltès's interest in Shakespeare further substantiates this idea, as he affirmed a great love for Shakespeare and cited him often in interviews. Explaining that he very rarely had a "shock" at the theater, Koltès included Chéreau's production of *Hamlet* among the few plays that had touched him (Costaz 62). In addition, he chose to translate *A Winter's Tale* (1988), which he calls "an incredible experience; I would do another translation of Shakespeare for my own pleasure. This guy taught me freedom. He really freed me from the rules of theater" ("une expérience incroyable; je referais une traduction de Shakespeare pour mon seul plaisir. Ce mec m'a appris la liberté. Il m'a beaucoup libéré par rapport aux règles du théâtre") (Regnault 330). Koltès's affinity for Shakespeare enriches the intertext, which undoubtedly resonates in the cultural memory of many of the play's spectators. More importantly, the parallels with *Hamlet* situate *Roberto Zucco* in the genre of great tragedy, placing Zucco amongst the celebrated characters of Shakespeare's legendary works. It is indeed an audacious move to suggest that a modern-day killer shares any relation with so momentous a figure in Western cultural history, and in doing so Koltès presents *Roberto Zucco* as a classic tragedy of inescapable fate.

Let us recall how *Hamlet* opens with two sentinels, Bernardo and Horatio, standing watch outside the castle. As they change shifts, they discuss whether or not they see the ghost of the king, Hamlet's recently slain father. While in the first scene of *Roberto Zucco* two *gardiens* stand in watch of a prison, rather than a castle, the action is plainly similar. Horatio sees the king ("Horatio: Before my God, I might not this believe/Without the sensible and true avouch/Of mine own eyes") (67–69), but Marcellus is unable to see the ghost. In the opening scene of *Roberto Zucco*, the first *gardien* also thinks that he sees and hears someone ("I thought I heard something") ("J'ai eu l'idée d'entendre quelque chose") (10) ("I thought I saw something")

("J'ai l'idée de voir quelque chose") (12); this moment recalls when Horatio thinks he sees a ghost. Like *Hamlet,* whose ghost's presence is not validated until it is seen for the second time ("Bernardo: 'Tis here!/ Horatio: 'Tis here!/ Marcellus: 'Tis gone! *Exit ghost*") (155–157), Zucco is not identified until he escapes: "Shit, you're right; it's an escape!" ("Putain, tu as raison: c'est une évasion") (13). Missing from *Roberto Zucco* is Marcellus's statement at the end of this scene, where, seeing that the ghost has disappeared, he laments, "we did it wrong, being so majestical. To offer it the show of violence; For it is as the air, invulnerable, And out vain blows malicious mockery" (158–160). By omitting a parallel statement, Koltès points to the guards' lack of circumspection, but at the same time he hints that Zucco does not warrant this kind of attention. It is important to note that Koltès does not place Zucco on par with Hamlet himself until later in the play (scene 8), when he questions his existence; in this first sketch, he instead seems more like Hamlet's father, who, like Zucco's, is already dead at the beginning of the play. In this sense, Zucco doubles as both his own father and himself.

The thirteenth scene, entitled "Ophelia," contains another implicit reference to *Hamlet,* except that in this case, Ophelia is associated with the sister in the play, rather than the girl. Poetic rather than violent, Koltès's Zucco also references his own grandeur by quoting Victor Hugo. In a drunken (or mad) state in scene 8, Zucco quotes eight lines from "Between giants and gods" ("Entre géants et dieux" *La Légende des siècles*) (45). This passage, as well as the name of the work from which it comes, explains Zucco's struggle in grandiose terms: "Strong and naked, my brow thrust into the abyss" ("Nu, fort, le front plongé dans un gouffre de brume") (22) Zucco is aware of his greatness.These intertextual literary references are not as improbable as they might appear, as the real Succo was known to quote authors such as Stendhal and Hugo at random. In addition to these literary intertexts, Koltès links Zucco to Greek mythology, Hinduism, and biblical figures. Once again, in Zucco's placement among great figures of world religions, his trajectory becomes eternal and thus contradicts the immediacy of the *fait divers*. Rather than being a sound bite on the news that will presumably be forgotten, Zucco is instead part of a cultural history that is both ageless and timeless. Zucco's trajectory thus functions as an allegory of the importance of the *fait divers:* eternal and mythical, Koltès gives Zucco's crimes a greater significance by placing them in a larger context.

In the beginning of the play and in the end, Koltès invokes the cult of Mithra. In the West, the cult of Mithra is heavily influenced by Greek and Roman mythologies, despite its Hindu origins. In Hinduism Mithra is the Lord of Heavenly Light and protector of truth, and he is invoked when an oath is taken; in Chinese mythology Mithra is represented in Chinese statues as a military general. He is considered to be the friend of man in this life and his protector against evil in the next. Representing an Aryan sun god in Sanskrit and Persian literature circa 1400 BCE, the cult of Mithra was introduced in the Roman empire in the first century BCE. Mithra is thought not to have died but to have ascended to heaven, where, it was believed, he would return at the end of time to raise the dead for the final judgment. There are seven degrees of initiation into the cult of Mithra, in which the neophyte proceeds through the celestial bodies, reversing the soul's entrance into the world at birth. These final stages of the ritual, when the neophyte ascends to heaven in the sun's chariot, parallel Zucco's disappearance at the end of the play and liken him to the sun god Mithra. To preface the play, Koltès cites the lithurgy of Mithra, as quoted by Jung in his last interview on the BBC. It is as follows: "After the second prayer you will see how the disc of the sun unfolds, and you will see hanging down from it the phallus, the origin of the wind, and if you move your face toward the East, it will move there, and if you move your face toward the West, it will follow you" ("Après la seconde prière, tu verras le disque solaire se déployer et tu verras pendre de lui le phallus, l'origine du vent; et si tu tournes ton visage vers l'Orient, il s'y déplacera, et si tu tournes ton visage vers l'Occident, il te suivra"). In scene 15, Zucco restates the liturgy of Mithra before falling from the prison roof. He beseeches the crowd below to "Look what's coming out of the sun. It's the sex of the sun; that's where the wind comes from" ("Regardez ce qui sort du soleil. C'est le sexe du soleil; c'est de là que vient le vent") (94). After he finishes the liturgy, the stage directions read *"A hurricane force wind rises. Zucco sways"* (*"Un vent d'ouragan se lève. Zucco vacille"*) (95). As Zucco disappears into the brightness, ostensibly awaiting the sun chariot his liturgy has invoked, the criminal takes on mythic proportions.

In his ascent to the light, Zucco also resembles the figure of Icarus, who flew towards the sun before plunging down to the earth. In this Greek myth, father and son Daedalus and Icarus were trapped in a maze by King Minotaur. When they could not escape, they decided to build a flying machine to flee. As they collected feathers to attach to Icarus' body, Daedalus warned his son not to fly too high or too close to the sun. Icarus, enchanted by the sun's dazzling beauty, flew so high that the sun's heat melted the wax holding his feathers, and he fell to his death. As if Zucco's destiny is inescapable, he falls as well, although unlike the real Succo, Koltès's Zucco never lands, a change that deeply disturbed readers who saw in the uncertain ending an apology of Succo.

In creating a timeless Zucco, Koltès also blends Christianity with Greek mythology to place Zucco in a biblical context. While not directly referring to Zucco as a Christ-figure, as Sarrazac claims (145), Koltès does liken him to two well-known biblical figures, Samson and Goliath. In an interview in 1988, Koltès stated that Zucco was "a hero like Samson or Goliath, monsters of force, finally defeated by a pebble or a woman" ("un héros comme Samson ou Goliath, monstres de force, abattus finalement par un caillou ou une femme") (back cover *Roberto Zucco*). In the eleventh scene, entitled "Delilah," Koltès assigns Zucco an allegorical past and provides a context for situating him in a broader historical perspective. Like the scene called "Ophelia," Koltès does not specifically associate Zucco with a biblical figure, but rather likens the girl to Delilah, thus intimating Zucco's likeness to Samson. "Delilah" alludes to the biblical parable of Samson and Delilah, in which Samson, an extraordinarily strong young man, is betrayed by his lover. As a young man, Samson's attraction to women distracted him from his mission to free his people. His enemies knew that his leadership was dangerous, and they enlisted beautiful Delilah to seduce him and uncover the secret of his power. After a week spent with Delilah, Samson confessed to her that his strength was in his hair, and thus Delilah was able to betray him. Samson was taken captive, blinded, and chained to pillars. Finally rediscovering his faith in God and his people, he summoned all his strength to send the temple crashing down on himself and his enemies. In the ninth scene of *Roberto Zucco,* the girl goes to the police station, and, pointing to Zucco's picture on the wall, announces that she knows him. Her brother is again behind the denunciation; she explains that "he's the one who told me to come see you because I recognized this picture in the street" ("c'est lui qui m'a dit de venir vous voir parce que j'ai reconnu cette photo dans la rue") (51). By associating the girl with Delilah (and her brother with Samson's enemies), Koltès places Zucco in the role of Samson without ever naming him. Resourceful in his cloaked comparisons, he hints at Zucco's greatness but never names it outright. In the final scene of the play, however, with Zucco perched on the prison roof like a poised Icarus, it is the crowd that likens Zucco to Samson (or Goliath). This is the first time in the play that the criminal is verbally equated with a mythical figure, as the previous examples consist of structural configurations that merely suggest this mythology. This new element distinctly depicts the crowd's admiration of the killer. In the scene, Zucco yells to the crowd below that he has no money and no need for it, a statement that affirms Zucco's refusal to take part in any form of exchange or "deal." A voice calls back to him, "You are a hero, Zucco" ("Tu es un héros, Zucco") (93). In a witty exchange that follows, the crowd, composed of prisoners and guards, tries to decipher what this label means: "A VOICE: It's Goliath. / A VOICE: It's Samson. / A VOICE: Who's Samson? / A VOICE: A truant from Marseilles. / A VOICE: I knew him in prison. A real beast. He could beat up ten people at once. / A VOICE: Liar. / A VOICE: With nothing but his fists. / A VOICE: No, with the jawbone of an ass. And he wasn't from Marseilles. / A VOICE: Delilah. Some story about hair. I know it. / A VOICE: There's always a woman to betray you. / A VOICE: We'd all be free if it weren't for women" ("UNE VOIX: C'est Goliath. / UNE VOIX: C'est Samson. / UNE VOIX: Qui est Samson? / UNE VOIX: Un truand marseillais. / UNE VOIX: Je l'ai connu en prison. Une vraie bête. Il pouvait casser la gueule à dix personne [*sic*] à la fois. / UNE VOIX: Menteur. / UNE VOIX: Rien qu'avec ses poings. / UNE VOIX: Non, avec une mâchoire d'âne. Et il n'était pas de Marseille. / UNE VOIX: Dalila. Une histoire de cheveux. Je connais. / UNE VOIX: Il y a toujours une femme pour trahir. / UNE VOIX: On serait tous en liberté sans les femmes") (94). This clever, somewhat absurdist dialogue conveys shrewdly how society fabricates popular heroes from its criminals, making them part of the common landscape through their association with mythical figures. The *marseillais* man with the Samson namesake evidently received his nickname from the original parable, and we may only wonder whether Succo's strange crimes will afford him a similar future. Koltès's depiction of Zucco thus reaches its pinnacle in this scene, suggesting that Zucco will become a mythical hero among the prisoners and public. At the same time, the playwright's wit (found in the crowd's crude search for Zucco's mythological counterpart, their ignorance of the biblical parable, and the coarseness of their responses) mocks society's fascination with the criminal. The crowd formulates knowledge in a fragmented manner to draw conclusions that only serve to echo preconceived notions. Rather than talking about how or why Zucco may be like Samson (or Goliath), for instance, the crowd extrapolates this information to condemn women, a particularly ironic conclusion given that the women in the play are most forgiving of Zucco. In Brechtian manner, Koltès is clearly poking fun at the public, whose hunger for a heroic figure leads them to ignore factual elements of the *fait divers*. Like the media that has created them, their light banter showcases their inability to process the events before them.

As in this last scene, *Roberto Zucco* is suffused with elements of comedy that call into question the overall tone of the play. Is *Roberto Zucco* a tragedy? A comedy? Both? From the first scene mocking the guards' inability to discern Zucco to the sixth scene, which shows the crowd's sarcasm and nonchalance, Koltès infuses dry humor into the seriousness of the play. As François Regnault writes, the play may be read in both ways: "*Roberto Zucco*, the play of absolute revolt if you take it as a tragedy, but as a comedy, the burlesque escape of a crazed killer" ("*Roberto Zucco*, la pièce de la révolte absolue si vous la prenez pour une tragédie, mais si pour une comédie, la cavale burlesque d'un tueur fou") (322). Other critics have referred to the play as "an action movie parody" (Wainwright 7), pointing to the dark humor that bubbles below the surface of the drama. The humorous notes further decenter many spectators by making light of a subject that is rarely treated by the media in this fashion. Koltès's comedy is especially seditious because in mirroring the public's complex fascination with the criminal spectacle, it reveals the pleasure of the spectacle and society's longtime endorsement of violence.

The Spectacle of Violence

The crowd's pleasure in the violent scene is perhaps the most profound social commentary of *Roberto Zucco*. Like Denis, Koltès does not blame the media for Zucco's allure, but instead points to a very natural affinity for and curiosity with the violent spectacle. In two scenes in particular, Koltès depicts the crowd's fascination with the criminal. Scenes 10 and 15 present "the crowd" ("la foule"), a collective of unnamed men and women who function like a Greek chorus, commentating Zucco's actions and the reaction of law enforcement. In both scenes, the crowd figures prominently and is seemingly representative of the public at large. Both of the scenes thus function as *mises-en-abîme* of the spectator's relationship with the theatrical production. As the audience watches the crowd onstage, which watches the criminal spectacle, Zucco's actions are doubly mediated, mimicking the media's diffused effect on the public. Displaying the fascination and banality of the spectacle, Koltès shows a public cynical towards violence, callous to human suffering, and skeptical of its law enforcers. Here again his depiction of Zucco parallels Denis's cool representation of Paulin. The banality of the crowd's reaction and the comedic elements of the scene combine to create a suspenseless episode that reflects the crowd's apathy.

At over fourteen pages—more than double the length of the majority of the scenes—the hostage scene (10) is clearly central to the play. In this scene, which takes place in a public park (a non-place), the elegant lady invites Zucco to sit down next to her. He immediately begins to mold himself into the image she desires, swearing that he has never been rough with a woman. Yet in the open space of the park at midday, where Zucco begins to feel visible (and thus vulnerable), he quickly changes tone and demands the woman's car keys. This scene recalls the first, in which he demands his military fatigues. As his mother did, the lady resists, and the scene escalates with Zucco placing a gun to her head. It is at this moment that the crowd approaches the scene, attracted to the violent spectacle like vultures. As they come closer, the lady chastises Zucco: "LADY—Stop creating a scandal. Look: these idiots are going to come closer and start making comments. They'll call the police. Look: they're already licking their lips. They love this kind of thing. I can't stand to hear what they think. Just shoot. I don't want to hear them, I don't want to hear" ("LA DAME.—Arrêtez de faire du scandale. Regardez: ces imbéciles vont s'approcher, ils vont faire des commentaires. Ils vont appeler la police. Regardez: ils s'en lèchent déjà les babines. Ils adorent ça. Je ne supporte pas les commentaires de ces gens-là. Tirez donc. Je ne veux pas les entendre, je ne veux pas entendre") (59–60). The spectacle provides what the crowd craves: drama, blood, and fear. It is not clear at first whether the crowd represents the media or simply the public at large, but this ambiguity is itself notable. The media has such a strong presence that the public recycles its discourse and generates its own spectacle that resembles the media's machine. In this scene Koltès best illustrates contemporary society's irreconcilable relationship with crime and the media, where the media has reinforced the public's ancient desire for the violent spectacle. In the lady's reaction to the crowd's advance, we see that she, too, comprehends the allure of the scene and is repulsed by the fascination it engenders. The crowd's farcically callous comments and proximity to the spectacle mirror its fascination but also an ignorance of the scene's gravity; in this way, the scene has an absurdist ring. This scene also demonstrates the criminal's pleasure in the crowd's attention. It is not until the end of the scene, when he is ready to kill the child, for instance, that Zucco signals the crowd to step back ("Ecartez-vous") (69). As in the *fait divers* and as echoed at the end of the play, Zucco has chosen a public place to stage his spectacle, creating the mediated opportunity for sensation.

It is important to note here that Koltès furnishes relatively few stage directions and gives no guidance to how the actors should read their lines. This absence of direction gives considerable interpretive freedom to the director and actors, but it primarily works to create a flatness in the characters' responses: neither shocked nor angry nor excited, their responses exude indifference and even poise. Likewise, in the crowd's analytical dialogue, Koltès points to their curious emotional distance from the crime despite their physical proximity to the spectacle. The draw of the dramatic spectacle tempts their voracious appetite for sensation, which is increased by their participation in a crowd. Intrigued by the drama, like the journalists in the *fait divers*, the crowd is also emotionally distant. At several moments, we witness the crowd's detachment from the violent scene, suggesting a desensitivity to violence and a difficulty in distinguishing reality from fiction. As if the man brandishing a gun were not standing in front of them but instead on a television screen, the crowd watches blandly: "ZUCCO (to the child)—Don't come any closer. / A MAN—Look how he's trembling. / ZUCCO—In the name of God, don't come any closer. Get down on the ground. / A WOMAN—It's the child that scares him. / ZUCCO—And now, put your hands down by your sides. Come here. / A WOMAN—But how's he supposed to crawl with his hands by his sides? / A MAN—It's possible, it's possible. If it were me, I'd figure it out" ("ZUCCO (*à l'enfant*).—N'approche pas. / UN HOMME.—Regardez comme il tremble. / ZUCCO.—N'approche pas, nom de Dieu. Couche-toi par terre. / UNE FEMME.—C'est l'enfant qui lui fait peur. / ZUCCO.—Et maintenant, les mains le long du corps. Approche-toi. / UNE FEMME.—Mais comment veut-il qu'il rampe avec les mains le long du corps? / UN HOMME.—C'est possible, c'est possible. Moi, j'y arriverais") (60). In pointing out how Zucco trembles, the man shows how the public focuses its attention on the criminal rather than on the victim. In this situation, Koltès presents archetypal examples of society's most protected and venerated citizens: women and children, who are traditionally the first to be released from hostage and to be saved in any dangerous situation. Yet here, a man deliberately ignores these victims, instead focusing on Zucco's fear. This is not clear at first, as the "he" in "he's trembling" could refer to the child, but a woman's subsequent comment ("it's the child that scares him") gives meaning to the man's vague pronoun. Referring not to these victims, but to Zucco, the crowd moreover demonstrates its superiority over the criminal by condescendingly analyzing and defining his actions. Coldly scrutinizing Zucco's fear, they are fascinated by his trembling, which does not seem consistent with their notion of a "cool killer." In this scene, where Zucco becomes an object of fascination for the crowd's inspection, he is their entertainment, their victim. And in the same way that the lady and the girl use Zucco to explore their own fantasies at the expense of blurring Zucco's identity, the crowd's commentaries do not in any way clarify Zucco's personage. Rather, they merely reflect a need to control and define the situation. Like the media's propensity for binary representations, the crowd reflects this predilection for the "will to know." In this way, Koltès demonstrates that the fascination with the killer does not lie in the killer himself, but instead reflects society's self-interest.

Desensitized to the reality of the violence before him, the man's comment in this scene reveals that he is content to gaze at the actions before him as a fictional spectacle; rather than turn away or endeavor to change the situation, he prefers to scrutinize it as if he were a journalist. This tendency is echoed by the words of "a woman," who measures the child's ability to place his hands at his sides while he lies on the ground. Indeed, the action is a rather difficult one, showing Zucco's amateurness in using a pastiche of one-liners from cinematic and televisual representations of crime. As in the *fait divers* when Succo stripped to his underwear to the crowd's surprise, Zucco's efforts to attract attention are flawed and impractical. Moreover, the woman's commentary demonstrates the emotionless practicality of her reasoning. She does not think of the child, but rather his movements; she watches the scene in an absurd and detached manner, like a puzzle of logic. As this scene progressively includes more voices, Koltès intensifies his social commentary by unraveling the public's numb fascination with violence. When Zucco places his foot on the child's head, the crowd's comments become increasingly removed from the scene at hand. A woman laments the burdens of today's children, and her remark is greeted with even greater coldness: "A WOMAN—Good lord, kids really see it all today. / A MAN—We did, too, when we were kids. / THE WOMAN—Because you were threatened by a maniac, too? / THE MAN—And the war, ma'am, have you forgotten the war? / THE WOMAN—Oh, really? Because the Germans put their foot on your head and threatened to kill your mother? / THE MAN—Worse than that, ma'am, worse than that. / THE WOMAN—In any case, here you are alive and well, and nice and fat" ("UNE FEMME.—Ah, mon Dieu, les enfants en voient de belles, de nos jours. / UN HOMME.—Nous aussi on en a vu de belles, quand on était gamins. / LA FEMME.—Parce que vous aussi avez été menacé par un fou, vous aussi? / L'HOMME.—Et la guerre, madame, vous avez oublié la guerre? / LA FEMME.—Ah bon? Parce que les Allemands posaient le pied sur votre tête et menaçaient votre mère? / L'HOMME.—Pire que cela, madame, pire que cela. / LA FEMME.—En tous les cas, vous voilà bien vivant, bien vieux, et bien gras") (63). In the increasing animosity of the scene, the crowd removes itself from the spectacle in front of them to create their own mini-drama. The man's arrogance, evident in his comparisons of the scene to World War II, prompts a dispute that breaks along gender lines when the woman unpleasantly contests the man's dismissiveness. Unlike the crowd in the fifteenth scene, which is a mélange of several characters named "a voice," Koltès divides the crowd in this scene by gender. In this distinction, Koltès shows that while the fascination with crime crosses gender lines, women tend to be more sympathetic to the victims; this view is highlighted throughout the play in the actions of the lady and the girl. In this particular scene, the crowd functions *not* as a heterogeneous group, but rather as a group of individuals (who each reads the crime in his or her own manner). In this way, Koltès meaningfully highlights the fluidity of the *fait divers* as a signifier, subverting assumptions that it is read in one way by the public.

Midway through this tenth scene of the play, the crowd begins to interact with the characters in the spectacle before them, encouraging the woman to give Zucco her keys. They are considerably disappointed by her aversion to their participation, however. When a man warns her, "He's going to blow your head off, my dear" ("Il va vous faire péter la gueule, ma petite dame"), she responds, "Just as well. I won't see your ugly faces anymore. Just as well" ("Tant mieux. Je ne verrai plus vos gueules à vous. Tant mieux") (65). A woman immediately remarks, "What a dreadful woman" ("Cette femme est affreuse"), and a man echoes, "She's mean. There are so many mean and cruel people" ("Elle est méchante. Il y a tant de gens méchants et cruels") (65). Witnesses to a drama, the crowd takes its role very seriously. They mediate the scene with an aloof interest and extrapolate the woman's actions to make suppositions about general society. And like the prisoners do in the crowd scene (15), this crowd blames a woman (in this case the elegant lady) instead of the criminal. When "a woman" asks the elegant lady how she feels, she replies dryly, "I'm fine, thanks, just fine. But I'd feel a lot better if you'd shut your mouths and go back to your kitchens and beat your kids" ("Ça va, merci, ça va. Mais je me sentirais tellement mieux si vous fermiez vos gueules et que vous retourniez dans vos cuisines et que vous partiez torcher vos mômes") (68). Her response addresses both the crowd's titillation at the violent scene and their hypocrisy (in suggesting that they are just as cruel with their own families). Like children, the crowd is excited by the potential violence and wants to participate in it, seemingly unaware of the vulgarity of their curiosity. When "a woman" accepts the lady's response as a reprimand ("She's mean, she's mean") ("Elle est dure. Elle est dure") (68), she crystallizes the naïveté and childlike image of the crowd. Moreover, the elegant lady's dry sarcasm ("I'm fine, thanks") deescalates the intensity of the scene for the crowd, especially as it is not reciprocated or even comprehended by them. In this way, *Roberto Zucco* addresses the crowd's inability to properly distinguish fiction from reality, as well as their fascination with the spectacle as a non-self-reflexive, detached interest.

While numb to the potential of violence, the crowd displays considerable cynicism toward the police, a theme echoed throughout both *J'ai pas sommeil* and *Roberto Zucco*. In scenes 1, 4, 9, 10, 14, and 15, Koltès underlines the law's incompetence in controlling crime: guards are unable to contain Zucco, inspectors cannot catch him, and the police do not recognize his presence among them. Fittingly, the crowd takes every opportunity to mock these defenders of discipline. In this representation of the police, Koltès reflects both the relative ineffectiveness of law enforcement and society's lack of faith in this organization: Zucco escapes, a citizen rather than policeman catches him, and an attempt to capture Zucco ends in giving him a sports car. Although many of these elements of the play are facts of the Succo *affaire*, the crowd's reaction to them is critical. Through their disrespectful sarcasm and nonchalance, Koltès presents the public's cynical view of police, which only further angered the Chambéry protesters.

As the policemen arrive at the hostage scene (10), a woman proclaims, "Now he'll have a reason to be scared" ("Maintenant, il va avoir des raisons de trembler"), and a man sarcastically replies, "This should make us laugh" ("On va rire, on va rire") (61). Symbolically further from the criminal than the crowd, the police do not immediately appear, and the crowd discusses whether or not they will be able to control the situation. A woman declares that they're scared ("ils ont la trouille"), while another man assures, "But of course not. It's a strategy. They know what they're doing" ("Mais non. C'est de la stratégie. Ils savent ce qu'ils font") (62). This remark seems to temporarily satisfy the crowd, which is newly intrigued by Zucco's increased aggressiveness toward the pair of hostages. When the police do not take any action, however, the crowd resumes its critique. I quote this scene at length to recreate the fluidity of the crowd's banter:

> A WOMAN—Well, mister, so that's what you call a special police tactic? You talk about tactic. They're on the other side of the park! They're scared. / A MAN—I said that it was a strategy. / A MAN—Strategy, my ass! / THE POLICE (*from afar*)—Put down your gun. / A WOMAN—Bravo. / A WOMAN—Now we're saved. / A MAN—Hell of a strategy. / A MAN—I'm telling you, they're planning to attack him. / A WOMAN—The only one I see planning to attack is that one. / A MAN—Actually, the attack is pretty much over. / A WOMAN—Poor kid. / A MAN—Lady, I'm going to slap you if you don't stop talking about that kid. / A MAN—Do you two really think this is the time to argue? A little dignity, please. We're witnessing a drama. We're staring into the face of death. / THE COPS (*from afar*)—This is the police. Put down your gun. You're surrounded. (*The crowd breaks into laughter*).
>
> UNE FEMME.—Dites, donc, monsieur, c'est cela que vous appelez la technique spéciale des flics? Tu parles d'une technique. Ils restent à l'autre bout. Ils ont la trouille. / UN HOMME.—J'ai dit que c'était de la stratégie. / UN HOMME.—Stratégie mon cul! / LES FLICS (*de loin*).—Lâchez votre arme. / UNE FEMME.—Bravo. / UNE FEMME.—Nous voilà sauvés. / UN HOMME. – Sacrée stratégie. / UN HOMME.—Ils préparent un coup, je vous dis. / UNE FEMME.—Moi, je ne vois que celui-là qui soit en train de préparer un coup. / UN HOMME.—Le coup est déjà pratiquement fait, d'ailleurs. / UNE FEMME.—Pauvre gosse. / UN HOMME.—Madame, je vais vous gifler si vous continuez à parler du gosse. / UN HOMME.—Vous croyez vraiment que c'est le moment de se disputer? Un peu de dignité. Nous sommes témoins d'un drame. Nous sommes devant la mort. / LES FLICS (*de loin*).—Nous vous ordonnons de lâcher votre arme. Vous êtes cerné. (*L'assistance éclate de rire*). (64)

This last man's rebuke ("do you two really think . . . ?") is typical of Koltès's humor throughout the play, present in the faux-seriousness of the characters' responses to violence. The absurdity of this comment allows the spectators to laugh at the man from a distance (what dignity is there in watching this scene?), but its accuracy (they are literally "staring into the face of death") encourages the theater audience to contemplate its own fascination in the spectacle.

Physically closer to Zucco than even the police, the crowd thus mediates the scene for the audience, commentating the police's actions and debating their ability to affect the outcome of this violence. Rather than reading the crowd as representatives of the media that present and debate information through their various interpretations of the spectacle, it is perhaps more accurate to say that the crowd has been influenced by the media: their cynicism and nonchalance are *effects* rather than illustrations of the media's influence, whose reports of criminals are sensationalized. The crowd's knowledge of popular culture depicting police (movies, television shows) is clear in their commentary of the scene; they understand that the police have a "technique," a "strategy," and an "attack" that they prepare. At the same time, several members of the crowd (including all of the women) are extremely cynical of the police's ability to alter the spectacle's outcome. Indeed, this derisive view of the police appears justified when in the conclusion of the scene the child is murdered. By mocking the police, the crowd counters the media's often flattering depiction of law enforcement. Demonstrating a (warranted) condescension to the police, the crowd presents itself as a savvy, cynical public. Although the crowd as a whole is extremely cynical of law enforcement, individual reactions vary significantly with regard to the hostages. Here, the female characters of *Roberto Zucco* are considerably less jaded than the men; they are the only characters that allow emotion to enter into the scene. This is evident in the remarks of a woman who repeatedly refers to "the poor kid." Similarly, on pages 60, 62, 63, 64, and 67, it is only a female voice that is able to break through the crowd's cynicism to make a personal connection with the hostages and the criminal. Despite these efforts to connect with the individual actors in the spectacle, however, the crowd will only tolerate cynicism; this is exemplified when a woman's mention of the child prompts a man to tell her to be silent or he will slap her (64). Emotional distance is imperative in the crowd, if only because this distance fosters some amount of control over the turbulent situation. The crowd turns the hostage scene into a spectacle for its own amusement, as if it were a television show or a movie. Viewed in this fashion, the crowd's cynical response to the police further increases its authority, while at the same time dismantling the police's subjectivity.

The antagonistic relationship with law enforcement witnessed in scene 10 is likewise recreated in the final scene of the play, which showcases the crowd's fascination with crime. In this fifteenth scene, Koltès seems at once caustic and curious, mocking the fascination with Zucco, yet at the same time fixing on the criminal's power to intrigue. Recreating the public's fascination with the *fait divers*, Koltès theoretically places the audience in the same position as the prisoners, where the public becomes the literal "prisoner" of Zucco's charade. Koltès thus presents a dual reading of *Roberto Zucco* in the form of a *mise-en-abîme* of Zucco's spectacle. On one level, the audience of spectators in the theater functions as a typical audience, watching the reaction of the crowd onstage, analyzing or enjoying the crowd's fascination with Zucco. From this vantage point, the spectator is relatively removed from the scene. On another level, which I would determine to be a "preferred reading," the audience of spectators blends with the prisoners on the stage, forming a larger crowd that watches Zucco. Koltès creates this possibility in the stage directions that frame this final scene: *"The prison rooftops, at midday. You cannot see anyone during the entire scene except for Zucco when he climbs to the top of the roof"* (*"Le sommet des toits de la prison, à midi. On ne voit personne, pendant toute la scène, sauf Zucco quand il grimpe au sommet du toit")* (90). In this description, only Zucco is visible, shrouded in bright light. Like the prisoners' indistinct voices, which emerge from the dark, the audience is also invisible, both groups awash in darkness. Looking up at Zucco from the perspective of the crowd, the audience is placed (both literally and symbolically) in the same position as the prisoners, who try to decipher Zucco's final words.

The final scene opens to the voices of prisoners and guards, whose banter reminds us of the crowd in the tenth scene. Like the leader in a Greek chorus, the first voice informs the audience that "Roberto Zucco has escaped" ("Roberto Zucco s'est échappé") (90). The mood is light, but mixed with tension, as the guards and prisoners react to his escape to the roof. The power relations between the prisoners and guards are especially apparent in this scene, where Zucco has managed to break from the grips of law enforcement. When an inmate escapes, the prisoners' sense of empowerment increases, and the guards' subjectivity is called into question. The first three voices in this excerpt appear to be guards, the fourth a prisoner, and the final a guard, but Koltès does not distinguish them in his stage directions. Rather they are readily discernible in their responses, the guards representing the status quo and the prisoners mocking the dominant ideology that upholds these binary systems; further character uncertainties are clarified by the use of *tu* and *vous*. As the crowd begins to grasp the reality of Zucco's escape, the first four voices (guards) together work to assure themselves that this is not possible. Here, the guards function as a single dominant voice of society, echoing the messages we receive about the penal system. The banter in the scene at once assures and subverts the prison system: the voices affirm each other in restating the impossibility of Zucco's escape, yet he *is* escaping. This act represents a subversion of the guards' power in a panoptic system where Zucco's largest fear is being visible. The last voice in this passage mocks the guards and their attempts to control Zucco through their language: Zucco may be "screwed," but he is nonetheless escaping. In this act, however, Zucco becomes even more visible, as evidenced by his presence onstage amidst the voices. As Zucco reaches the top of the roof, the voices call out to him. Based on the stage directions "laughter," as well as the formal address of Zucco, it is clear which voices represent the guards and which the prisoners. One guard tells Zucco to get down from the roof ("descendez immédiatement") (91) to laughter. One prisoner beseeches Zucco to "tell us what you did to stay in prison for less than an hour?" ("dis-nous comment tu fais pour ne pas rester une heure en prison?") (91), and another asks, "How did you get out? Show us the way" ("Par où as-tu filé? Donne-nous la filière") (92). Like the reactions of the old gentleman, the elegant lady, and the girl, who were attracted by Zucco's ability to detach himself from society, the crowd of prisoners is intrigued by Zucco's ability to literally free himself from the confines of society. Zucco's philosophical response to the men recalls other nebulous statements, but here he is at his most eloquent and assured. When asked how he managed to escape, he explains: "ZUCCO—From above. You don't have to try to scale the walls, because beyond the walls, there are other walls, there's always a prison. You have to escape by the rooftops, towards the sun. They'll never put a wall between the sun and the earth. / A VOICE—And the guards? / ZUCCO—Guards don't exist. All you have to do is not see them. In any case, I could take up five of them with just one hand and crush them in one blow" ("ZUCCO.—Par le haut. Il ne faut pas chercher à traverser les murs, parce que, au-delà des murs, il y a d'autres murs, il y a toujours la prison. Il faut s'échapper par les toits, vers le soleil. On ne mettra jamais un mur entre le soleil et la terre. / UNE VOIX.—Et les gardiens? / ZUCCO.—Les gardiens n'existent pas. Il suffit de ne pas les voir. De toute façon, je pourrais en prendre cinq dans une seule main et les écraser d'un coup") (92). Exaggerating his own strength as mythical, Zucco likens himself to someone like Goliath, constructing his own heroism and demonstrating his awareness of how to use the crowd to achieve his self-empowerment. Proof of this tactic's success is just twenty lines later when a man echoes Zucco's claim to boast that Zucco can crush ten men in one blow. The crowd's almost instantaneous transformation of the "facts" showcases the role of rumor in constructing the criminal's heroism.

Zucco's declaration reflects a vision of a complexly contrived society that functions to imprison its inhabitants. Resembling the maze-like metro in scene 6, the prison emerges as a multilayered, enclosed structure that echoes Zucco's view of life. In this last scene, spectators witness Zucco's dilemma as a struggle with a society whose structures do not make sense to him. As Heed suggests, Zucco's ascension from the prison to the metaphorical light of the sun becomes a means for society's castoffs to head towards a greater light and towards death ("l'ascension de Zucco par dessus les toits de la prison vers la forte métaphore du soleil et de la lumière devient le parcours de l'exclu de la société vers une plus grande clarté et vers la mort") (58). Heed's association of Zucco with the excluded in society exemplifies how Koltès's play resonates with far more than the *fait divers* itself. The ambiguous ending captures best how the play challenges the core structures of society. At the end of the play, as Zucco stands atop the prison roof, the voices below try to decipher his language in hopes of giving meaning to his actions. Rather than addressing the media, as he does in the *fait divers*, Zucco instead addresses a group of prisoners: a captive crowd. In this interesting shift, we may read the media as a captive audience, at the mercy of the criminal. In an attempt to interpret the meaning of Zucco's discourse, the crowd empowers the criminal. As their heads turn toward the sky in a posture of reverence, silently awaiting his speech, the crowd appears in awe of Zucco; they seem sure his words contain some hidden meaning. Here we may return to Foucault, who defines madness as one of the systems of exclusion used to order society. He writes: "From the depths of the Middle Ages, a man was mad if his speech could not be said to form part of the common discourse of men. His words were considered nul and void, without truth or significance, worthless as evidence . . . and yet, in contrast to all others, his words were credited with strange powers, of revealing some hidden truth, of predicting the future, of revealing, in all their naiveté, what the wise were unable to perceive" (*Archaeology of Knowledge* 216–17). As Foucault emphasizes, the mad person's words are either rejected or espoused. In this scene, rather than dismissing Zucco's words as those of a madman, the crowd comes to see in him a figure of freedom and authority, and their inquisitiveness demonstrates their desire to believe him. Similar to Duras's valorization of the language (or non-language) of the criminal in works like *L'Amante anglaise* and *Les Viaducts de la Seine-et-Oise*, Koltès allows the public to experience the criminal's discourse outside the knowledge machines that would normally exclude him. In the last part of the scene, as Zucco explains the liturgy of Mithra to the crowd, he instructs them to "Look at the sun." Zucco seems to command the play's audience, as well as the prisoners and guards, again correlating the spectators with the crowd onstage. The stage directions that follow this command read *"A complete silence falls over the courtyard"* (*"Un silence complet s'établit dans la cour"*) (94). In the quiet that ensues, the play's audience melds into the faceless voices onstage, and the spectators further disappear into the crowd onstage. High above the obliging crowd, he continues his explanation, correlating the light of the sun with freedom ("you have to escape by the rooftops, towards the sun") ("il faut s'échapper par les toits, vers le soleil") (94). Like Caligula's wish for the moon, Zucco's desire to reach the sun reflects a vain, absurd effort to reach immortality. Symbolically, the crowd has trouble seeing him, blinded by the total freedom Zucco envisions: "There's too much light" ("Il y a trop de lumière") (94). Moreover, they appear confused by Zucco's speech, and for every idea that Zucco expresses, a voice in the crowd responds that he does not understand Zucco. In this last scene, society appears incapable of deciphering the implications the criminal offers. Capable only of comprehending literal meanings, the general public does not learn from the criminal's struggle. As Zucco loses his balance (*"Zucco sways"*) (*"Zucco vacille"*) (95), two voices declare, "He's mad" ("Il est fou") (95), closing him into a category. The sun's brightness blinds the crowd and the audience, and a final voice screams, "He's falling" ("Il tombe") (95). The play ends on this note.

The last scene of the play brings the reader back to the beginning, to an invisible Zucco on the prison rooftops; yet at the end of *Roberto Zucco*, the audience—like the crowd onstage—is no closer to understanding his motive than at the play's start. As Wainwright notes, "what is so unsettling is that Zucco remains unpredictable and inscrutable" (7). Koltès has shrewdly portrayed Zucco's ability to command a crowd and to attract the admiration of excluded others like himself.

He has moreover critiqued the very core structures of society, assailing not only law enforcement and the judicial system (whose efforts to define and confine Zucco have failed miserably), but also the binary systems of exclusion that blind us from the metaphorical sun he describes in the last scene. *Roberto Zucco* thus challenges dominant views of the criminal in the rupture of the dichotomy of good and evil, in the comparison of the criminal with mythological and heroic figures, and in the complex interactions between Zucco and characters of the play. Through all these interchanges, the criminal remains inscrutable. By focusing the play's attention on society, Koltès reverses the media's representation of crime, which centers blame uniquely on the criminal. He instead transforms the spectator's distant gaze and correlates it with the crowds who watch Zucco with fascination and awe. *Roberto Zucco* revisits the crime in a way that captures contemporary society's love affair with the criminal. Similar to Camille's character in *J'ai pas sommeil*, we never come closer to understanding why Zucco killed, and like Denis, Koltès steers his audience from posing this question. Directed away from the why and toward the how, we are guided to probe how the criminal serves society as a whole. Koltès does not allow us to blame the bewildered and confused Zucco for this frightening, detached view of the world, but instead turns the mirror on the audience, who plays a part in its construction. This interpretation of the *fait divers* touches a collective nerve, as evidenced by the public reaction to the play. What the public failed to grasp was that the media's representations of Succo's crimes did more to sensationalize the murders than Koltès's play, and ironically, their own protests generated international interest in the production that has secured the play's place in history. Its censorship attests to the theater's power to rattle the public consciousness, and its worldwide popularity proves its brilliance in speaking to a global community fascinated with meaningless crime and violence.

Chapter Six

Rewriting History

Throughout this project, I have sought to underline how the contemporary *fait divers* functions as an important site of struggle for the control of social meaning. As evidenced by the Paulin and Succo *affaires* of the 1980s, media, politicians, and law enforcement vie with each other to influence public sentiment about crime, *insécurité*, and the Other. In these representations of the crime story, dominant institutions encrust the *fait divers* with their particular ideologies, often sensationalizing the crime story to generate public outrage and influence public policy about controversial issues such as immigration laws and the death penalty. For these reasons, it is important to examine how the *fait divers* embodies these struggles for meaning, particularly given its increasing circulation and mounting importance in contemporary society. Like these *affaires*, the literary or cinematic works that rearticulate the crime story quickly become a struggle for meaning about the public's relationship to crime, manifest in the criticism and even the censorship of these works. As examples of how powerful groups (politicians, law enforcement, social organizations) use the media to impose their particular visions of reality, the Paulin and Succo *affaires* thus raise fundamental questions about representation and reception. Through an analysis of historical, cultural, and social factors that have shaped the varied representations of these two *faits divers*, I conclude that the artistic rewritings of these crime stories represent contested sites of resistance that question the ideology that constructs the criminal as a dangerous Other. In this way, they reflect growing resistance to the dominant knowledge machines of media, the police, and politicians.

In this final section, I return to several questions raised throughout this project. First I summarize how Denis's and Koltès's works subvert the media's representation of the *fait divers*. Next I examine two common threads in these rewritings that raise provocative questions about the public's relationship to the criminal: the role of female characters who interact with the criminal and the notion of the criminal as a hero. These two thrusts exemplify how Denis and Koltès resist the traditional depiction of the *fait divers* by presenting characters who refuse to comply with the warnings of the media and the police. Finally I discuss the larger implications of these rewritings, which function as important precursors to a growing public resistance to media sensationalism about crime.

Subverting the System: *Media Culpa*?

The Paulin and Succo *affaires* share several important similarities that warrant their close comparison. Despite their relative rarity, violent crimes committed by young immigrants represent some of the most feared criminal exploits in contemporary society, a feeling heightened by the media's disproportionate focus on these acts. As "motiveless" crimes, the Paulin and Succo *affaires* thus reflect the least common but most conspicuous crimes in the media. During the late 1980s, a time of perceived growing insecurity in France, these two crimes and their activations became easy targets for the Right's campaigns against crime and immigration. The Paulin and Succo *affaires* were thus used as examples of the Left's failure to ensure public safety, a tactic justified by law enforcement's relatively ineffective efforts to catch the killers: in the Paulin *affaire*, it was pure coincidence that a policeman stumbled upon the criminal, and in the Succo *affaire*, a young woman turned Succo in to authorities. While the rare circumstances of these captures do not imply the police's inability to fight crime, they do contrast the image of reliable investigative tactics depicted by media, film, and television, where the police's methodical efforts never fail to pay off in criminal convictions. Instead, these two cases reveal how law enforcement actually functions (as Ferrell notes, science is secondary to chance in catching criminals), thus presenting a divergent view of the justice system that conceivably drains public confidence in law enforcement. Denis and Koltès capture this public wariness in their rewritings, most notably through the diminished importance of law enforcement and the public's cynical attitude towards policemen and prison guards.

In addition to the modest importance of law enforcement in these works, the rewritings of these *affaires* portray a considerably subdued media presence, one whose role falls secondary to the public's first-hand knowledge. This representation of the media radically contests the media's self-representation as the public's guardian. In *J'ai pas sommeil* and *Roberto Zucco*, characters interact directly with the criminal, erasing the media's intermediary role in transmitting the crime story. This new way of relaying the *fait divers* is significant in that it denies many of the ideological battles that take place over meaning. As Foucault suggests, "we must not imagine a world of discourse divided between accepted discourse and excluded discourse, or between the dominant discourse and the dominated one; but as a multiplicity of discursive elements that can come into play in various strategies" (*History of Sexuality* 100). In bypassing the media's interpretive stance that separates the public from the criminal, these artists subvert systems of exclusion and allow for a direct interaction between the criminal and the public, proving that it is possible to envision the world of discourse that Foucault describes. In *J'ai pas sommeil*, characters outrightly ignore the media: Daïga looks past sensational headlines, female characters ignore clear warnings to stay inside, and televisions warning of public danger go unwatched. Despite the omnipresence of these varied media channels, then, characters plainly disregard their presence. In *Roberto Zucco*, on the other hand, there is a distinct absence of the media, whose realistic presence in the play is noted only in Zucco's wanted poster in scene 6.

Without the media in this intermediary role that encrusts the criminal with cultural and political battles, the public is freed to create its own meanings. So on the one hand, we see that without these fear-driven warnings so present in media reports on crime, individuals *choose* to interact with the criminal. This omission of the media's influence thus valorizes the public's autonomy by suggesting that the public does not listen to the media or rely on it to make meaning and choices. On the other hand, like Denis's examples of the media's strong presence in society, *Roberto Zucco* also reflects how the public as a whole has internalized the media's messages about crime and violence. Although the media is not specifically invoked in the play, Koltès shows us how it functions as a covert ideologue. Scene 10, for instance, demonstrates how the public and the criminal act out clichés of violent scenes seen on television. Despite the inevitable presence and influence of the media, however, Denis's and Koltès's protagonists do not listen to or search out the media's authority about these events. Significantly, they choose to make their own judgments about the criminal's virtue. By ignoring police and media to act autonomously, these characters radically reject dominant sources of information. We can see a similar resistance of media forms in postmodern horror films, where authority is undermined and institutionalized knowledges are subverted. *Halloween* (1978), the *Scream* franchise (1996, 1997, 2000), *The Blair Witch Project* (1999), *Ring* (1998), and *Tesis* (1999) all contest symbolic forms of knowledge (the media, the police, the university system). They do not, however, present a "cool" attitude toward the criminal. In all of these works, characters greatly fear the criminal, who is to be avoided at all costs; terror, rather than personal gain, motivates these individuals. *J'ai pas sommeil* and *Roberto Zucco* thus go a step further by critiquing the machines of knowledge in the context of a real crime story and presenting the criminal's point of view.

J'ai pas sommeil and *Roberto Zucco* reflect not only a devaluing of the media and law enforcement in the public eye, but also a deliberate subversion of the criminal's representation in the media. It is due in part to the characters' direct and often positive interactions with the criminal that Denis and Koltès have been accused of presenting "nonjudgmental" representations of the criminal. They fundamentally subvert the media's fear-driven view of crime by reducing public insecurity and presenting a nonjudgmental view of the criminal that rewrites Otherness. As I have shown, this desensationalized view of crime is accomplished in several principal ways: (1) by refusing the sensational cause and effect of crime. Neither Denis nor Koltès focuses on why the man becomes a criminal. Both artists emphasize that they do not wish to psychologize the criminal, thus subverting audience expectations of a resolution. Refusing the comfort of knowledge, Denis and Koltès do not offer their audiences a cathartic release at the end of their works; (2) by breaking down binary representations of evil/good and mad/sane. These rewritings present well-rounded criminals in the context of a fallible public. Gone are the clear divisions between the public and the criminal, a depiction that radically contrasts the media's efforts to classify the criminal through sensational labels, psychological evidence, and police testimony. Instead, Denis and Koltès provide the criminal with a subjectivity commonly denied by the media's focus on his Otherness; and (3) by depicting the public's fascination with the criminal. Whether through camera shots that linger on the criminal body or via the crowd's interest in the criminal spectacle, Denis and Koltès show that we remain fascinated by crime. The nonmediated fascination of Daïga and the elegant lady furthermore place the criminal in a broader historical context, which is brought out in *Roberto Zucco* through intertextual mythological and literary references. In these three primary ways, Denis and Koltès reorient their audience towards a more balanced view of crime that, in its uniqueness, is highly subversive. Within this nonjudgmental representation of the criminal lie thorny questions raised by critics about how the public may interpret these neutralized representations of the criminal, namely: what happens when the element of fear is removed from depictions of crime? Here let us examine the role of female characters, whose presence undeniably dominates both stage and screen. It is through these characters that liberation and catharsis are equated with the removal of the fear and panic generated by prevailing media reports.

Seeking the Criminal: Female Characters and Empowerment

The powerful presence of female characters in *J'ai pas sommeil* and *Roberto Zucco* underscores the importance of examining how they are represented in these works: as the largest cluster of potential victims of the criminal—and thus a group specifically targeted by the media—the role of female characters is pivotal to the rewriting of the *fait divers*. In each of these rewritings, Denis and Koltès present female protagonists who radically subvert the media's presentation of weak, fearful victims, offering readers a model of empowerment and resistance. As I stated at the beginning of this study, I had not intended to look at the role of women in the *fait divers* specifically, either as characters or as readers; I had no preformed hypotheses about women's relationship to crime, as my theoretical goals lay elsewhere. As this project developed, however, I repeatedly noticed that they maintained a distinct relationship with the criminal that was plainly more open and inquisitive. This unique rapport with the criminal reflects research that posits women's greater interest in crime stories. Auclair has shown that women make up the single largest group of readers of the *fait divers,* and they see these *faits divers* as reflections of their inferior social status. He explains that the interest in the crime story is in "direct relation to the isolation of the individual, or in inverse relation to their social, political and cultural integration" ("l'intérêt pour le chronique varie en raison directe de l'isolement des individus ou, si l'on veut inverse de leur intégration à la vie sociale, politique, et culturelle") (152). In addition, Auclair explains that women are stricter at criminal judgments: "more fascinated by murder stories, they are just as merciless when it comes to punishing" ("plus fascinées par le récit des meurtres, elles sont également plus implacables quand il s'agit de punir") (152). Auclair's information must be interpreted carefully, however: over thirty years have passed since his research, with women's roles steadily shifting and ethnographic studies showing that people read much differently than researchers had previously imagined. We do not want to fall into the trap of creating pockets of ideal readers by assuming that all women read the *fait divers* in the same way. Female characters in *J'ai pas sommeil* and *Roberto Zucco*, for instance, do not appear to use the *fait divers* to reflect their dismal lives, as Auclair suggests, but rather to realize their dreams and desires. Looking at these female characters, we note several shared characteristics: an intrigue with the criminal that exceeds that of the male characters, a recklessness with regard to personal safety and law, a history of abuse or victimization, and a cynicism towards police and the media. In the context of these personal stories, we can begin to see how and why women in these works appear charmed by the criminal.

Female characters figure prominently in *J'ai pas sommeil* and *Roberto Zucco*, interacting in key, often positive ways with the criminal. Daïga follows Camille, Ninon endearingly calls him and Raphaël nice boys, and Camille has several female friends; likewise, the girl, the elegant lady, and the prostitute of *Roberto Zucco* all display their physical and psychological interest in Zucco. All of these women are considerably reckless in their choices and actions. Although the criminals are males who clearly break social codes, the women in these works do not dramatically oppose them; in not adhering to standards of morality, these female characters rupture the binary divisions that separate the "good" public from the "evil" criminal. In *J'ai pas sommeil* Daïga deliberately wrecks a car, smuggles caviar over the border, and steals from Camille; Mona kidnaps her child; and Ninon permits illegal workers and nonpaying residents in her hotel. In *Roberto Zucco*, the girl runs away from home, the mother violently threatens her children, and the elegant lady leaves her husband for a killer. Not content to follow social mores, these women have minds of their own and use them accordingly. Many of them, moreover, deliberately ignore society's unwritten rules about being in the company of strange men, and even when they know that the object of their affection is a criminal, they refuse to follow decorum, instead pursuing the killer. Victims of abuse (the girl), sexual exploitation (the prostitute, the girl), harassment (Daïga), and neglect (the elegant lady), the women in these rewritings often act courageously out of a need to flee their environments. Yet rather than passively delighting in the *fait divers* before turning to condemn the murderer (as Auclair suggests), these female characters pursue the criminal's company. Unfulfilled and often mistreated in their homes (whether this is represented as a family or a country), these women become risk-takers who gamble on the criminal rather than rely on a more passive form of protection, the police. This unique choice again projects a cynical view of law enforcement, which has clearly failed to protect women in adequate ways; this dynamic results in an affiliation with the criminal rather than the institutions that theoretically protect her from him, again blurring the distinction between good and evil. This cynicism toward law enforcement is most clearly manifested in Daïga's numerous run-ins with the police and the woman's sarcastic comments about the police's inability to catch Zucco in scene 10 of the play. Other instances in these works show that these women have reason to be apprehensive about the police's ability to protect them: screams by women go unheard, police condescend to and harass female characters, several women are killed despite police efforts to protect them, and it is only by chance that these criminals are caught. In both works, it is a female character who turns in the criminal, proving that women are equally if not more capable of taking care of themselves. The police's subjectivity thus overturned, female characters emerge as competent subjects in their own right. Most of all, *J'ai pas sommeil* and *Roberto Zucco* present women who are strikingly similar to the criminal, an affinity which seems to come from a shared feeling of isolation and rejection. An Other herself, the female character functions on the same plane as the criminal. Each character that seeks out the criminal does not fit comfortably into her surroundings (family, job, culture), and until meeting the killer, she has been incapable of realizing her dreams. Her attraction to him thus functions to construct a less critical representation of the criminal. Rather than buckling to the media's fear tactics, they are in some instances able to use criminals to realize their desires, as Daïga does in *J'ai pas sommeil* when she flees Paris with all of Camille's money. In Koltès's work, however, this is not the case. While female characters are critical of law enforcement, they are also desperate Others whose powerless position in society draws them to the criminal in a pathological way. Whereas Daïga represents an empowered woman who does not need Camille but rather uses him to realize her financial independence, the girl and the elegant lady show us women whose fearlessness more closely parallels desperation, drawing them to anyone who seems capable of delivering them from their immediate problems. Given Auclair's hypothesis that women read *faits divers* because the stories reflect their inferior status, this portrayal of desperate female characters is perhaps more realistic than critical, but it is nonetheless disappointing to see women type-cast in such well-worn stereotypes. Looked at in another way, however, Koltès (like Denis) presents women who are not motivated by fear and insecurity, but rather by self-preservation and improvement. Their independence (whether we view it positively or negatively) likewise manifests cynicism with larger institutions such as police and the media. What stands out in both *J'ai pas sommeil* and *Roberto Zucco*, then, is a representation of women that sharply contrasts the media's presentation of weak, fearful victims of insecurity.

The Criminal as Hero

Here I would like to return to the question of the criminal as a hero, which I raised in the beginning of this project and have touched upon throughout my examination of the two *affaires*. The core of this question is raised primarily by the texts that encrust the *faits divers*, although *Roberto Zucco* directly confronts this notion in the final scene when a character ("a voice") calls Zucco a hero. Essentially, this debate of the criminal-as-hero may be divided into two primary—and diametrically opposed—ideas: (1) that these works mark the end of the heroization of the criminal and (2) that they signal the emergence of the criminal as depicted as a hero. In chapter 2, I examined Baudrillard's claims that the Paulin *affaire* signifies the end of the "héroisation des criminels." The public, he pronounced, is bored by the *fait divers*, and Baudrillard used Paulin to explain that from this moment on, a "fascination ordinaire" enshrouds the *fait divers*. In my analysis, I delineated several flaws in Baudrillard's arguments, but here I would like to briefly return to his statements in reference to this project as a whole. Again, it is important to address these issues, as they form part of the incrustations of the *fait divers*, thus contributing to its meaning in the public arena; as Bennett reminds us, "the text is only available for analysis in the context of its activations" (14). First of all, we know from Denis's film that Paulin did not disappear, as Baudrillard claimed; quite contrarily, the criminal was resurrected by a reader of the *fait divers* (Denis) who found the crime sufficiently fascinating to write and direct a screenplay about it. Paulin's resurrection in the media following the cinematic adaptation of his crimes thus signals his resurgence in the public consciousness as well; in this way, *J'ai pas sommeil* effectively overturns Baudrillard's (mis)reading of the *fait divers*. Looking at the Succo *affaire* and the public's immense interest in it, made explicit through media reaction and public controversy to the play, Koltès's play also suggests that Baudrillard's conclusion that Paulin marks the end of the criminal-hero is erroneous. As I have shown, Succo was consistently referred to as a hero by both journalists and non-media individuals; given that the Succo *affaire* occurred just after the Paulin case, Paulin clearly did not signal the end of the heroization of criminals. Moreover, Succo continues to be an object of worldwide interest: *Roberto Zucco* has been staged in over thirty countries, Kahn's film *Roberto Succo* has been released on DVD, and filmmakers such as the Taviani brothers have announced their plans to work on another film about his crimes. Froment also reports that at the time of her book's publication, four years after Succo's death, his grave remained covered with flowers (468). Most recently, in the summer of 2004, *France 2* broadcast a special series of *Faites entrer l'accusé* (Bring in the accused), made up of six one-hour programs about French serial killers. Paulin was the subject of the first, and Succo the last. Each program drew over three million viewers, gaining the second-largest audience at that prime-time slot. Online forums further attest to the interest in these killers. On Com.live's website about the Paulin program, "Boss" wrote to a friend, "you're going to love it" ("tu vas te régaler"). Regarding the Succo program, "Chantou" admits being "totally moved and seduced by [Succo's] mysterious and crazy personality" ("j'avoue que moi, j'ai été coplètement émue et je suis séduite par son mystérieux et fou caractère"). "Gus78" even posted a photo of Succo that could be downloaded to a mobile phone, adding that it was too bad that Succo had died so young ("dommage qu'il soit mort si jeune") (*Faites entrer l'accusé*). These examples attest to

Succo's recent popularity, if not his heroization. Yet, for all the references to these criminals' perseverance in the media, Koltès and Denis *do* portray the public's relative apathy with the *fait divers* as a mediated story, suggesting that Baudrillard is at least partially correct in his conclusions. As I have shown, Daïga's consistent disregard for the media and the older women characters' self-assured response to crime in *J'ai pas sommeil* display a cynicism with the presentation of the *fait divers* in the media that might be used to determine the banality of the crime story. Yet if we look closely at the characters' interactions with the criminal, we see that this banality does not lie with the criminal, but rather with the media and the larger institutions that construct him. In other words, the public's "banal" reaction to the *fait divers* is a reaction to the criminal's sensational representation in the media as a signifier for cultural, political, and social issues. In *J'ai pas sommeil*, for instance, we see Daïga shrug off the police and ignore media representations of the criminal, yet she follows Camille. Likewise, in *Roberto Zucco*, we see characters attracted to Zucco, but cynical of the police. In the hostage scene (10), for instance, the crowd is drawn to Zucco's spectacle but mocks the police's efforts to take charge of the scene; the prisoners in scene 15 are likewise mesmerized by Zucco's figure on the roof but laugh at the guards' inability to catch him. Radically, the characters of these works side with the criminal rather than with the larger institutions that are created to separate and protect the public from the "monster." While the criminal still functions in a sensational manner, attracting the public, it is the representation of and interference with the *fait divers* that generates the most "banal" public reaction. Baudrillard is thus partially correct in stating that there exists a degree of banality in the *fait divers*, but he is erroneous in presuming the public's boredom with the criminal.

In diametric opposition to Baudrillard's claims that the criminal-hero has disappeared, other spokespersons in France and the United States claim that society is witnessing a startling new trend that venerates the criminal. In addition to the protesters and journalists who make this claim, psychologists and philosophers have bemoaned this contemporary trend. In the 1970s, for instance, psychiatrist Thomas Millar decried the tendency of contemporary Western society to glamorize hedonism and antisocial behavior, and to confuse psychopathy with heroism (cited in Black 28). Citing the "popularity" of the criminal, these critics condemn the criminal's sensationalized diffusion in contemporary society, pointing fingers at fictional representations of the crime. Rather than blaming media for outrageous acts of sensationalism that deliberately manipulate public sentiment, angry reviewers and citizens instead focus blame on artistic productions. As a result, artists who rewrite the crime story become the focus of these recriminations and blame. Reaching an apex of censorship, the extreme public discomfort with these "heroic" depictions of the criminal emphasizes how clearly Denis and Koltès subvert typical representations of the criminal. In several interviews, Koltès likened Zucco to a hero, and in the play, Zucco's twisted logic shows how the criminal constructs himself as a hero. In *J'ai pas sommeil* as well, while Camille does not overtly speak of his greatness, his flashy manner of flaunting the stolen money and his fixation with his own image as a performer (being looked at, photographed, or watching himself) suggest that he very much enjoys being the center of attention. Following his arrest, Paulin also reportedly collected pictures of himself in newspapers. Despite Baudrillard's claims that the public is not interested, then, these fictionalized criminals show that they know how to stoke public fascination (which we see reflected in the real *faits divers* as well). By manipulating the forces around him, the criminal constructs his own image, which is then validated by the public's fascination. Even more than heroic representations, however, many critics lament the neutrality with which the criminal is depicted, suggesting that any representation other than that of total condemnation is unacceptable. Not responding to Kooistra's definition of a criminal-hero, or to the non-hero of Baudrillard's claims, the criminals of these two *faits divers* seem to float between fascination and banality, depending on their representation and their readers. As I have emphasized throughout this work, perhaps a better approach than debating whether and to what extent society glorifies the criminal, we ought instead to probe how the criminal *serves* the media and society as a whole, looking at how we use his existence to frame larger debates. Rather than focusing on sensational and provocative questions, we learn much more by examining these crimes through a context-activated theory that attempts to go beyond the primary levels of meaning.

Determining Artistic Influence

A fundamental question that arises, then, is exactly how *J'ai pas sommeil* and *Roberto Zucco* have influenced the meaning of these *faits divers*. Throughout this research, I have repeatedly demonstrated how the criminal and his acts shift in meaning according to the discourse and events that frame his actions. The heightened reactions to the rewritings of these *affaires* signal a concern that the actual events will be altered in the public memory, and certainly, these fears are not unfounded. As Bennett has theorized and demonstrated, texts are "constantly inscribed within different contexts and caught up in an ever shifting set of relations with other texts, such that it is productive of variable effects and meanings" (5). In *Roberto Zucco* especially, the public protests demonstrated a genuine fear that Koltes's vision of Zucco would alter or replace the image of the real Succo. With *J'ai pas sommeil*, we see how the film did indeed affect the "truth" of the events; recent reviewers have referred to Denis's film to cite criminal details, with one reviewer erroneously stating that Raphäel was Caucasian, an error that is particularly significant given the racial overtones that characterized coverage of the Paulin *affaire*.

In the years following the artistic rewritings of these *faits divers*, then, we begin to ask which particular activations of the crime story become privileged in the dominant discourse of crime. Certainly, the *fait divers* is privileged because it comes closest to the "truth" and because it came first. Yet for the broader public, *J'ai pas sommeil* and *Roberto Zucco* are clearly privileged because of their circulation; their worldwide distribution allows a larger population to access these rearticulations, exceeding the reach of the original crime stories. In addition, however, the reviewers and protestors of these two works have touched perhaps more people than the actual film and play. Ironically, while one might argue that Koltès's play has made famous the violent actions of a madman, it is just as likely that the play's censors are "to blame"; it was they who created the conflict that seared Succo's name in the minds of citizens who would not have otherwise seen the play. In other words, because the play and its censorship have become inextricably linked, it is impossible to determine whether the international success of *Roberto Zucco* is due to the brilliance of the play or to the controversy it stirred. We see how these incrustrations function, for example, when protestors picketed *Roberto Zucco* without having seen the play; its hype preceded its representation, encrusting it with a meaning that stemmed from its activation (or the threat of this activation, since *Roberto Zucco* was not actually staged in Chambéry). In a reverse effort in favor of the play, reviewers of *Roberto Zucco* encrusted the play with Koltès's biography, shifting focus from the criminal to the artist. The rival efforts of the protesters and the play's reviewers highlight the power of these incrustations to influence meaning. Thus, while it is clear that Koltès's play is about more than a patricidal cop-killer, and worthy of watching regardless of its controversy, the employment of these controversial elements to attract spectators has also had the effect of resuscitating theater as an art form. When a literary work can cause a controversy of this proportion, it is testimony to its importance, and at a time when public support for literary studies and cultural activities is at a low, this kind of press reminds the public that art and literature play an important role in defining and shaping our cultural values.

Given that these kinds of debates strongly influence public opinion (and thereby polls and votes), the struggle to control the meaning of the *fait divers* is paramount. This is evidenced by the battles between *Le Monde* and *Le Figaro* during the Paulin *affaire*, where newspapers fought to control the printed representation of Thierry Paulin. As John Fiske elaborates, "to make sense of the world is to exert power over it, and to circulate that sense socially is to exert power over those who use that sense as a way of coping with their daily lives" (3). Fiske emphasizes that the ability to control discourse often signals a parallel capacity to control public sentiment. Recent battles over the depiction of crime have even been blamed for affecting the outcome of the 2002 French presidential race. After the Left's shocking loss to National Front leader Le Pen in the first round of the elections, *Le Monde* made an investigation into the mediatization of *insécurité*. The paper found that between January and May of 2002, there were 987 "*faits divers-police-justice*" stories released every week over the sixty-five newspapers studied. In other words, *insécurité* was treated twice as often as employment and eight times as much as unemployment, even though there was no rise in crime during this period ("Pourquoi les faits divers fascinent"). These findings corollate the hypermediatization of the crime story with the poitical outcome of the elections, leading us to the conclusion that the public's internalization of the media-driven fear led it to ignore the real issues at stake. But what about the public that *does not* use this information to make sense of the world? Denis's and Koltès's works are unique in that they present characters who *ignore* these discourses presented by media, politicians, and law enforcement. Although the media and police influence the lives of these characters in subtle ways, there is a meaningful lack of attention paid to these powerful media of the message; in this neglect of legal and political powers, we may be able to best determine the significance of these artists' work. As I have shown, the public in *J'ai pas sommeil* and *Roberto Zucco* sharply contrasts with the media-constructed public. It does not follow the media's mini-soap opera of the killer's crimes, and it does not sit at home frightened to venture outside. Unlike *Le Figaro*'s claims that "France is scared," no one in these works seems afraid. Denis and Koltès instead show us individual characters who are fascinated with the criminal and who search him for solutions to their problems and fantasies; for these characters, the criminal symbolizes a liberating rupture with society's rules. In this way, these artists radically advocate ignoring the dominant knowledge machines.

Throughout my analyses, I have sought to theorize a way of examining these crimes in the context of their activations, and of analyzing their rewritings amidst battles over social, political, and cultural meaning. By closely examining these contexts, I have shown how dominant media and political groups use the *fait divers* to magnify public fear through sensationalized, immediacy-driven depictions of crime and insecurity. In response, Denis and Koltès subvert this dangerous combination of immediacy and insecurity by initiating a dialogue with the criminal that serves to reduce the public fear. Through this unique exchange, these artists provide a new model of contesting dominant readings, of confronting fears, of ignoring the media, and of taking individual risks. By providing an alternative representation of crime and of its audiences, these artists create a forum that valorizes a multiplicity of voices and a diversity of knowledges and readings. Recent trends suggest that these battles over crime will proliferate and continue to characterize political and cultural discussions in the media. Due to more accurate methods of reporting and documenting crime, the sheer number of "motiveless" killers in France is increasing. As the central direction of the French police declared regarding the increase in serial killers, "Between 1985 and 1995, we had one more every year. For the last five years, we've discovered one every six months. Something's going on, it's clear" ("Entre 1985 et 1995, on en avait un de plus chaque année. Depuis cinq ans, on en découvre un tous les six mois. Il se passé quelque chose, c'est clair") (Vezard 37). Among the French serial killers who occupied the front pages of France's newspapers in the years spanning the turn of the twentieth century are Guy George, Louis Poirson, Sid Ahmed Rezzala, Pierre Navelot, Francis Heaulme, Patrice Alègre, and Emile Louis. The media (and the public) continue to show a steady interest in these crimes, with the continued popularity and increase of reality shows, docudramas, and journalistic rewritings of the *affaires* attesting to the public's thirsty fascination. In the face of this undying interest, we may only hope that artists like Denis and Koltès will remain engaged in these battles over the meaning of crime, contesting dominant discourses that obscure important social issues with sensational fear tactics.

Significantly, there is a growing body of literature based on criminal affairs that do just this. Several recent films from the United States have rewritten sensational murder stories from the point of view of the criminal with considerable acclaim. Rob Marshall's wildly successful *Chicago* (2002) accentuates the media's role in sensationalizing crime, and Patty Jenkins's *Monster* (2003) presents the human side of female serial killer Aileen Wuornos (although the actor's portrayal of the killer was praised more than the film itself). Gus Van Sant's *Elephant* (2003) is loosely based on the Columbine High School murders, but the director refuses to explain how disturbingly normal high school kids became motiveless killers. Like *J'ai pas sommeil*, it was a critical success, winning Cannes's best picture and best director awards in 2003, but some reviewers called it "irresponsible," and the general (American) public seemed disturbed by its refusal to judge the criminal acts. In Canada, Québécoise Hélène LaLiberté's play *Le Piège: Terre des hommes* (1996) tackles motiveless murder by retelling the story of a young man killed because he was wearing a cowboy hat. It was voted the best theatrical staging in Québec in 1996. Québécois Robert Lepage's play and film of the same name (*Le Polygraphe* 1997) examine how different versions of the truth affect our understanding of a murder. In France, there have been a number of artistic rewritings of sensational crimes, and they have met with somewhat varied success. Bertrand Tavernier based his film *L'Appât* (1995) on Morgan Sportes's journalistic account of the same title (1990), which I referenced in my introductory chapter. His film won the Golden Bear Award at the Berlin International Film Festival, but he has yet to find an American distributor to reach a larger audience. François Ozon's treatment of the banal killing of a young Arab in his film *Les Amants criminels* (1999) received lukewarm reviews, as did Catherine Breillat's *A ma sœur* (2001), which was banned by the Ontario Film Review Board for offending "contemporary provincial moral standards." Franck Evard's play *Faits divers pour un non lieu* (2001) is inspired loosely by the Guy George *affaire* and strongly criticizes the media's role in hyping crime; it has yet to find a director. Two novels written for the young adult public present highly mediated *faits divers* that are similar to the works in this study. In *Tant pis pour le sud* (1990), Lehmann fictionalizes the *affaire Carpentras* to call into question the National Front's role in defacing the Jewish cemetery, and in *La Bombe humaine* (1994) Jonquet relates the Neuilly-sur-Seine hostage *affaire* from the point of view of a sympathetic child who finds humanity in his captor. Finally, the *affaire Romand*, in which a man lived a false professional life for eighteen years before killing his entire family, has inspired several recent works: Philippe Minyana's play *Habitations* (2001), Emmanuel Carrère's novel *L'Adversaire* (which was staged in 2001), and two films—Nicole Garcia's journalistic *L'Adversaire* (2001) and Laurent Cantet's *Emploi du temps* (2001), a liberal interpretation of the events that sympathizes with the murderer by omitting the final violence.

Notable additions to this list are works by Francophone authors from North Africa. Rather than treating sensational *grandes affaires*, however, these works tend to focus on murders that are racially or ethnically motivated. Similar to Kassovitz's *La Haine*, which was based on a forgotten *fait divers* in which a sixteen-year-old Zairean youth was shot in police custody, these rewritings endeavor to make the public aware of crimes quickly forgotten by the media. Ahmed Kalouaz's novel *Point kilométrique 190* (1986), for instance, recounts the 1983 Grimzi *affaire* in which a young Algerian on vacation in France was severely beaten and thrown out of a train to his death by three French Legionnaire candidates. The Grimzi *affaire,* sparked a fiery but brief discussion about racism in the media, particularly as it occurred during the first national march led by the *beur* community, made up primarily of second-generation immigrants of North African descent. In the novel, journalist Sabine returns to the night of Grimzi's murder on the train to try to understand the cowardly reactions of its witnesses. *Point kilométrique 190* provides an in-depth look into media sensationalism, public apathy, and the wrongful analysis that plagues crime, in particular racial crimes. Incorporating direct quotes from the media, Kalouaz struggles against the banality of this crime, yet in focusing on the victim rather than the murderers, his work finds itself part of the very banality he denounces; it is out of print and rarely studied. Based on the same crimes, Roger Hanin's film *Train d'enfer* (1984) received poor reviews and was criticized for presenting an overly simplistic, Manichean analysis of the events that was attributed to a political move to denounce racism (Hanin is Mitterand's brother-in-law) (Guetney 64). Other writers have also had difficulty marketing their work. Algerian writer Hafsa Zinai-Koudil based her film *Le Démon au féminin* (1993) on a *fait divers* in which a woman who refused to wear the *hijab* was exorcised and permanently disfigured by her husband and brother. The crime itself never received national attention, but her film was shown at the Festival of Amiens, where it received the Audience Choice Award (1995). Banned in Algeria and no longer available in France, however, the film has reached only a small audience. While these works do not always detail the *fait divers* from the point of view of the criminal, instead giving their victims a voice by making them into posthumous protagonists, they do follow trends in expressing nonjudgmental depictions of the crime story. Already in Kalouaz's and Zinai-Koudil's works, the media is shown to be either unreliable or ineffective in influencing the public, and like Denis and Koltès, these artists explore the possibility of resisting the discourse of institutions that feed on fear and racism. A study of these works has yet to be done and would contribute significantly to scholarship on the Francophone *fait divers*.

While the resistant stance to these artistic productions will undoubtedly continue—simplistic explanations of crime that blame popular culture are in step with contemporary society's short attention span—the resulting controversies can serve to encourage public dialogue about how meaning is constructed. As Tavernier advocated when *L'Appât* was televised amidst controversy that it would glorify the crimes, fiction can be an enlightening part of the discussion about crime. Indeed, it invites us to what Todorov calls "a dialogue in which no one has the last word" (250). For this reason, it is more important than ever to support works that create and enrich this dialogue, that challenge dominant thought, and that work to decrease knee-jerk, fearful reactions that contribute to a dangerous monoculture.

Works Cited

Abgrall, Jean-François, and Samuel Luret. *Dans la tête du tueur, sur les traces de Francis Heaulme*. Paris: Albin Michel, 2002

Alcoff, Linda. "The Problem of Speaking for Others." *Cultural Critique* 20 (1991–92): 5–32.

Ambroise-Rendu, Marc. "Trop peu de policiers à Paris pour protéger les personnes âgées." *Le Monde* (22 January 1986): 13.

Amenábar, Alejandro. *Tesis*. New Yorker Films, 1996.

d'Arrigo, José. "L'Étonnante confession du tueur de Toulon." *Le Figaro* (8 February 1988): 17.

"Les Assassins du XVIIIe: sans doute des drogués." *Le Figaro* (10–11 November 1984): 12.

Attoun, Lucien. "*Roberto Zucco* de Bernard-Marie Koltès. Il était une voix." *Le Monde* (6 February 1992): 24.

Auclair, Georges. *Le "Mana" quotidien. Structures et fonctions de la chronique des faits divers*. Paris: Anthropos, 1970.

Augé, Marc. *Non-places. Introduction to an Anthropology of Supermodernity*. 1992. Trans. John Howe. New York: Verso, 1995.

Baillon, Jean-Claude. "Jeu de chacals et de chiens." *Autrement* 104 (1989): 6–7.

Barak, Gregg. "Media, Crime, and Justice: A Case for Constitutive Criminology." *Cultural Criminology*. Ed. J. Ferrell and C. Sanders. Boston: Northeastern UP, 1995. 132–60.

Barillaud, Marie-Christine, Jacqueline Bieque, and Patrick Dahlet. "Le Fait divers. Aspects théoriques, pédagogiques." *Le Français dans le monde*. Paris: Hachette & Larousse, 1990. 76–89.

Barthes, Roland. "Structure of the *Fait-Divers*." *Critical Essays*. Trans. Richard Howard. Evanston: Northwestern UP, 1972. 185–95.

Barthes, Roland. "The Death of the Author." *Image, Music, Text*. Trans. Stephen Health. London: Flamingo, 1977. 142–48.

Barthes, Roland. *S/Z*. 1970. Trans. Richard Miller. New York: Hill and Wang, 1974.

Baudrillard, Jean. *Consumer Society: Myths and Structures (Theory, Culture and Society)*. Trans. George Ritzer. London: Sage, 1997.

Baudrillard, Jean. "Cool Killers." *Autrement* 104 (1989): 143–45.

Baudrillard, Jean. *Cool Memories: 1980–1985.* Trans. Chris Turner. New York: Verso, 1990.

Baudrillard, Jean. *The Perfect Crime.* 1995. Trans. Chris Turner. New York: Verso, 1996.

Baudrillard, Jean. *The Transparency of Evil: Essays on Extreme Phenomena.* New York: Verso, 1993.

Bedarida, Catherine. "Bernard-Marie Koltès, contemporain de référence." *Le Monde* (17 March 1999): 17.

Belleret, Roger. "Z, comme Succo. L'Evocation théâtrale du 'monstre de Mestre' sur le lieu de ses crimes, en Savoie, est très contestée." *Le Monde* (2 November 1991): 17.

Belleret, Roger. "*Roberto Zucco* déprogrammé à Chambéry." *Le Monde* (9 January 1992): 19.

Benjamin, Sonja. "Claire Denis, une cinéaste curieuse de toutes les cultures." *Journal Français d'Amérique* (August 1995): 10.

Bennett, Tony. "Text and Social Process: The Case of James Bond." *Southern Review: Literary and Interdisciplinary Essays* 16 (1983): 3–16.

Berenstein, Rhonda. "Spectatorship as Drag: The Act of Viewing and Classic Horror Cinema." *Viewing Positions: Ways of Seeing Film.* Ed. Linda Williams. New Brunswick: Rutgers UP, 1995. 231–63.

Bernard, Jean-Jacques. Review of *J'ai pas sommeil,* by Claire Denis. *Première* (June 1994): 64.

Besson, Louis. Reply to Letter of Roger Planchon. *Le Monde* (12–13 January) 1992: 13.

Black, Joel. *The Aesthetics of Murder: A Study in Romantic Literature and Contemporary Culture.* Baltimore: The Johns Hopkins UP, 1991.

Bommer, Lawrence. "*Zucco* Tells Young Murderer's True Story." *Chicago Tribune* (20 January 1995): 8.

Bonvoisin, Samra, and Mary-Anne Brault-Wiart. Interview with Claire Denis. *L'Aventure du premier film.* Ed. Bonvoisin and Brault-Wiart. Paris: Bernard Barrault, 1989. 33–45.

Bourdieu, Pierre. *On Television.* Trans. Priscilla Parkhurst Ferguson. New York: The New P, 1998.

Bourgeois, Nathalie. "Les Vieilles Dames du *Figaro.*" *Autrement* 104 (1989): 70–75.

Bourgoin, Stéphane. *Le Nouvel Almanach du crime et des faits divers.* Paris: E-dite, 2001.

Bourgoin, Stéphane. *Serial killers. Enquête sur les tueurs en série.* Paris: Grasset, 2004.

Bradby, David. "Bernard-Marie Koltès: Chronology, Contexts, Connections." *New Theatre Quarterly* 13.49 (1997): 69–90.

Brustein, Robert. "On a Cold Planet." *New Republic* (22 May 1995): 29–30.

Butler, Judith. "The Body You Want" [Interview with Liz Kot]. *Artforum* (November 1992): 84.

Caplan, Betty. "Vive Koltès." *Glasgow Herald* (22 November 1994): 10.

"Citoyens français." *Le Monde* (8 December 1987): 16.

Clover, Carol J. *Men, Women, and Chain Saws: Gender in the Modern Horror Film.* Princeton: Princeton UP, 1992.

Costaz, Gilles. "Retour au désert: Bernard-Marie Koltès: 'j'écris des pièces pas des spectacles'." *Acteurs* 3 (1988): 61–66.

Curtiss, Thomas Q. "Murderer as Hero: Koltès' Legacy." *International Herald Tribune* (9 January 1992): 5.

Dauncey, Hugh. "Reality Shows on French Television: Télé-vérité, télé-service, télé-civisme or . . . télé-flicaille?" *French Cultural Studies* 5 (1994): 85–98.

Davis, R.G. "The Sense of the Real in English Fiction." *Comparative Literature* 3 (1951) 200–17.

Debieuvre, Jean-Louis. "Assassins, vous avez dit assassins!" *Le Figaro* (7 December 1987): 12.

"La Déclaration de la Mairie de Paris." *Le Monde* (12–13 January 1992): 13.

Deleuze, Gilles. *Cinema 2: The Time Image*. 1985 Trans. Hugh Tomlinson and Robert Galeta. Minneapolis: U of Minnesota P, 1989.

Delsol, Catherine. "Jean-Pierre Pierre-Bloch: le Ministre de l'Intérieur doit démissionner . . .'." *Le Figaro* (13 November 1984): 13.

De Palma, Brian. *Dressed to Kill*. MGM/UA, 1980.

Demme, Jonathan. *Silence of the Lambs*. MGM/UA, 1991.

Denis, Claire, dir. *J'ai pas sommeil*. New Yorker Films, 1994.

Dion, Sylvie. "Le Fait divers comme genre narratif." *Imprévue. Théorie du Texte et du Genre* 2 (1988): 45–54.

Dumont, Bruno, dir. *L'Humanité*. Arte Video, 1999.

Duplouich, Jacques. "Maman ne m'aimait pas . . ." *Le Figaro* (10 February 1988): 8.

Duplouich, Jacques. "Le Tueur fou tombe du toit." *Le Figaro* (2 March 1988): 42.

Dupochonelle, Valérie. "La Grande Peur des vieilles dames." *Le Figaro* (17 January 1986): 11.

Duras, Marguerite. *Les Viaducs de la Seine-et-Oise*. Paris: Gallimard, 1960.

Duras, Marguerite. *L'Amante anglaise*. Paris: Gallimard, 1967.

Ehrenberg, Alain. "La Vie en direct ou les shows de l'authenticité." *Esprit* (January 1993): 13–35.

Epstein, Su C. "The New Mythic Monster." *Cultural Criminology*. Ed. J. Ferrell and C. Sanders. Boston: Northeastern UP, 1995. 66–79.

Erickson, Steve. Review of *I Can't Sleep,* by Claire Denis. *Cinéaste* (June 1994): 64.

"Faites entrer l'accusé." Online Forum (2004): <http://www.comlive.net/sujet-32827-0.html>.

Ferenczi, Thomas. "Faits divers." *Le Monde* (17 November 1984): 2.

Ferrell, Jeff. "Criminalizing Popular Culture" *Popular Culture, Crime, and Justice.* Ed. F. Bailey and D. Hale. Boston: Wadsworth, 1998: 71–83.

Fiske, John. *Media Matters: Race and Gender in U.S. Politics.* Minneapolis: U of Minnesota P, 1996.

Foucault, Michel. *The Archaeology of Knowledge.* 1969. Trans. A.M. Sheridan. New York: Pantheon, 1972.

Foucault, Michel, ed. *I, Pierre Rivière, Having Slaughtered My Mother, My Sister, and My Brother . . . A Case of Parricide in the Nineteenth Century.* 1973. Trans. Frank Julinek. New York: Pantheon, 1975.

Foucault, Michel. *The History of Sexuality.* Volume 1: *An Introduction.* 1976. Trans. Robert Hurley. New York: Random House, 1978.

Foucault, Michel. *Discipline and Punish: The Birth of the Prison.* 1975. Trans. Alan Sheridan. New York: Vintage Books, 1979.

"La France a peur." *Le Figaro* (13 November 1984): 1.

Froment, Pascale. *Je te tue. Histoire vraie de Roberto Succo, assassin sans raîson.* Paris: Gallimard, 1991.

Froment, Pascale. "Zucco contre Succo." *Nouvel Observateur* (30 January 1992): 65–66.

Gaines, Jane. "White Privilege and Looking Relations: Race and Gender in Feminist Film Theory." *Screen* 29 (1988): 12–27.

Gendre, Bertrand Le. "L'Opposition et la peine de mort. La peur exploitée." *Le Monde* (15 November 1984): 1+.

Genet, Jean. *Les Bonnes.* Paris: Folio, 1986.

Girard, René. *La Violence et le sacré.* Paris: Grasset, 1972.

Godard, Colette. "Le Chemin qui conduit à la mort." *Le Monde* (21 April 1990): 24.

Guardian (London). Review of *I Can't Sleep,* by Claire Denis (17 May 1994): 18.

Guilledoux, Dominique le. "Démons et merveilles du politique. Entretien avec Pierre Joxe." *Autrement* 104 (1989): 178–88.

Hall, Stuart. "Culture, the Media and 'The Ideological Effect'." *Mass Communication and Society.* Ed. J. Curran, M. Gurevitch, and J. Woollacott. London: Arnold, 1977.

Heed, Sven Åke. "Le Regard de l'autre dans le théâtre de Bernard-Marie Koltès." *Moderna Språk* 88 (1994): 52–59.

Hickey, Eric W. *Serial Murderers and Their Victims.* Belmont: Wadsworth, 1991.

"Historique des prime time. Juillet 2004." (2005): <http://fan2tv.webheberg.com/audiences/historique_07juillet2004.htm>.

Hobsbawm, Eric J. *Bandits.* London: Weidenfeld & Nicolson, 1969.

Huet, Sophie. "Le Pen dénonce une politique pénale laxiste." *Le Figaro* (14 November 1984): 6.

Hyatt, Ralph. "Criminals: An American Obsession." *USA Today Magazine* (May 1995): 36–38.

Imbrohoris, Jean-Pierre. *Démences meurtrières*. Paris: Filipacchi, 1993.

"Insécurité. Le Pouvoir au pied du mur." *Le Figaro* (14 November 1984): 1.

Jenkins, Philip. *Using Murder: The Social Construction of Serial Homicide*. Hawthorne: Aldine de Gruyter, 1994.

Jonquet, Thierry. *La Bombe humaine*. Paris: Syros, 1994.

Jousse, Thierry. "Entretien avec Claire Denis." *Cahiers du Cinéma* (May 1994): 25–30.

Jurgenson, Caroline. "*Roberto Zucco* au théâtre de la ville. La Solitude des champs de la mort." *Le Figaro* (7 February 1992): 25.

Kahn, Cédric. "La longue traque de Cédric Kahn." *Télérama à Cannes* (31 December 2004): <http://cinema.telerama.fr/edito/cannes01/magazine/kahn/ITV_kahn.asp>.

Kalouaz, Ahmed. *Point kilométrique 190*. Paris: Harmattan, 1986.

Kaplan, E. Ann. *Looking for the Other: Feminism, Film, and the Imperial Gaze*. New York: Routledge, 1997.

Kassovitz, Mathieu. *La Haine*. New Yorker Films, 1992.

Katz, Jack. "What Makes Crime 'News'?" *Media, Culture, and Society* 9 (1987): 47–75.

Kellerman, Jonathan. *Savage Spawn: Reflections on Violent Children*. New York: Ballantine, 1999.

Klausner, Emannuelle, and Brigitte Salino. "Les Rages de Bernard-Marie Koltès." *L'Evénement du Jeudi* (12–18 January 1989): 84–85.

Koltès, Bernard-Marie. *Roberto Zucco* (suivi de *Tabataba* et *Un Hangar à l'ouest*). Paris: Minuit, 1990.

Kooistra, Paul. *Criminals as Heroes: Structure, Power, and Identity*. Bowling Green: Bowling Green SU Popular P, 1989.

Kristeva, Julia. *Strangers to Ourselves*. Trans. Leon S. Roudiez. New York: Columbia UP, 1991.

Lagrange, Hughes. "L'Etre de sécurité." *Autrement* 104 (1989): 122–27.

Lantéri, Jean. "L'Oiseau et la labyrinthe." *Alternatives Théâtrales* 35–36 (1990): 58–69.

Lee, L. "Brian DePalma's *Carlito's Way* Joins the Gangster-film Pantheon." *ETC: Times Union* (2 December 1993): 8.

Lehmann, Christian. *Tant pis pour le sud*. Paris: L'Ecole des loisirs, 2000.

Lejeune, François. "Le Monstre." *Paris-Match* (18 December 1987): 11 pp.

Lemoine, Françoise. "XVIIIe. Le temps de la peur." *Le Figaro* (12 November 1984): 10.

Léridon, Yves. "L'Insupportable Provocation de Zucco-le-fou." *Le Figaro* (2 January 1992): 22.

Lesinge, Jacques. "'On tue pour voler sans risque.'" *Le Figaro* (17 January 1986): 11.

Létourneau, Jacqueline. "Les Contextes de signification d'un fait divers." *Tangence* 37 (1992): 46–55.

Lever, Maurice. *Canards sauvages. Naissance du fait divers*. Paris: Fayard, 1993.

Levin, Jack, and James Alan Fox. *Mass Murder: America's Growing Menace*. New York: Berkeley Books, 1991.

Lhomeau, Jean-Yves, and Edwy Plenel. "Violences. La Réponse du pouvoir." *Le Monde* (14 November 1984): 1+.

Lillo, Gaston. "De Quelques modulations et usages du fait divers." *Tangence* 37 (1992): 16–28.

Lippy, Tod. "Writing and Directing *I Can't Sleep*" (interview with Claire Denis). *Scenario* 3 (1997): 87.

Lyon, Eleanor, and Clinton R. Sanders. "Repetitive Retribution: Media Images and the Cultural Construction of Criminal Justice" *Cultural Criminology*. Ed. J. Ferrell and C. Sanders. Boston: Northeastern UP, 1995. 25–44.

Macabru, Pierre. "*Roberto Zucco* de Bernard-Marie Koltès. Portrait d'un inconnu." *Le Figaro* (8 February 1992): 23.

Martinelli, Jean-Louis. "Notes." *Séquences 2* (1995): 14.

Merigeau, Pascal. "Festival de Cannes. Un Certain regard." *Le Monde* (18 May 1994): 22.

Met, Philippe. "Looking for Trouble: The Dialectics of Lack and Excess." *Kinoeye: New Perspectives on European Cinema* 3.7 (June 2003): <http://www.kinoeye.org/03/07/met07.php>.

Le Monde. Review of *J'ai pas sommeil,* by Claire Denis (26 May 1994):22.

M'sili, M. *Fait divers en République: Histoire sociale de 1870 à nos jours*. Paris: CNRS, 2000.

Mucchielli, Laurent. *Violences et insécurités. Fantasmes et réalités dans le débat français*. Paris: La Découverte, 2001.

Muller, Marie. "L'Assassin à la boucle d'oreille." *Nouvel Observateur* (11–17 December 1987): 104–06.

Mulvey, Laura. "Visual Pleasure and Narrative Cinema." *Screen* 16.3 (1975): 305.

Nash-Stedlicki, Richard Erin. "Searching for *Roberto Zucco*." *American Theatre* (1995): 6–7.

Nichols, Bill. *Blurred Boundaries: Questions of Meaning in Contemporary Culture*. Bloomington: Indiana UP, 1994.

Nirascou, Gérard. "Les Bornes franchies." *Le Figaro* (13 November 1984): 1.

Nirascou, Gérard. "Les 'Bons' Morts et les autres." *Le Figaro* (7 December 1987): 12.

O'Reilly-Fleming, Thomas. *Serial and Mass Murder: Theory, Research, and Policy*. Toronto: Canadian Scholar's P, 1996.

Parenti, Michel. *Inventing Reality: The Politics of the Mass Media*. New York: St. Martin's, 1986.

Pasqual, Lluis. "Démultiplier le regard" [Interview with Jean-Claude Llalas]. *Koltès. Combats avec la scène*. Paris: CNDP, 1996. 110–14.

"Peine de mort: nouvelles controverses." *Le Figaro* (15 November 1984): 1.

Peralva, Angelina, and Eric Macé. *Médias et violences urbaines*. Paris: La Documentation française, 2002.

Peyrefitte, Alain. "Confiance perdue." *Le Figaro* (12 November 1984): 1.

Peyrot, Maurice. "La Sinistre routine des agresseurs de vieilles dames." *Le Monde* (20 December 1991): 10.

Piatzszek, Stéphane, and Olivier Seguret. "De telles histoires se traitent à l'aveugle, sans théorie" [interview with Claire Denis]. *Libération* (2004): <http://www.liberation.fr/page.php?Article=259927>.

Planchon, Roger. "Résister aux malfaiteurs." *Le Monde* (10 January 1992): 12.

"La Polémique autour de la pièce de Bernard-Marie Koltès. *Roberto Zucco* sera jouée à Paris." *Le Monde* (12–13 January 1992): 13.

"Pourquoi les faits divers fascinent." *France 5: C dans l'air* (17 December 2004): <http://www.france5.fr/cdanslair/D00063/274/>.

Puyalte, Francis. "Les Aveux hallucinants des deux assassinats." *Le Figaro* (3 December 1987): 10.

Quinney, Richard. *Criminology: Analysis and Critique of Crime in America*. Boston: Little, Brown, 1975.

Regnault, François. "Passage de Koltès." *Nanterre Amandiers. Les Années Chéreau 1982–1990*. Ed. Sylvie de Nussac. Paris: Imprimerie Nationale, 1990. 320–34.

Rémy, Jacqueline. "De quoi frémir?" *Les Cahiers de L'Express. Les Nouveaux visages du crime* 33 (1995): 4.

Riou, Alain. "Erreurs d'aiguillage." *Nouvel Observateur* (26 May 1994): 66.

"Roberto Succo arrêté en Italie." *Le Figaro* (1 March 1988): 1.

"Roberto Succo pourrait être jugé en Italie." *Le Monde* (2 March 1988): 12.

"Roberto Succo se blesse au cours d'une tentative d'évasion." *Le Monde* (13 March 1988): 12.

"*Roberto Zucco* sera joué à Paris." *Le Monde* (12–13 January 1992): 13.

Rose, Tricia. "Rap Music and the Demonization of Young Black Males." *Black Male: Representations of Masculinity in Contemporary American Art*. Ed. T. Golden. New York: Whitney Museum of American Art, 1994. 148–57.

Salino, Brigitte. "Mais qui a peur de Roberto Zucco?" *L'Événement du Jeudi* (28 November–4 December 1991): 100–02.

Sarrazac, Jean-Pierre. "Résurgences de l'expressionisme: Kroetz, Koltès, Bond." *Etudes Théâtrales* 7 (1995): 139–53.

Schmitt, Olivier. "*Roberto Zucco* à Barcelone. Visages du crime." *Le Monde* (13 October 1993): 11.

Schmitt, Olivier. "Rencontre avec Bruno Boëglin, metteur en scène de *Roberto Zucco*." *Le Monde* (6 February 1992): 19.

Schwartz, Vanessa. "Cinematic Spectatorship before the Apparatus." *Viewing Positions: Ways of Seeing Film*. Ed. Linda Williams. New Brunswick: Rutgers UP, 1994. 87–113.

Schwarzbaum, Lisa. "I Can't Sleep" (review). *Entertainment Weekly*, 8 Sept. 1995.

Seidler, Victor. "Masculinities, Culture, and Difference." Keynote speech. *La(s) Retórica(s) de la Masculinidad*. Sevilla (2 March 2000).

Siclier, Jacques. "Le Temps des assassins." Review of *J'ai pas sommeil*, by Claire Denis. *Le Monde* (30 March 1998): 19.

Sister, My Sister. Screenplay by Wendy Kesselbaum. Dir. Nancy Meckler. Unapix, 1994.

Sportes, Morgan. *L'Appât*. Paris: Seuil, 1990.

Staiger, Janet. *Interpreting Films: Studies in the Historical Reception of American Cinema*. Princeton: Princeton UP, 1992.

Stein, Peter. "Pourquoi es-tu devenu fou, Roberto?" [interview with Anne Laurent]. *Alternatives Théâtrales* 35–36 (1990): 146.

Surette, Ray. "Prologue: Some Unpopular Thoughts about Popular Culture." *Popular Culture, Crime and Justice*. Ed. F. Bailey and D. Hale. Belmont: Wadsworth, 1998. xiv–xxiv.

Tavernier, Bertrand. *L'Appât*. TF1 Vidéo, 1995.

Théolleyre, Jean-Marc. "Morbide fascination." *Le Monde* (5 December 1987): 13.

Tithecott, Richard. *Of Men and Monsters: Jeffrey Dahmer and the Construction of the Serial Killer*. Madison: The U of Wisconsin P, 1997.

Todorov, Tzvetan. *The Conquest of America: The Question of the Other*. 1982. Trans. Richard Howard. Norman: U of Oklahoma P, 1999.

Tötösy de Zepetnek, Steven. "From Comparative Literature Today toward Comparative Cultural Studies." *Comparative Literature and Comparative Cultural Studies*. Ed. Steven Tötösy de Zepetnek. West Lafayette: Purdue UP, 2003. 235–67.

Tristan, Anne. "Marseille. Conversations en lambeaux." *Autrement* 104 (1989): 30–34.

"Les Tueurs avouent treize meurtres de vieilles dames." *Le Figaro* (3 December 1987): 1, 10.

"Les Tueurs de vieilles dames." *Le Figaro* (12 November 1984): 1.

Tunnell, Kenneth D. "Reflections on Crime, Criminals, and Control in Newsmagazine Television Programs." *Popular Culture, Crime and Justice*. Ed. F. Bailey and D. Hale. Belmont: Wadsworth, 1998. 111–22.

Ubersfeld, Anne. *Bernard-Marie Koltès*. Paris: Actes Sud, 1999.

Vargas Llosa, Mario. "El Contrapoder de la literatura." *El País Semanal* (5 March 2000): 15–24.

Vandendorpe, Christian. *De la fable au fait divers*. Montréal: CIADEST, 1991.

Vertigo: Esthétique et histoire du cinema. Hors série (July 2004). Paris: Seuil, 2004.

Vézard, Frédéric. *La France des tueurs en série*. Paris: Flammarion, 2002.

Violette, Gérard. Reply to Letter of Roger Planchon. *Le Monde* (12–13 January 1992): 13.

Wainwright, Jeffrey. "The Bruce Lee of Drama: Words Were Like Weapons in the Hands of Bernard-Marie Koltès." *London Independent* (11 March 1998): 7.

Walker, David H. *Outrage and Insight: French Writers and the "Fait divers."* Oxford: Berg, 1995.

Willis, Ellen. "Beyond Good and Evil: Crime and Cultural Politics." *Tikkun* 9 (1994): 51–57.

Young, Deborah. Review of *I Can't Sleep,* by Claire Denis. *Variety Film Reviews* (23 May 1994): 210.

Zinai-Koudil, Hafsa, dir. *Le Démon au féminin*. Zinai-Koudil, 1993.

Index